Ladakh

Ladakh

A PHOTO TRAVELOGUE

NARRATION AND PHOTOGRAPHS

SOHINI SEN

NIYOGI
BOOKS

Published by

NIYOGI BOOKS

D-78, Okhla Industrial Area, Phase-I
New Delhi-110 020, INDIA
Tel: 91-11-26816301, 49327000
Fax: 91-11-26810483, 26813830
email: niyogibooks@gmail.com
website: www.niyogibooksindia.com

Design: Sohini Sen, Shashi Bhushan Prasad (Niyogi Books)

ISBN: 978-93-85285-02-8
Publication: 2015

Printed at: Niyogi Offset Pvt. Ltd., New Delhi, India

To my Dad,
who had wished to
see the world through
my eyes

Contents

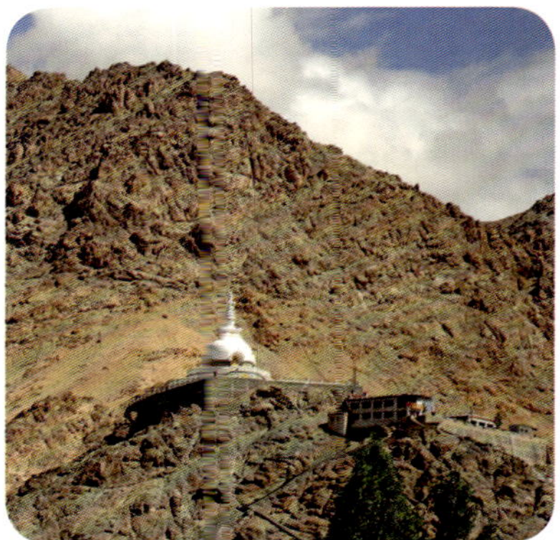

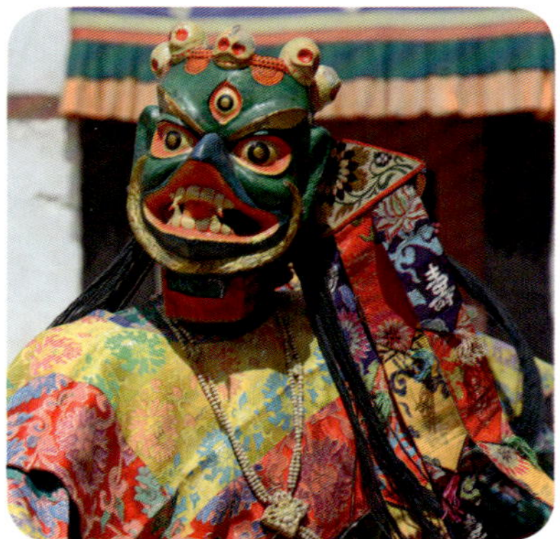

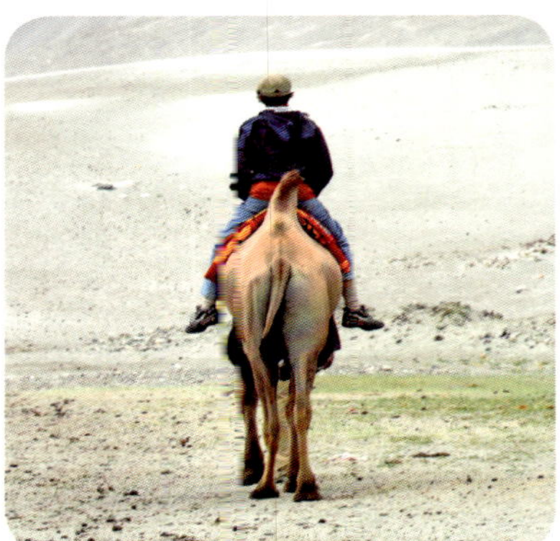

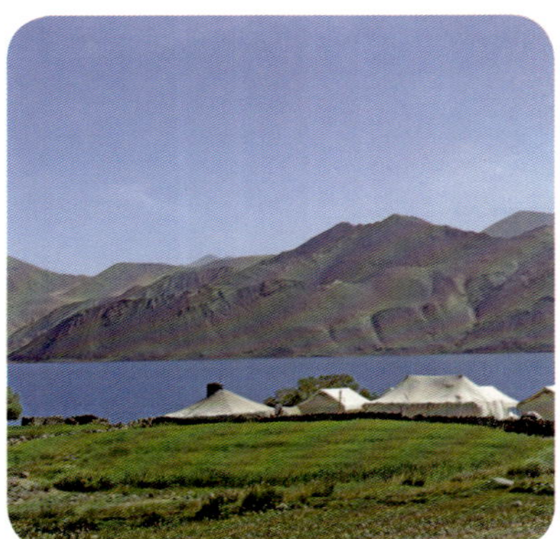

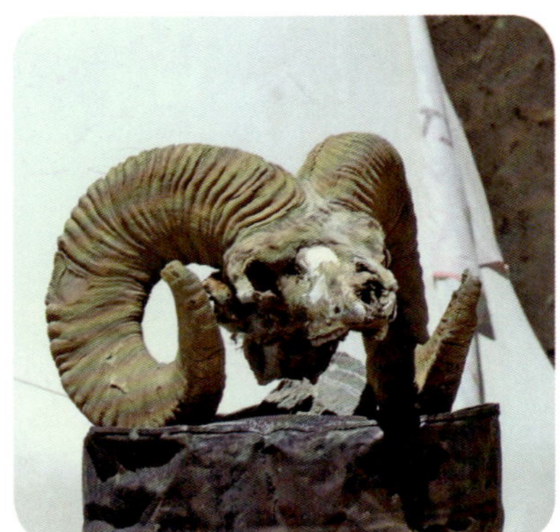

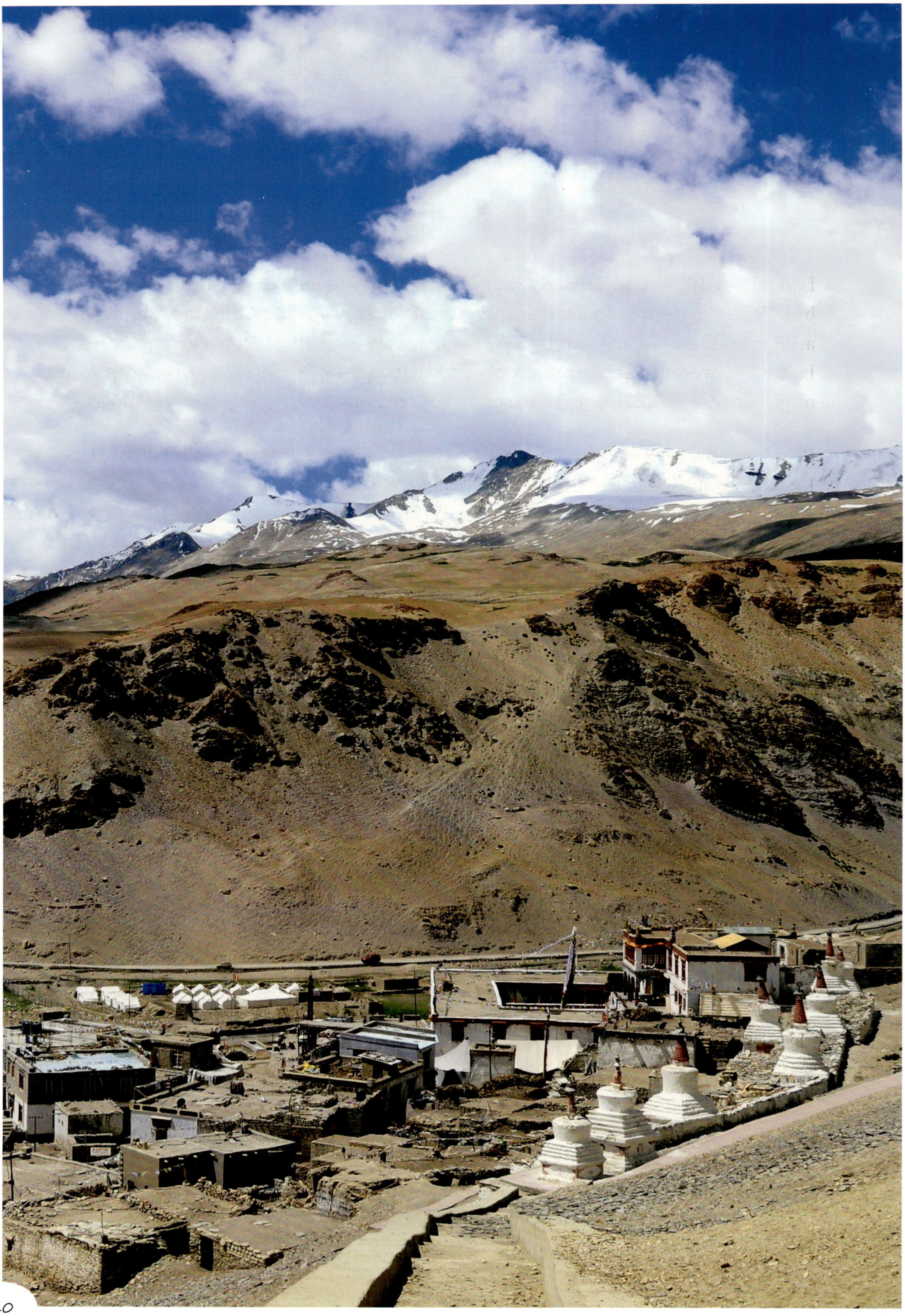

Why this book is unique

Ladakh—with its dramatic terrain of larger-than-life mountains, unbelievably blue lakes, ancient monasteries and quaint villages—offers the traveller such a high that he wishes to hashtag it for the rest of his life. One cannot handle Ladakh's ever-changing million-pixel landscapes without using up a couple of gigabytes worth of text just to say what an overwhelming experience it was.

But no amount of text can ever—truly ever—capture the enchantment that is Ladakh. One needs to see it to believe it. Some travellers have published their collection of photographs of Ladakh. From these, we know that Ladakh is harshly sunlit, breathtakingly beautiful, and freezing cold.

Every journey is a tale. My long Ladakhi journey with a friend was one as well. A tale about the midnight-blue magpie streaking past the car window, the curious marmot popping out of its hole, and masked lamas deliberately creating a humorous interlude in a serious ritual. After all, between pummelling Romans and guzzling boar, the indomitable Gauls too had fun. Our journey was also about those cups of hot, syrupy tea downed to survive at high passes, the ice-cold wind sneaking into the tent at night, the first encounter with a Ladakhi toilet, and the dogged pursuit of a couple of waddling Tibetan Sand Grouse in the hope of a good photograph.

Just photos or just text would not have been enough to share those moments of discovery and spontaneous laughter. So, I had to come up with this new genre: a photo travelogue in a comic-book format.

Since the main characters are real people, and one of them was consistently behind the camera, one wouldn't get to 'see' much of them in the book. And while the protagonists' conversations are real, the same cannot be said for that of some other characters. Most of them spoke Ladakhi, some spoke Shelduck, and some, Gull. I had to interpret these into their nearest English equivalent. I tried my best.

Sohini Sen
January 2015

LADAKH

(A ROUGH MAP OF AREAS MENTIONED IN THE BOOK)

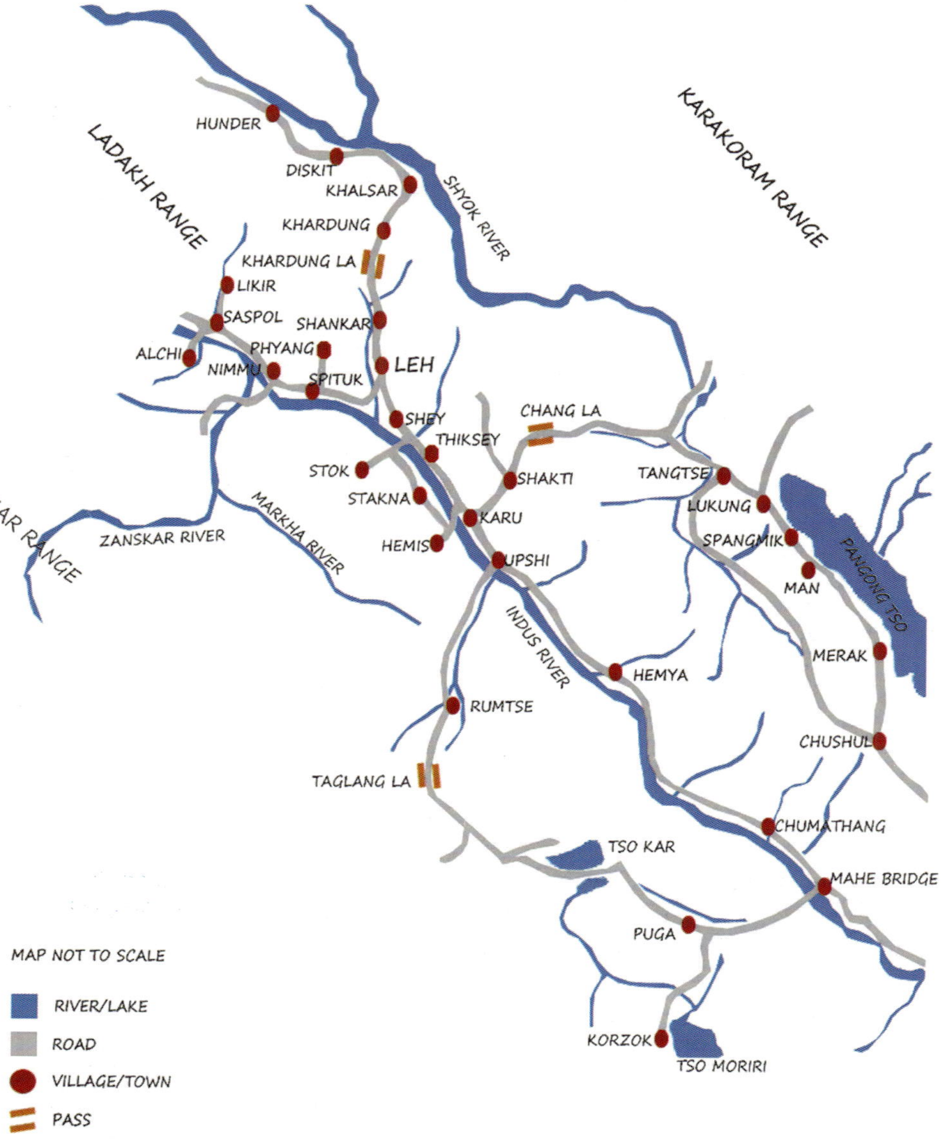

Chapter 1: Leh

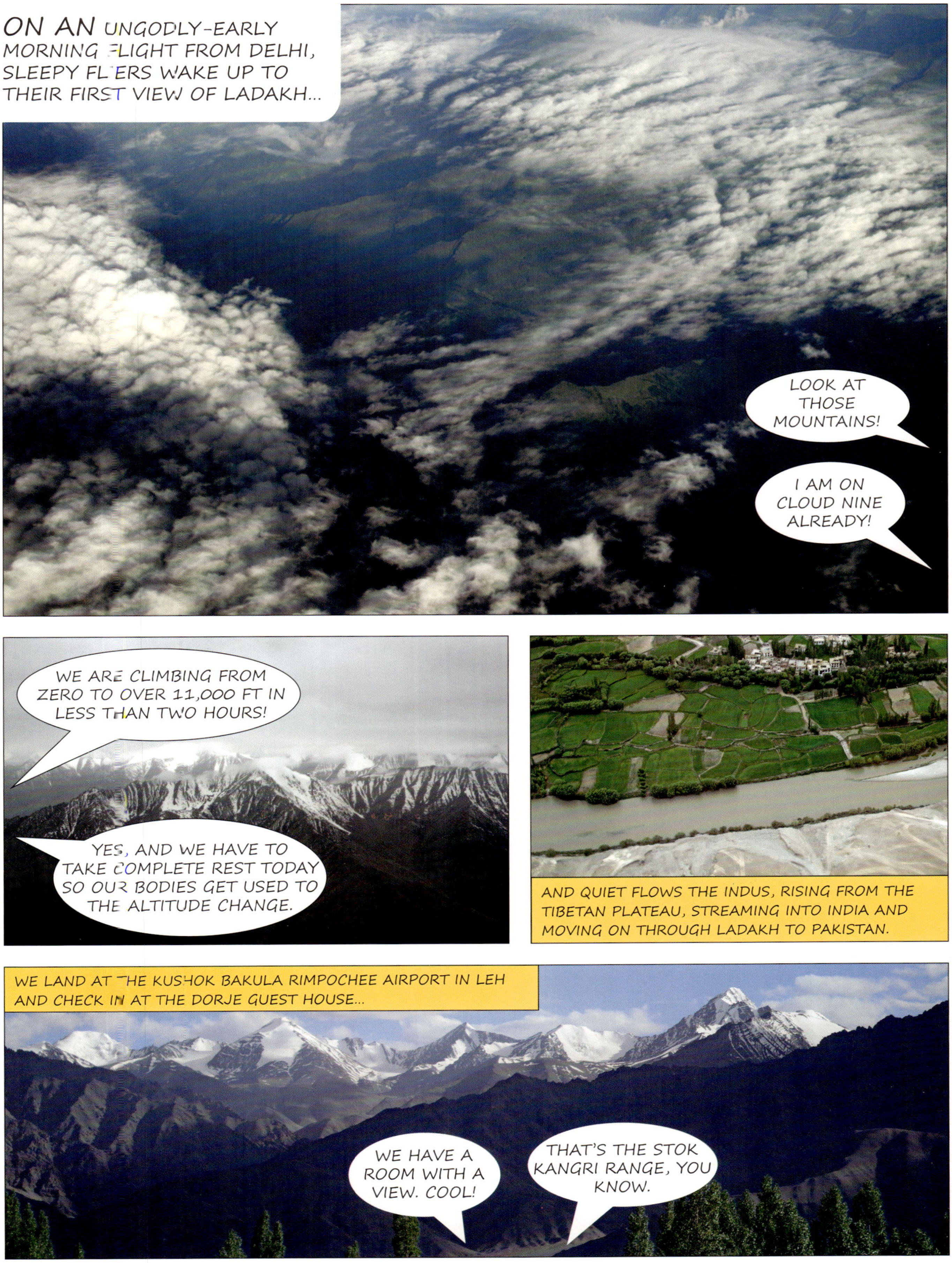

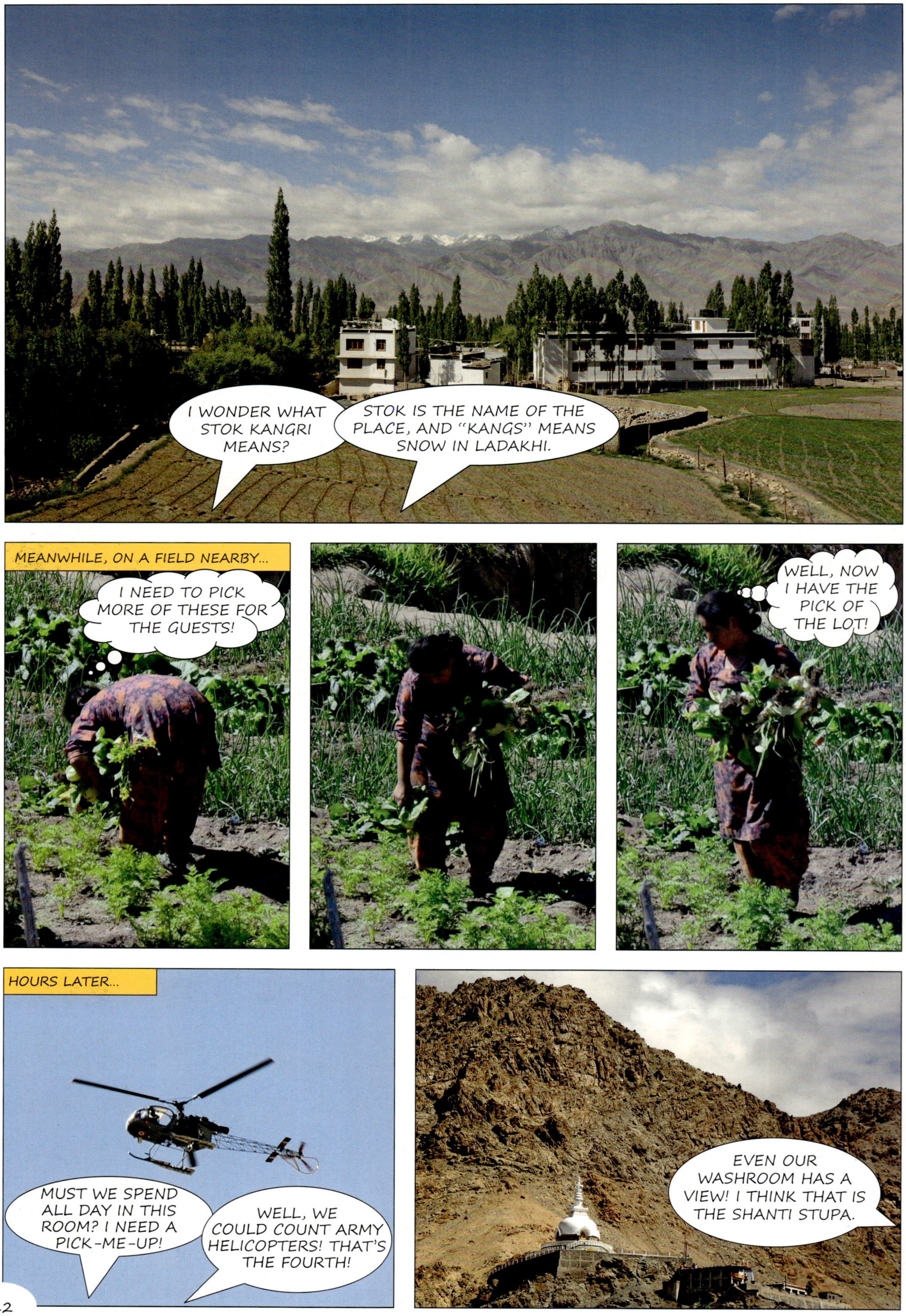
I WONDER WHAT STOK KANGRI MEANS?
STOK IS THE NAME OF THE PLACE, AND "KANGS" MEANS SNOW IN LADAKHI.
MEANWHILE, ON A FIELD NEARBY...
I NEED TO PICK MORE OF THESE FOR THE GUESTS!
WELL, NOW I HAVE THE PICK OF THE LOT!
HOURS LATER...
MUST WE SPEND ALL DAY IN THIS ROOM? I NEED A PICK-ME-UP!
WELL, WE COULD COUNT ARMY HELICOPTERS! THAT'S THE FOURTH!
EVEN OUR WASHROOM HAS A VIEW! I THINK THAT IS THE SHANTI STUPA.

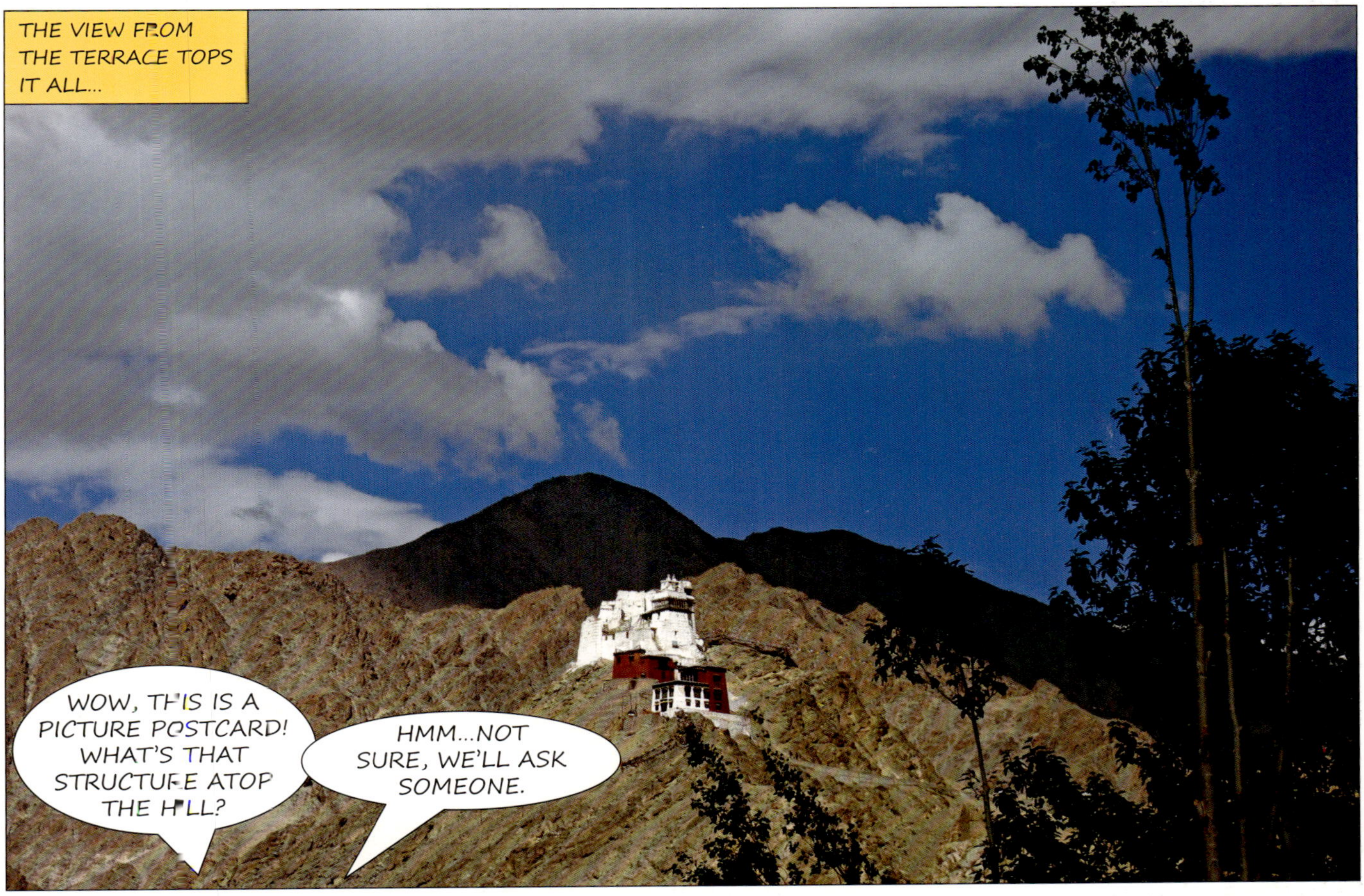
THE VIEW FROM THE TERRACE TOPS IT ALL...
WOW, THIS IS A PICTURE POSTCARD! WHAT'S THAT STRUCTURE ATOP THE HILL?
HMM...NOT SURE, WE'LL ASK SOMEONE.

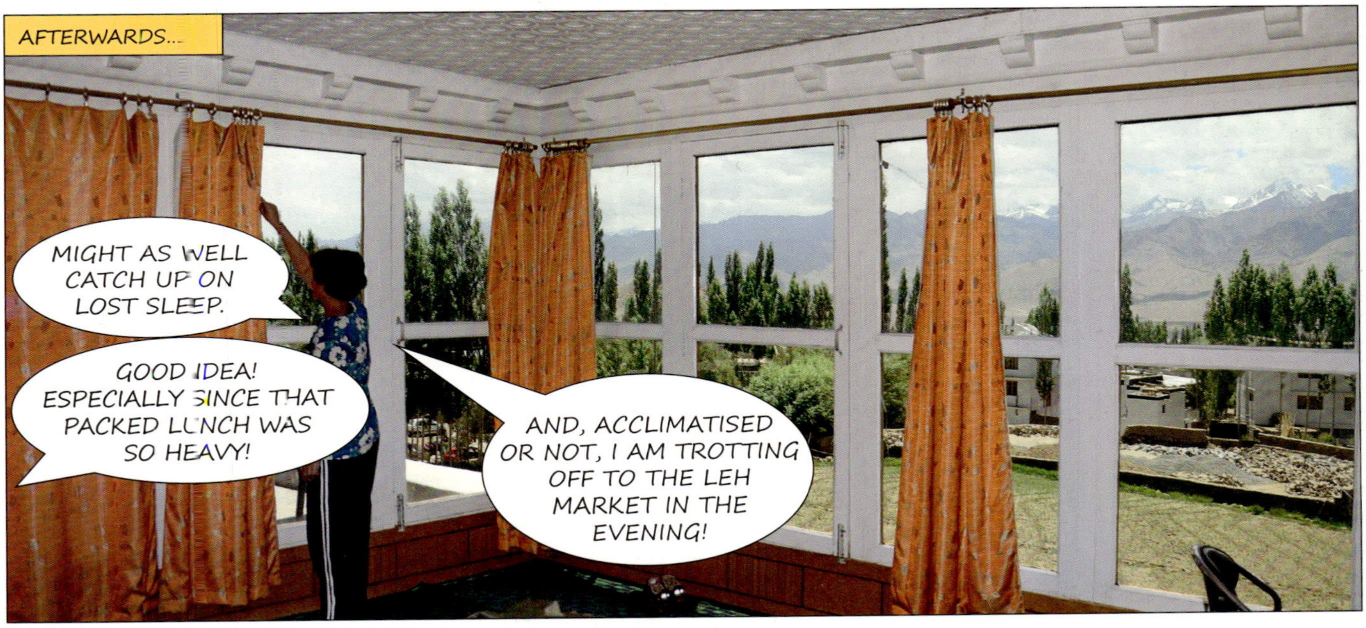
AFTERWARDS...
MIGHT AS WELL CATCH UP ON LOST SLEEP.
GOOD IDEA! ESPECIALLY SINCE THAT PACKED LUNCH WAS SO HEAVY!
AND, ACCLIMATISED OR NOT, I AM TROTTING OFF TO THE LEH MARKET IN THE EVENING!

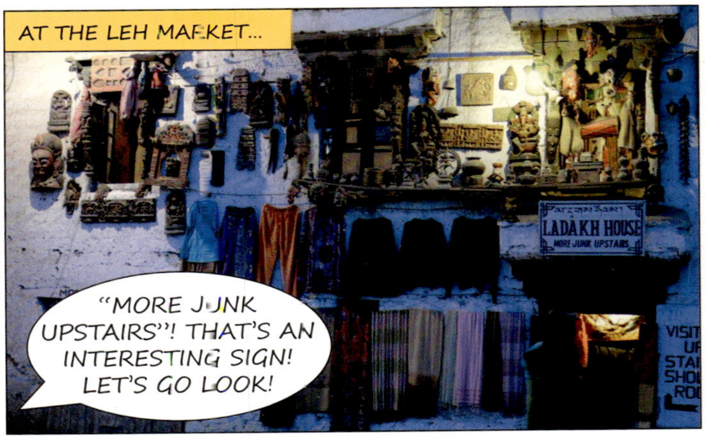
AT THE LEH MARKET...
LADAKH HOUSE
MORE JUNK UPSTAIRS
"MORE JUNK UPSTAIRS"! THAT'S AN INTERESTING SIGN! LET'S GO LOOK!

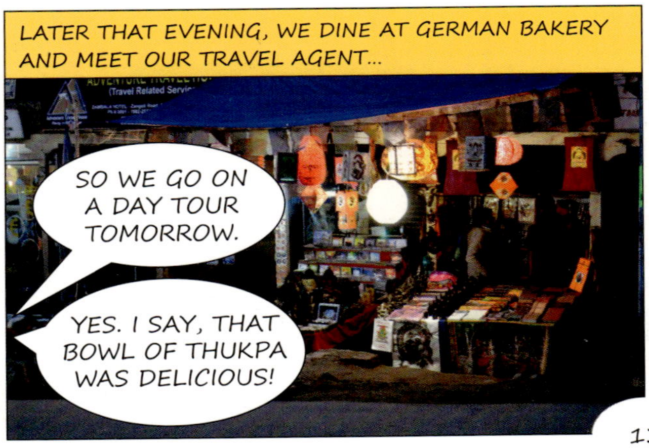
LATER THAT EVENING, WE DINE AT GERMAN BAKERY AND MEET OUR TRAVEL AGENT...
SO WE GO ON A DAY TOUR TOMORROW.
YES. I SAY, THAT BOWL OF THUKPA WAS DELICIOUS!

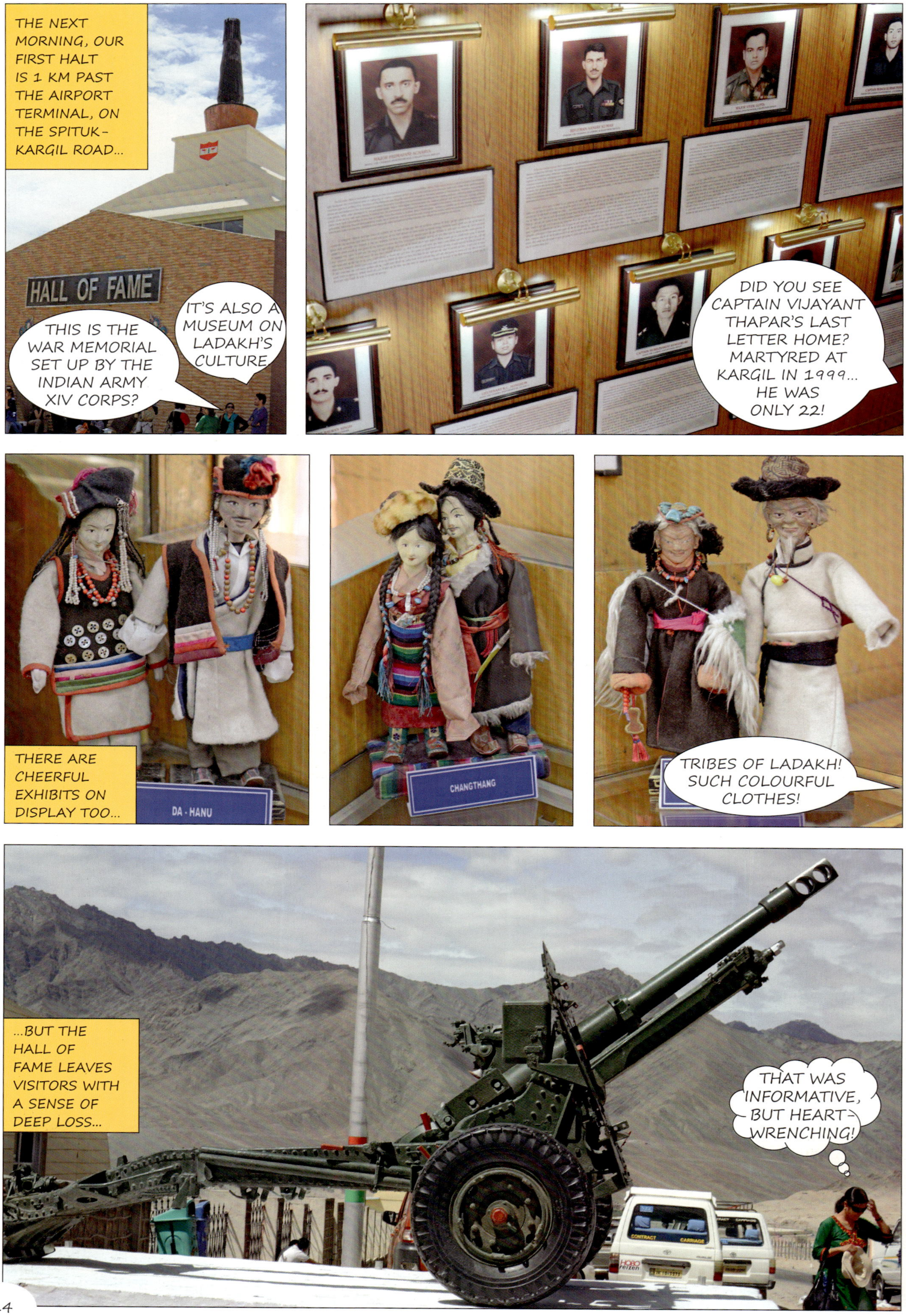
THE NEXT MORNING, OUR FIRST HALT IS 1 KM PAST THE AIRPORT TERMINAL, ON THE SPITUK-KARGIL ROAD...
HALL OF FAME
THIS IS THE WAR MEMORIAL SET UP BY THE INDIAN ARMY XIV CORPS?
IT'S ALSO A MUSEUM ON LADAKH'S CULTURE.
DID YOU SEE CAPTAIN VIJAYANT THAPAR'S LAST LETTER HOME? MARTYRED AT KARGIL IN 1999... HE WAS ONLY 22!
THERE ARE CHEERFUL EXHIBITS ON DISPLAY TOO...
DA - HANU
CHANGTHANG
TRIBES OF LADAKH! SUCH COLOURFUL CLOTHES!
...BUT THE HALL OF FAME LEAVES VISITORS WITH A SENSE OF DEEP LOSS...
THAT WAS INFORMATIVE, BUT HEART-WRENCHING!

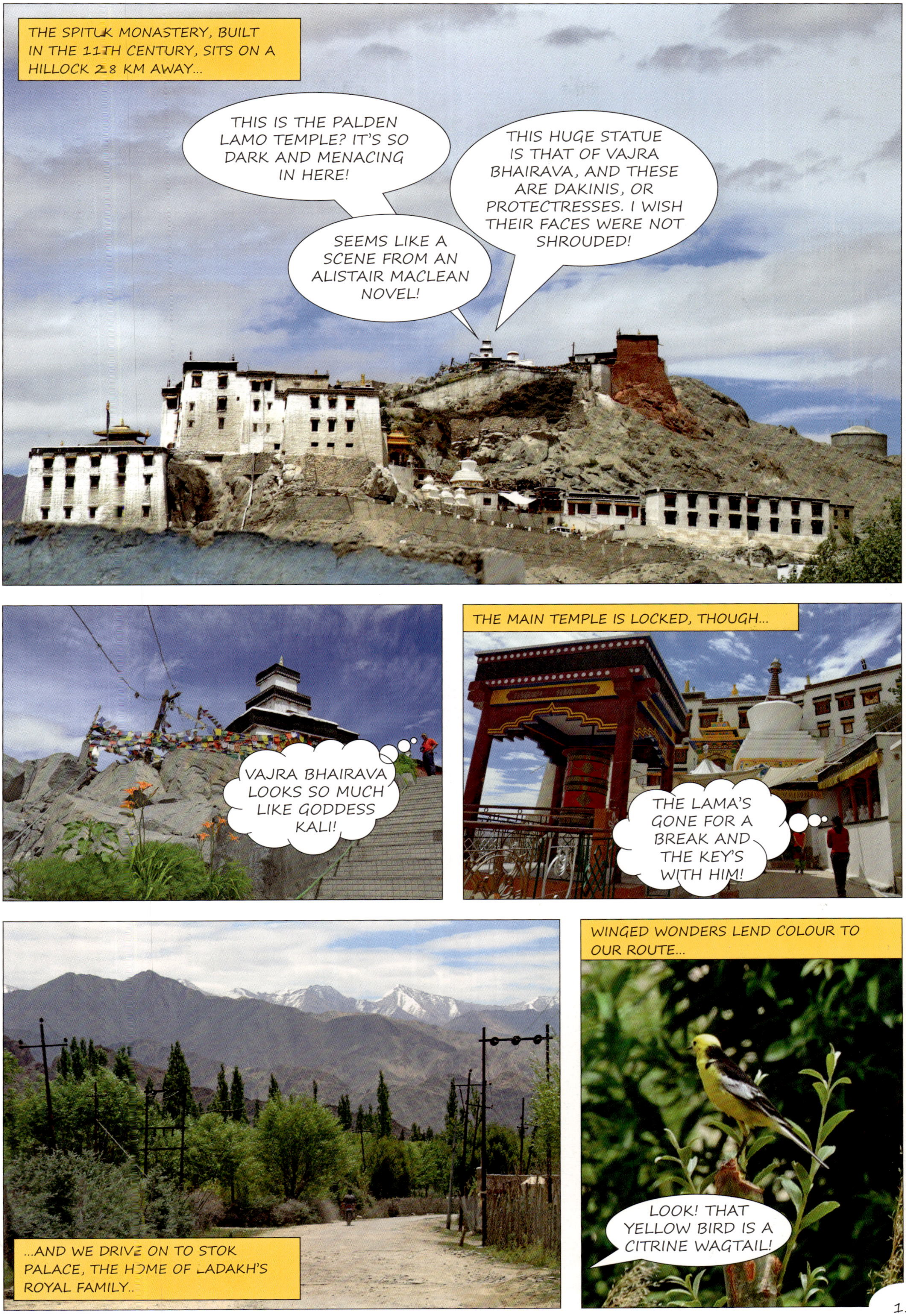

THE SPITUK MONASTERY, BUILT IN THE 11TH CENTURY, SITS ON A HILLOCK 28 KM AWAY...
THIS IS THE PALDEN LAMO TEMPLE? IT'S SO DARK AND MENACING IN HERE!
SEEMS LIKE A SCENE FROM AN ALISTAIR MACLEAN NOVEL!
THIS HUGE STATUE IS THAT OF VAJRA BHAIRAVA, AND THESE ARE DAKINIS, OR PROTECTRESSES. I WISH THEIR FACES WERE NOT SHROUDED!
VAJRA BHAIRAVA LOOKS SO MUCH LIKE GODDESS KALI!
THE MAIN TEMPLE IS LOCKED, THOUGH...
THE LAMA'S GONE FOR A BREAK AND THE KEY'S WITH HIM!
...AND WE DRIVE ON TO STOK PALACE, THE HOME OF LADAKH'S ROYAL FAMILY..
WINGED WONDERS LEND COLOUR TO OUR ROUTE...
LOOK! THAT YELLOW BIRD IS A CITRINE WAGTAIL!

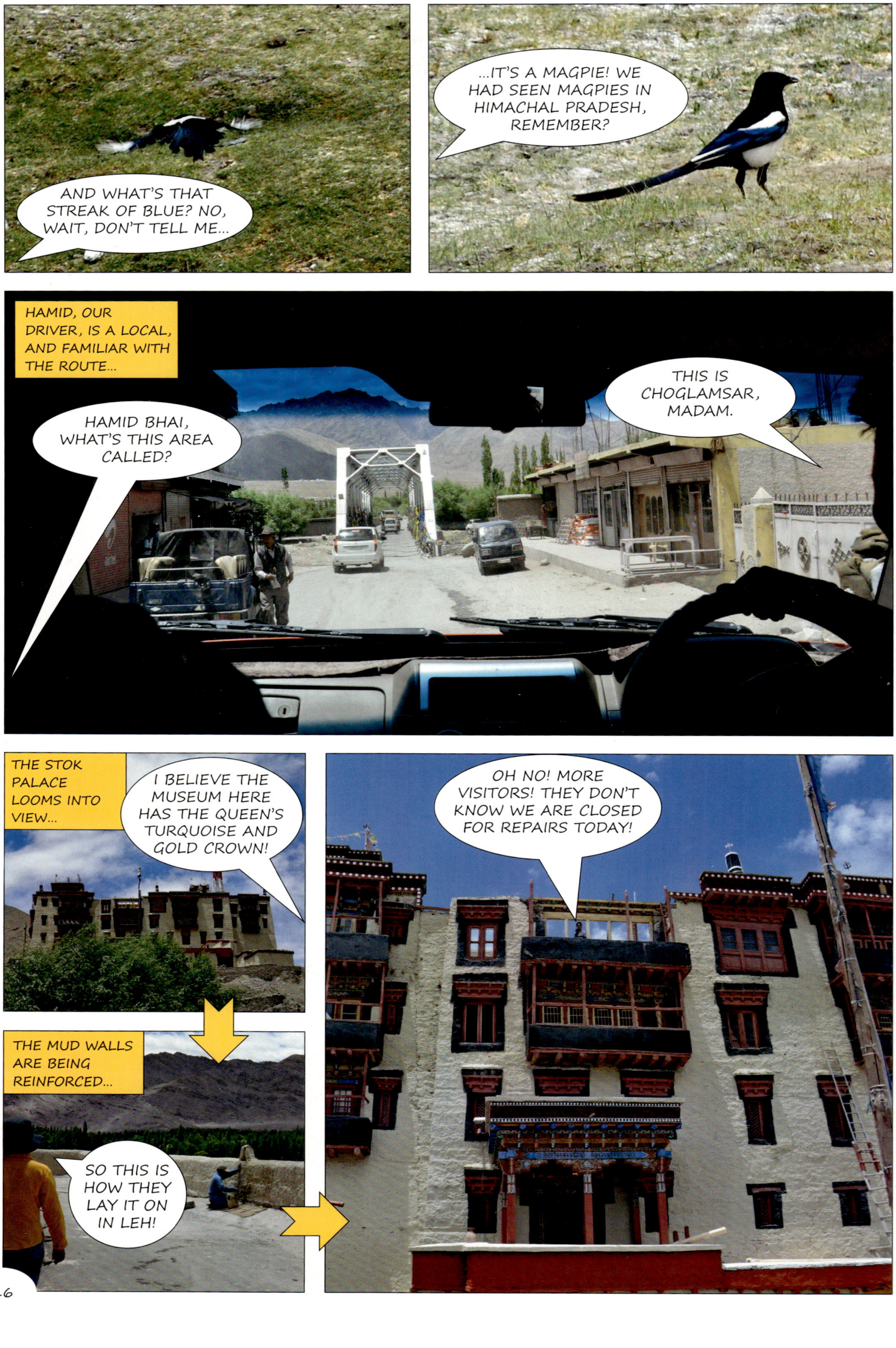
AND WHAT'S THAT STREAK OF BLUE? NO, WAIT, DON'T TELL ME...
...IT'S A MAGPIE! WE HAD SEEN MAGPIES IN HIMACHAL PRADESH, REMEMBER?
HAMID, OUR DRIVER, IS A LOCAL, AND FAMILIAR WITH THE ROUTE...
HAMID BHAI, WHAT'S THIS AREA CALLED?
THIS IS CHOGLAMSAR, MADAM.
THE STOK PALACE LOOMS INTO VIEW...
I BELIEVE THE MUSEUM HERE HAS THE QUEEN'S TURQUOISE AND GOLD CROWN!
THE MUD WALLS ARE BEING REINFORCED...
SO THIS IS HOW THEY LAY IT ON IN LEH!
OH NO! MORE VISITORS! THEY DON'T KNOW WE ARE CLOSED FOR REPAIRS TODAY!

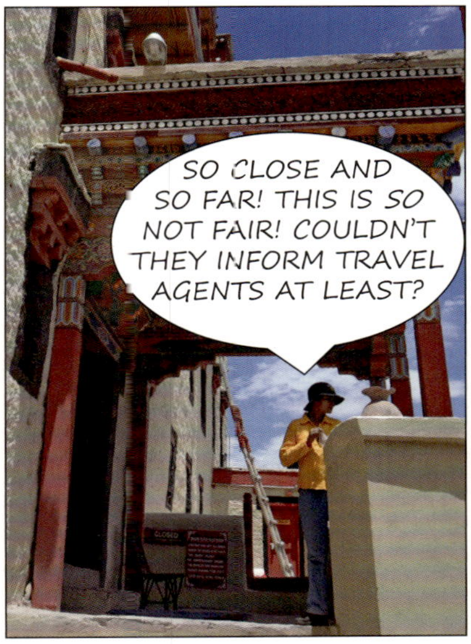
SO CLOSE AND SO FAR! THIS IS SO NOT FAIR! COULDN'T THEY INFORM TRAVEL AGENTS AT LEAST?

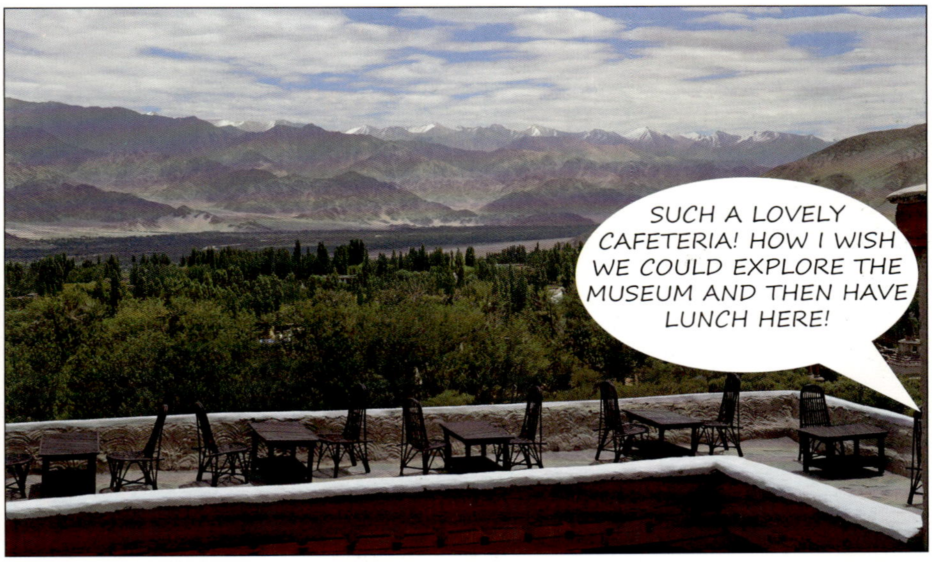
SUCH A LOVELY CAFETERIA! HOW I WISH WE COULD EXPLORE THE MUSEUM AND THEN HAVE LUNCH HERE!

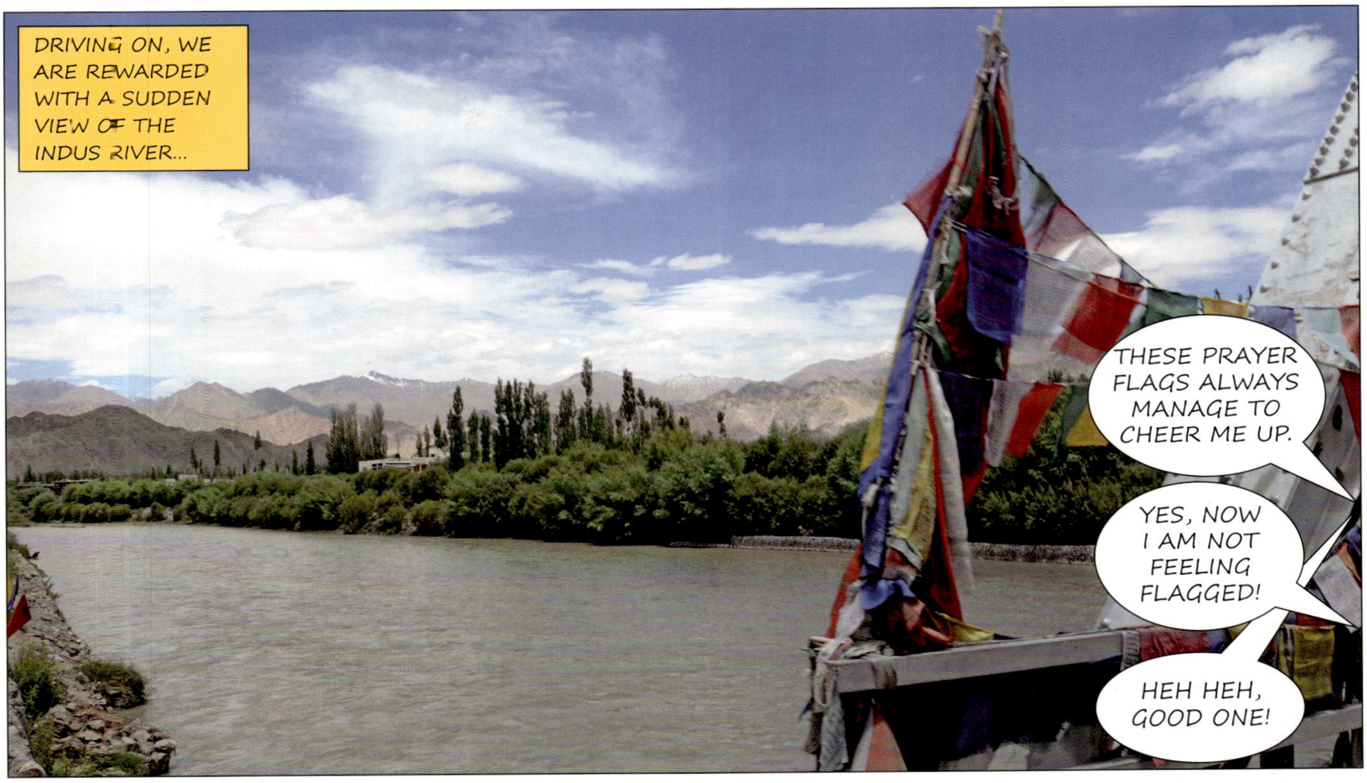
DRIVING ON, WE ARE REWARDED WITH A SUDDEN VIEW OF THE INDUS RIVER...
THESE PRAYER FLAGS ALWAYS MANAGE TO CHEER ME UP.
YES, NOW I AM NOT FEELING FLAGGED!
HEH HEH, GOOD ONE!

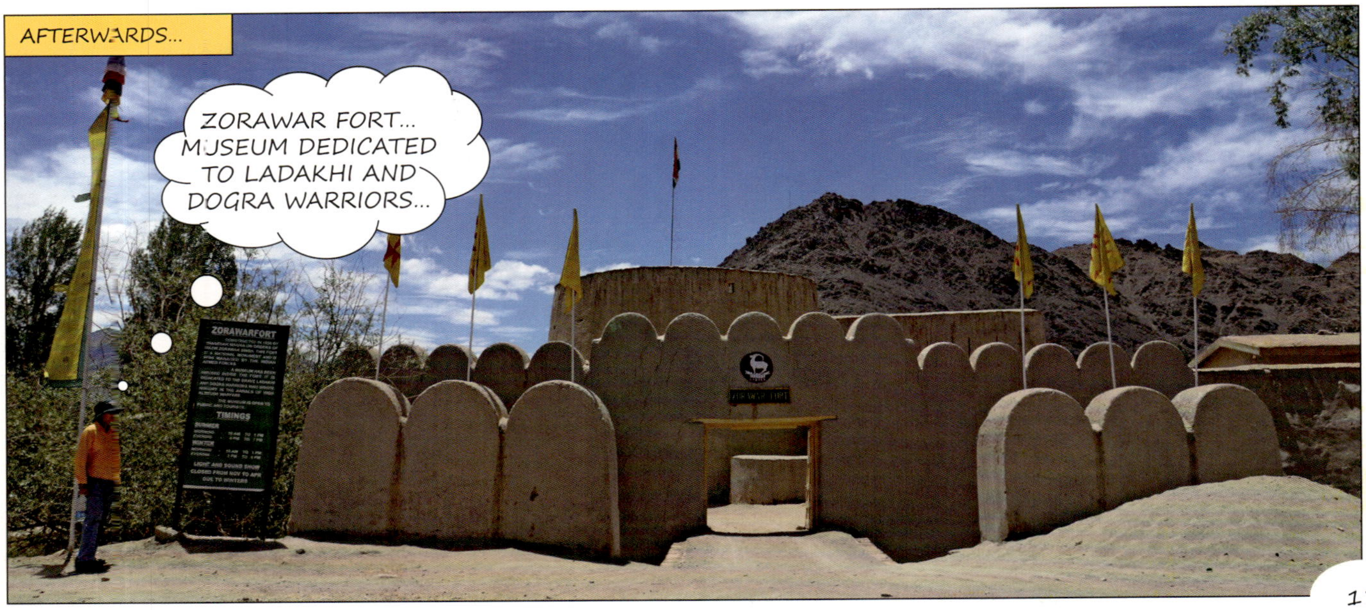
AFTERWARDS...
ZORAWAR FORT... MUSEUM DEDICATED TO LADAKHI AND DOGRA WARRIORS...

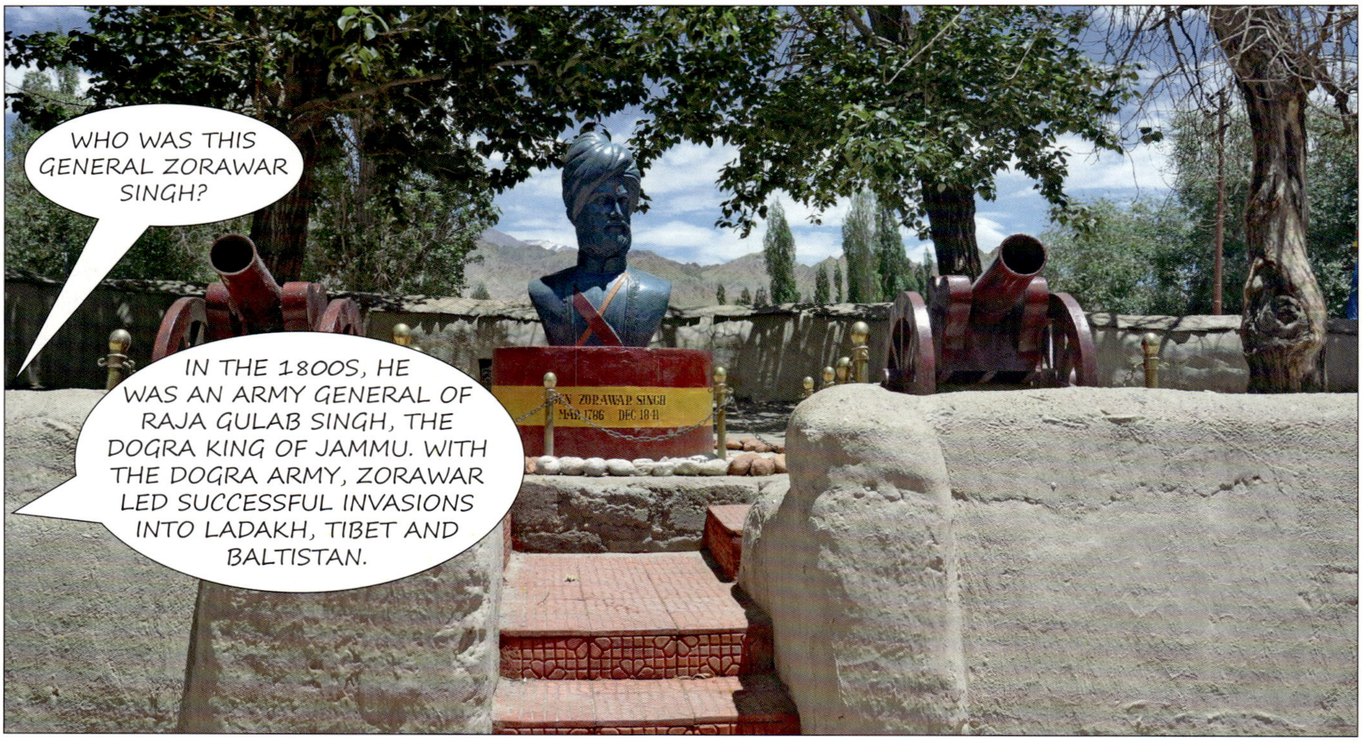
WHO WAS THIS GENERAL ZORAWAR SINGH?
IN THE 1800S, HE WAS AN ARMY GENERAL OF RAJA GULAB SINGH, THE DOGRA KING OF JAMMU. WITH THE DOGRA ARMY, ZORAWAR LED SUCCESSFUL INVASIONS INTO LADAKH, TIBET AND BALTISTAN.

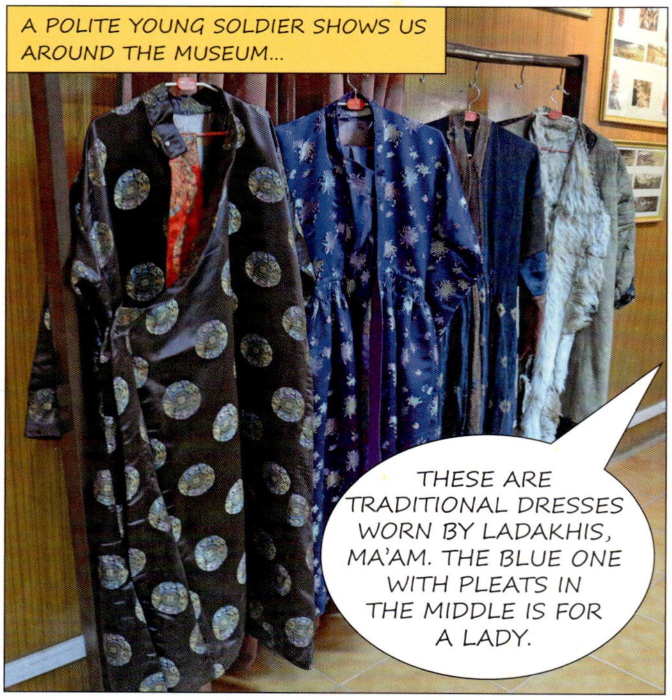
A POLITE YOUNG SOLDIER SHOWS US AROUND THE MUSEUM...
THESE ARE TRADITIONAL DRESSES WORN BY LADAKHIS, MA'AM. THE BLUE ONE WITH PLEATS IN THE MIDDLE IS FOR A LADY.

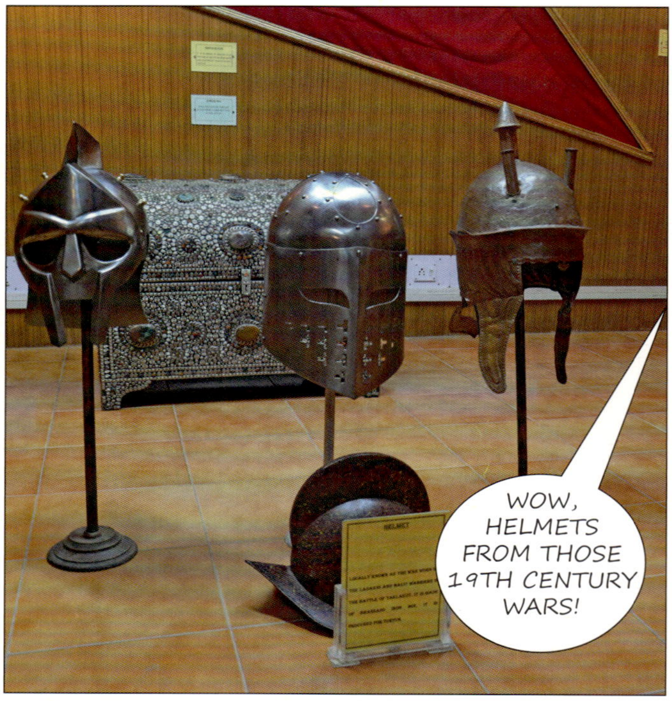
WOW, HELMETS FROM THOSE 19TH CENTURY WARS!

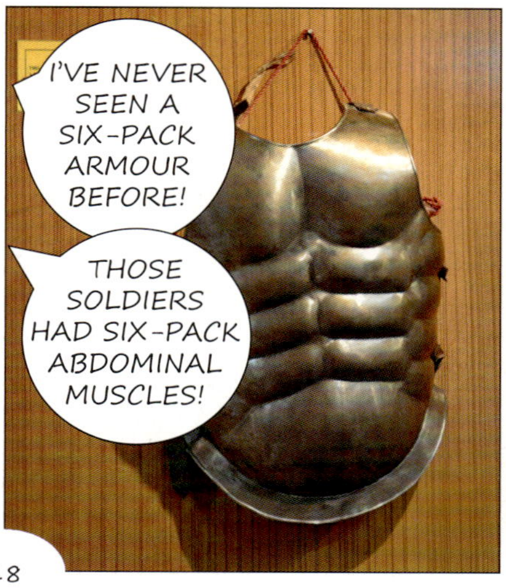
I'VE NEVER SEEN A SIX-PACK ARMOUR BEFORE!
THOSE SOLDIERS HAD SIX-PACK ABDOMINAL MUSCLES!

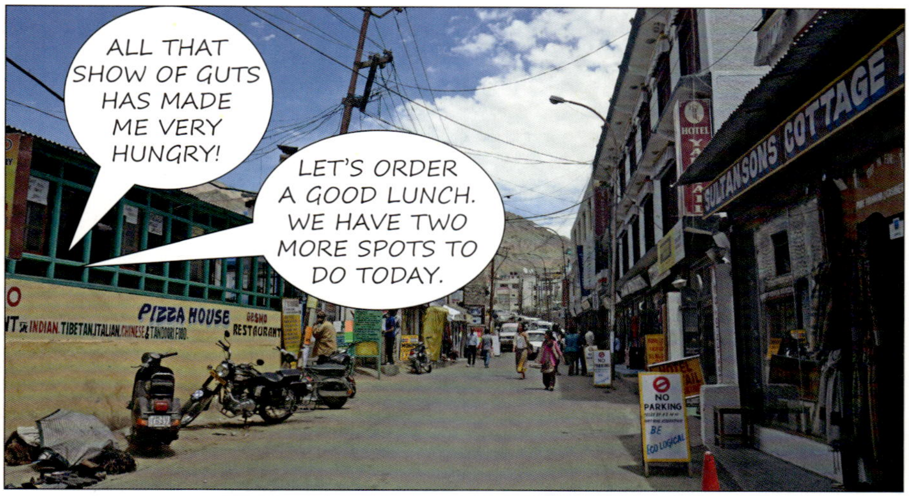
ALL THAT SHOW OF GUTS HAS MADE ME VERY HUNGRY!
LET'S ORDER A GOOD LUNCH. WE HAVE TWO MORE SPOTS TO DO TODAY.
PIZZA HOUSE
SULTANSONS COTTAGE
NO PARKING

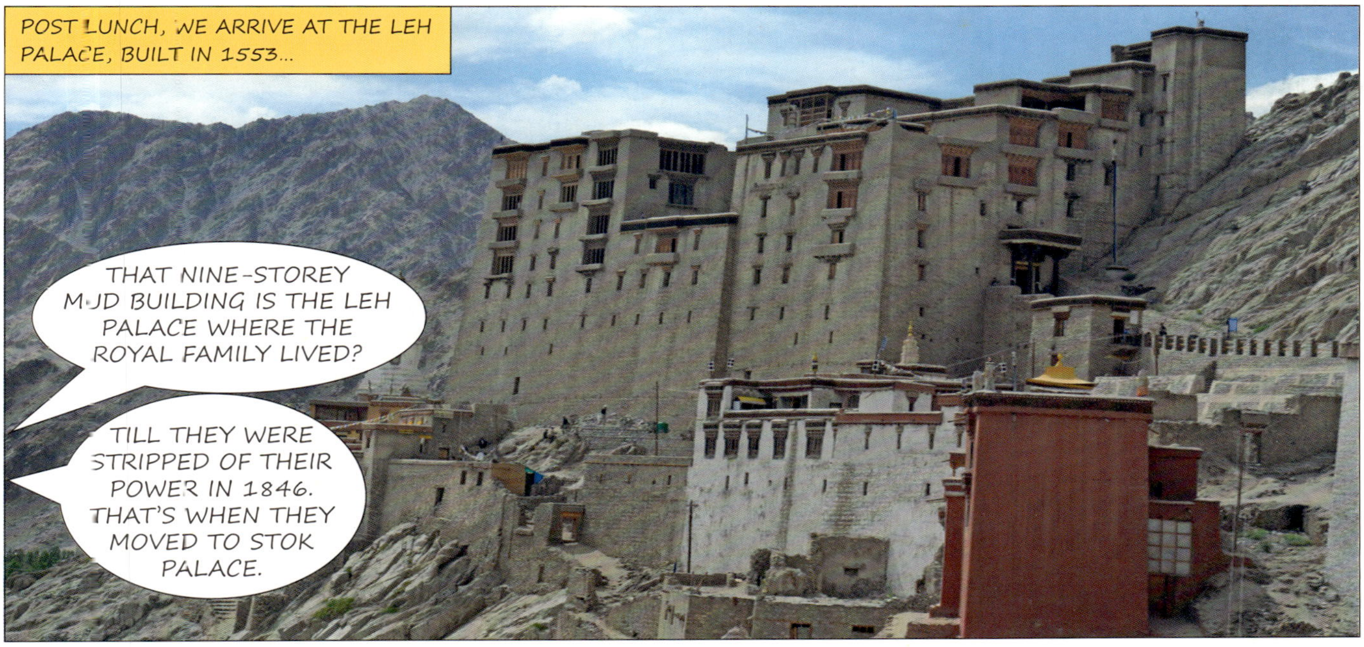
POST LUNCH, WE ARRIVE AT THE LEH PALACE, BUILT IN 1553...
THAT NINE-STOREY MUD BUILDING IS THE LEH PALACE WHERE THE ROYAL FAMILY LIVED?
TILL THEY WERE STRIPPED OF THEIR POWER IN 1846. THAT'S WHEN THEY MOVED TO STOK PALACE.

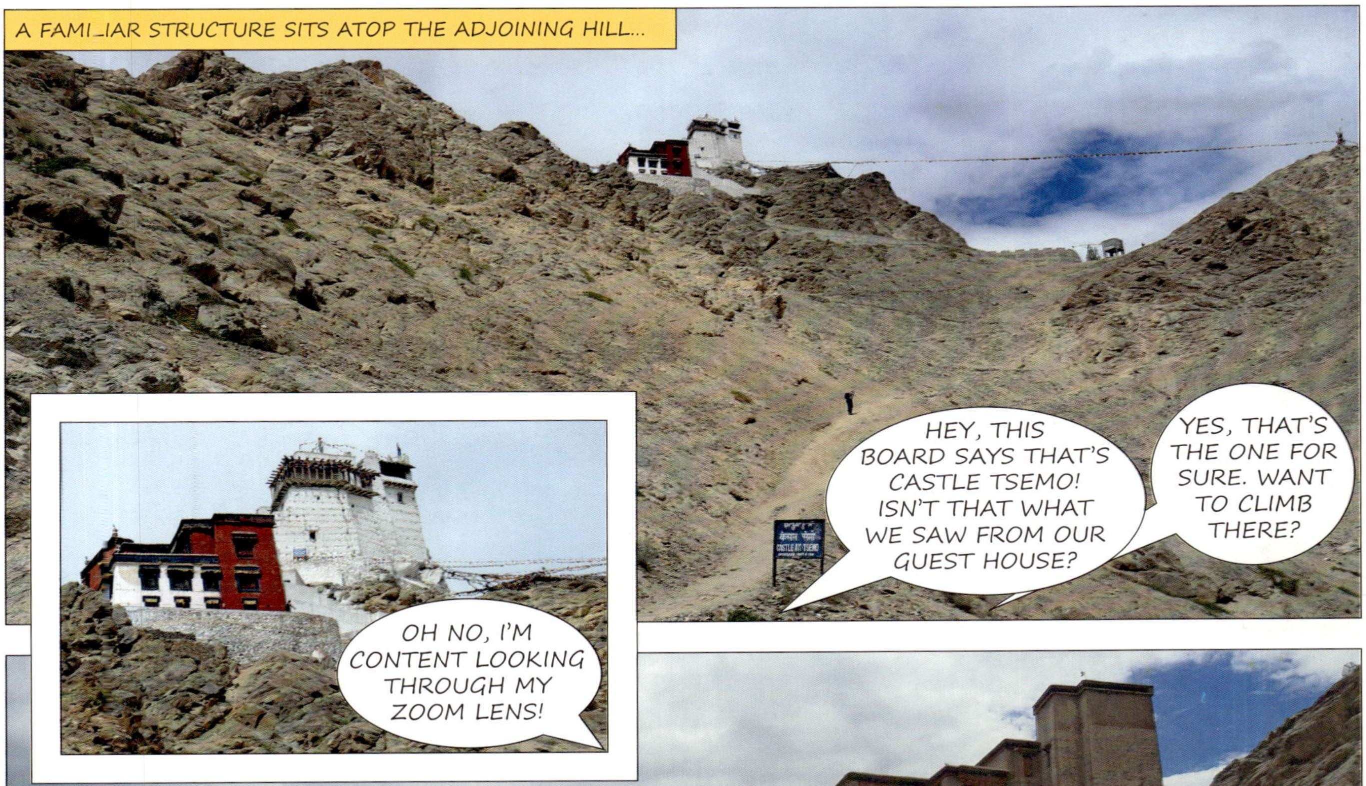
A FAMILIAR STRUCTURE SITS ATOP THE ADJOINING HILL...
HEY, THIS BOARD SAYS THAT'S CASTLE TSEMO! ISN'T THAT WHAT WE SAW FROM OUR GUEST HOUSE?
YES, THAT'S THE ONE FOR SURE. WANT TO CLIMB THERE?
OH NO, I'M CONTENT LOOKING THROUGH MY ZOOM LENS!

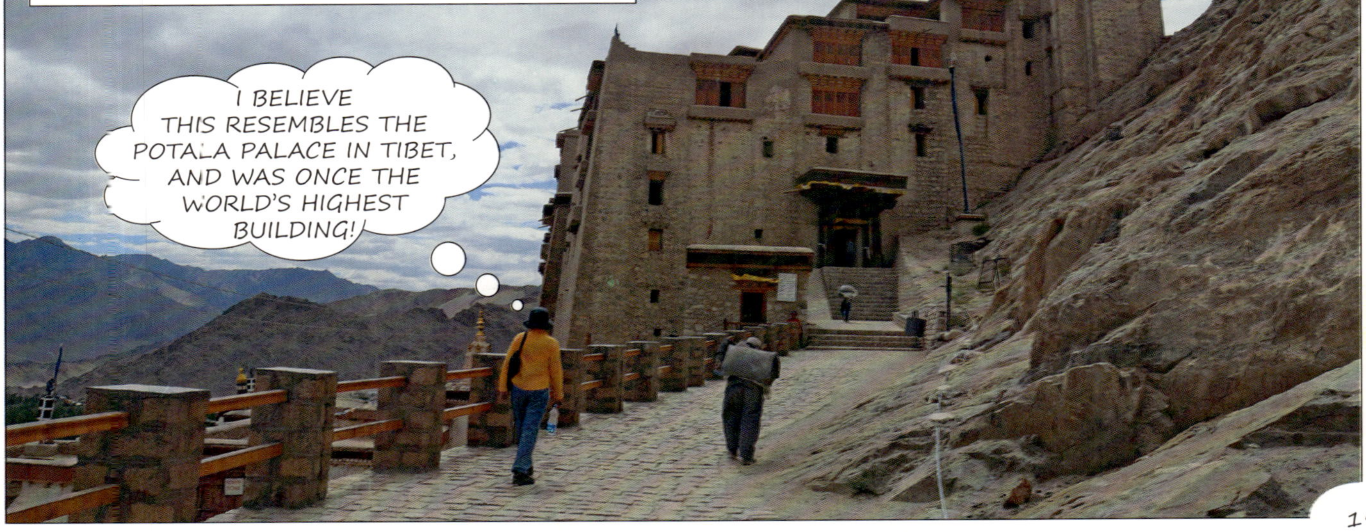
I BELIEVE THIS RESEMBLES THE POTALA PALACE IN TIBET, AND WAS ONCE THE WORLD'S HIGHEST BUILDING!

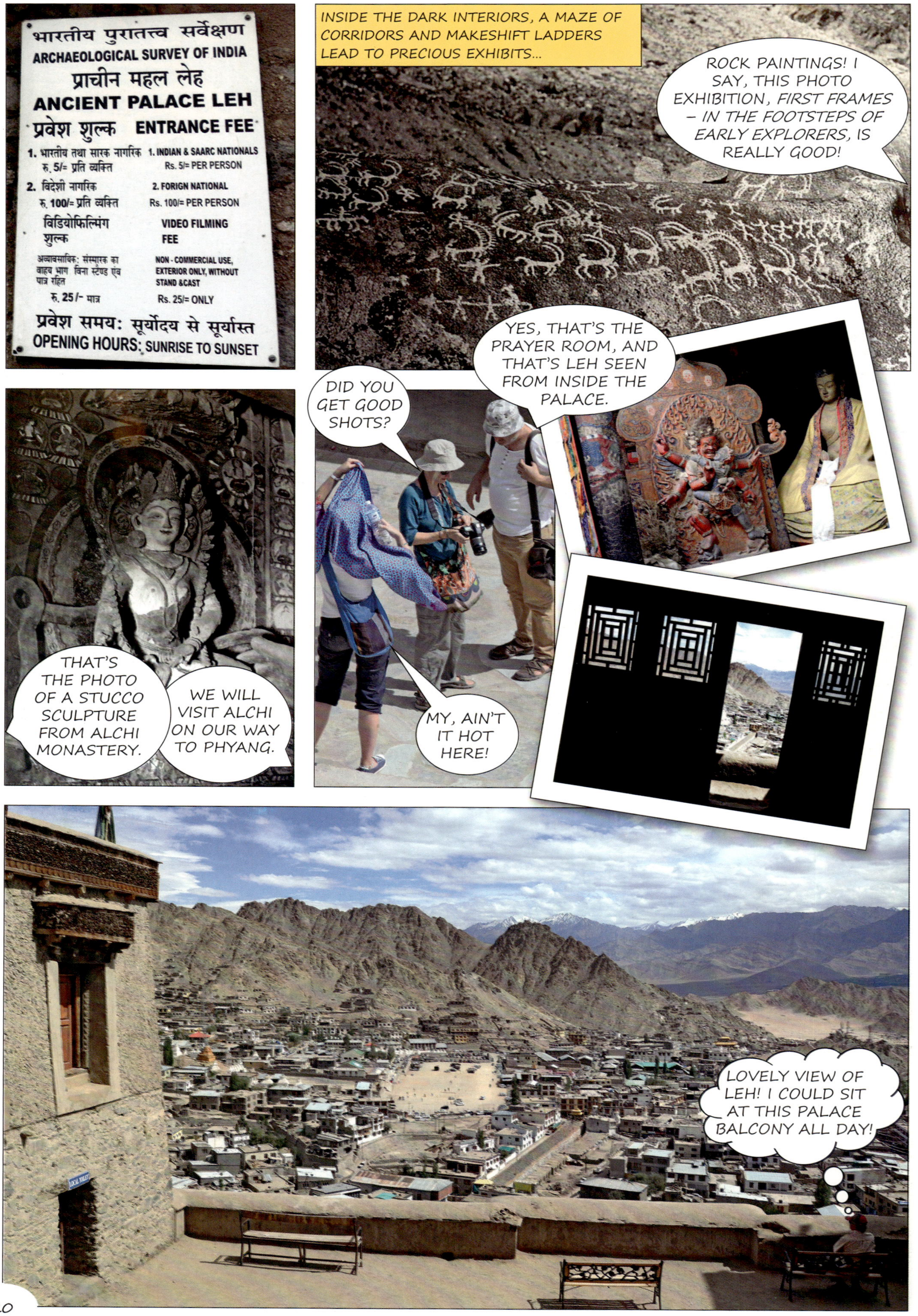
भारतीय पुरातत्त्व सर्वेक्षण
ARCHAEOLOGICAL SURVEY OF INDIA
प्राचीन महल लेह
ANCIENT PALACE LEH
प्रवेश शुल्क ENTRANCE FEE
1. भारतीय तथा सारक नागरिक रु. 5/= प्रति व्यक्ति
1. INDIAN & SAARC NATIONALS Rs. 5/= PER PERSON
2. विदेशी नागरिक रु. 100/= प्रति व्यक्ति
2. FORIGN NATIONAL Rs. 100/= PER PERSON
विडियोफिल्मिंग शुल्क
VIDEO FILMING FEE
NON - COMMERCIAL USE, EXTERIOR ONLY, WITHOUT STAND &CAST
रु. 25/- मात्र
Rs. 25/= ONLY
प्रवेश समय: सूर्योदय से सूर्यास्त
OPENING HOURS: SUNRISE TO SUNSET
INSIDE THE DARK INTERIORS, A MAZE OF CORRIDORS AND MAKESHIFT LADDERS LEAD TO PRECIOUS EXHIBITS...
ROCK PAINTINGS! I SAY, THIS PHOTO EXHIBITION, *FIRST FRAMES – IN THE FOOTSTEPS OF EARLY EXPLORERS*, IS REALLY GOOD!
THAT'S THE PHOTO OF A STUCCO SCULPTURE FROM ALCHI MONASTERY.
WE WILL VISIT ALCHI ON OUR WAY TO PHYANG.
DID YOU GET GOOD SHOTS?
YES, THAT'S THE PRAYER ROOM, AND THAT'S LEH SEEN FROM INSIDE THE PALACE.
MY, AIN'T IT HOT HERE!
LOVELY VIEW OF LEH! I COULD SIT AT THIS PALACE BALCONY ALL DAY!

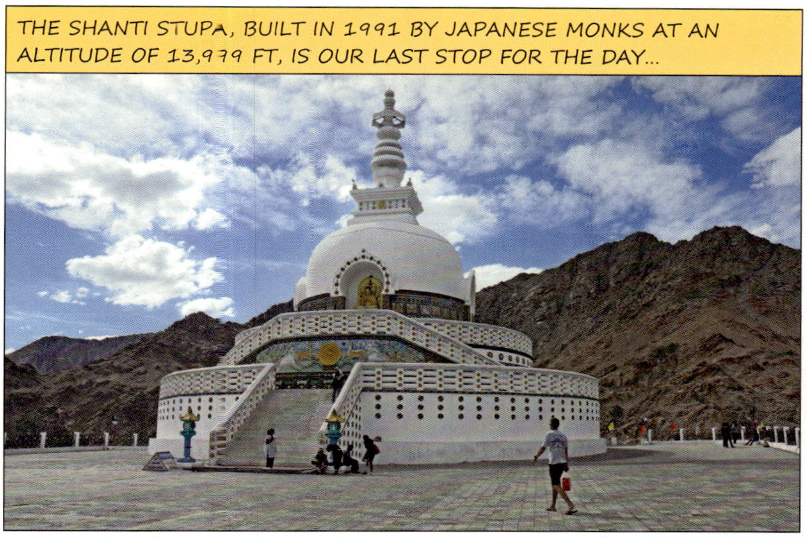
THE SHANTI STUPA, BUILT IN 1991 BY JAPANESE MONKS AT AN ALTITUDE OF 13,979 FT, IS OUR LAST STOP FOR THE DAY...

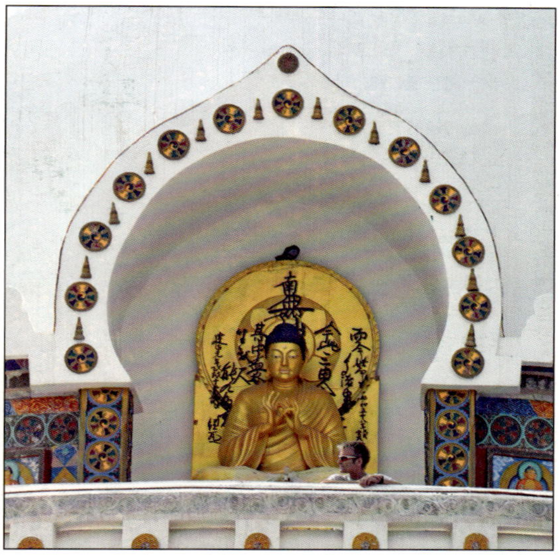

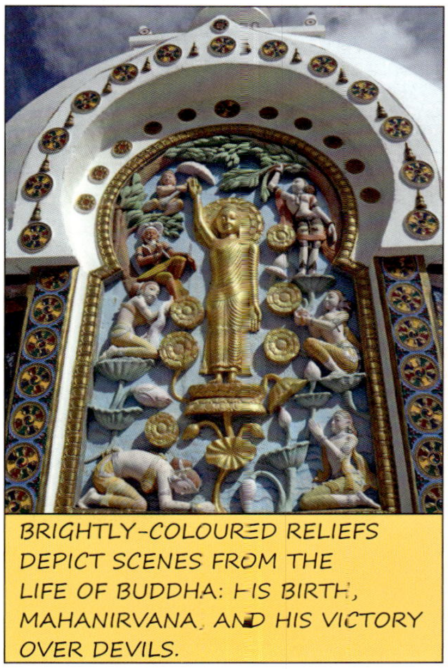
BRIGHTLY-COLOURED RELIEFS DEPICT SCENES FROM THE LIFE OF BUDDHA: HIS BIRTH, MAHANIRVANA, AND HIS VICTORY OVER DEVILS.

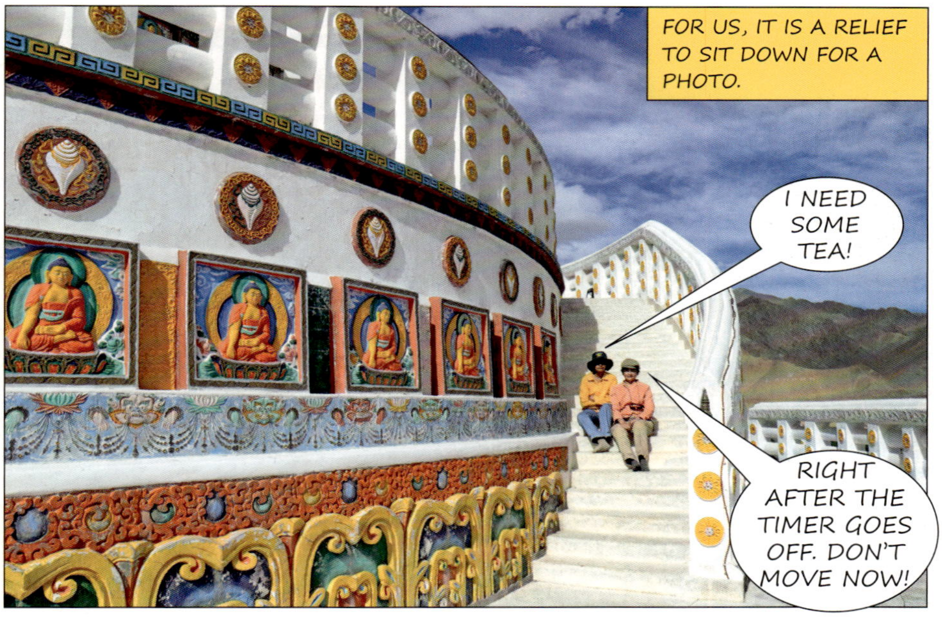
FOR US, IT IS A RELIEF TO SIT DOWN FOR A PHOTO.
I NEED SOME TEA!
RIGHT AFTER THE TIMER GOES OFF. DON'T MOVE NOW!

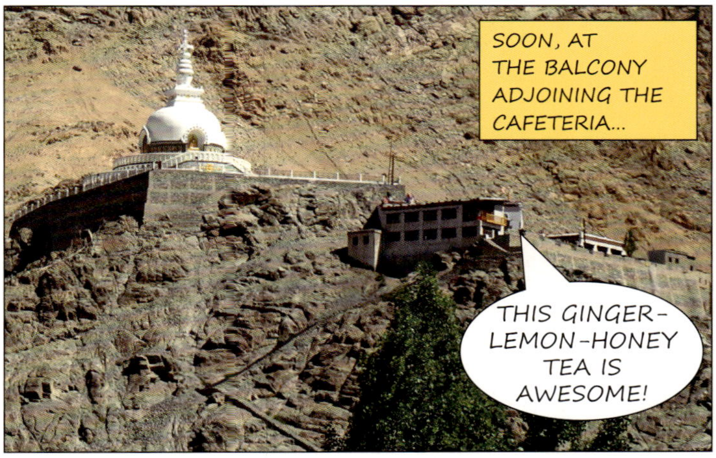
SOON, AT THE BALCONY ADJOINING THE CAFETERIA...
THIS GINGER-LEMON-HONEY TEA IS AWESOME!

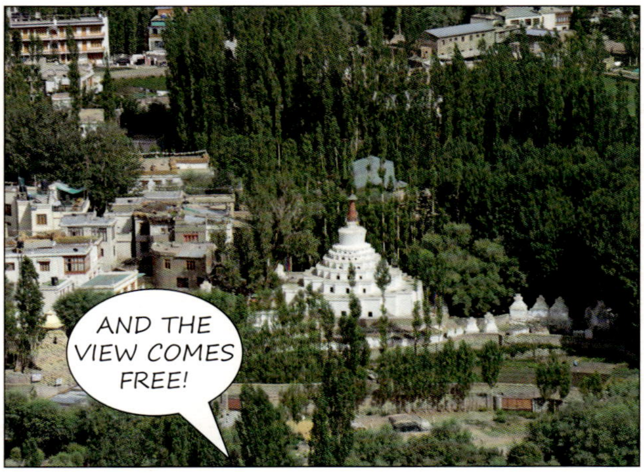
AND THE VIEW COMES FREE!

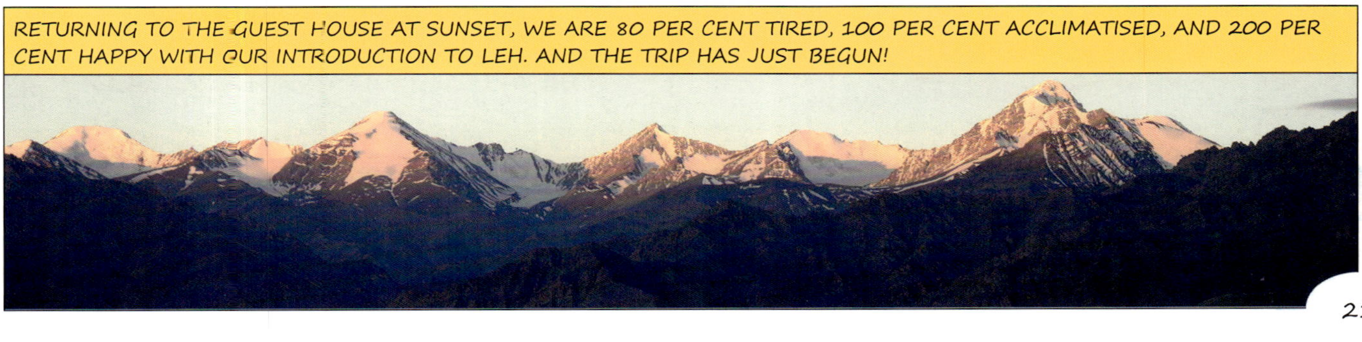
RETURNING TO THE GUEST HOUSE AT SUNSET, WE ARE 80 PER CENT TIRED, 100 PER CENT ACCLIMATISED, AND 200 PER CENT HAPPY WITH OUR INTRODUCTION TO LEH. AND THE TRIP HAS JUST BEGUN!

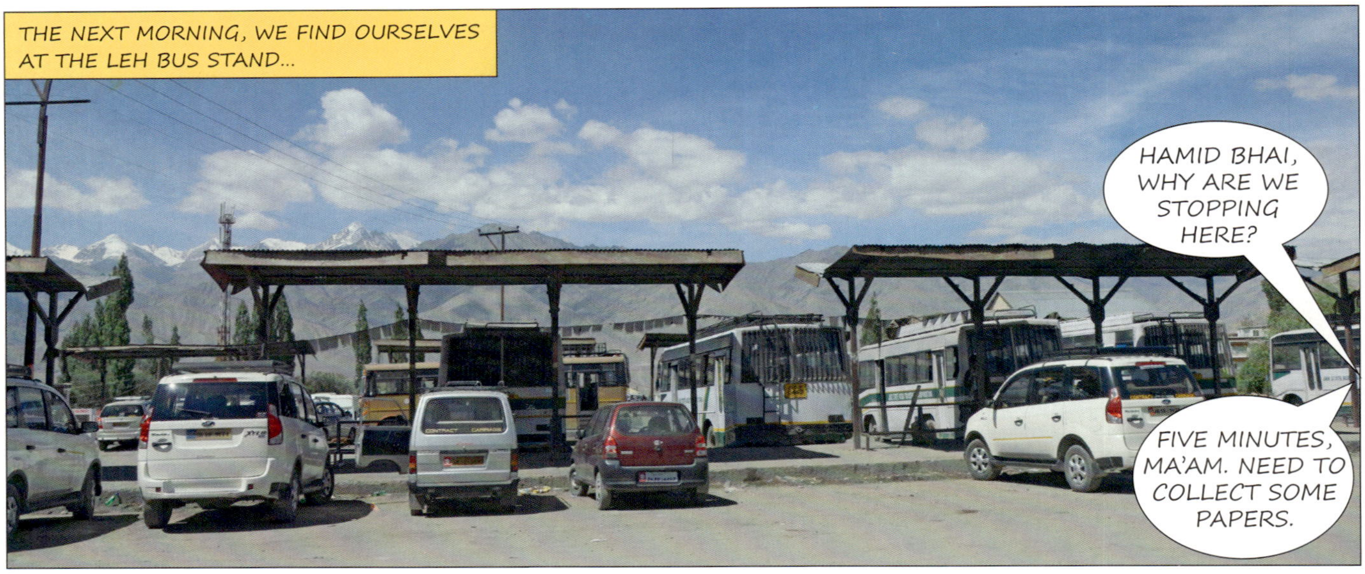

THE NEXT MORNING, WE FIND OURSELVES AT THE LEH BUS STAND...
HAMID BHAI, WHY ARE WE STOPPING HERE?
FIVE MINUTES, MA'AM. NEED TO COLLECT SOME PAPERS.

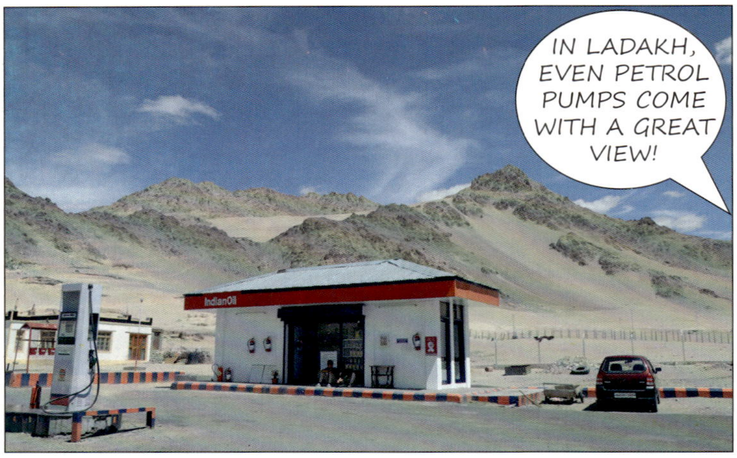

IN LADAKH, EVEN PETROL PUMPS COME WITH A GREAT VIEW!
IndianOil

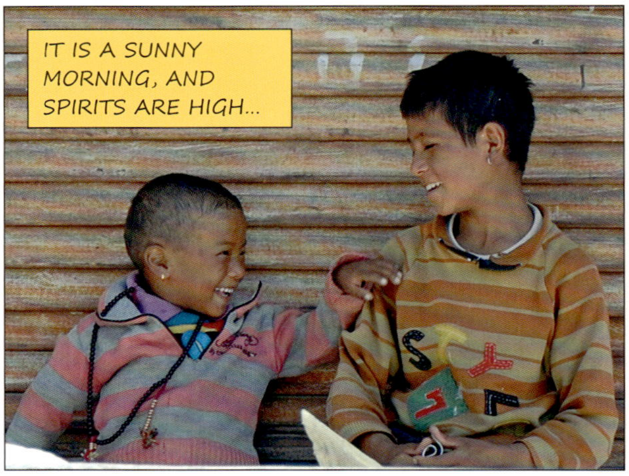

IT IS A SUNNY MORNING, AND SPIRITS ARE HIGH...

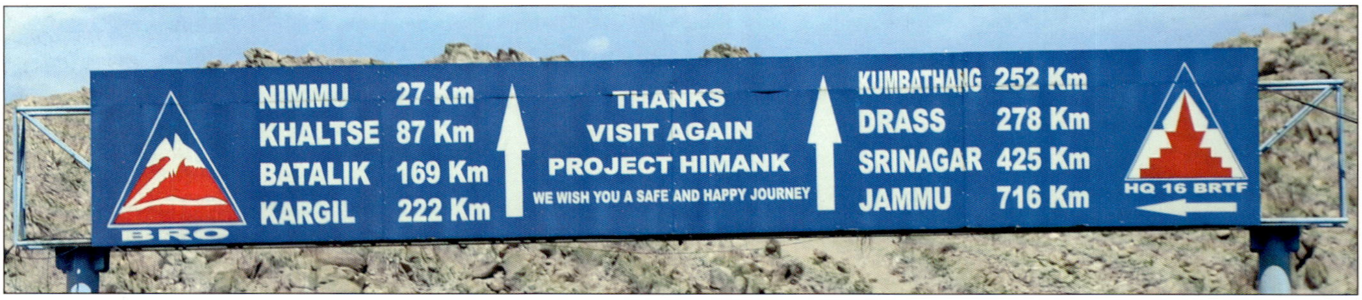

NIMMU 27 Km
KHALTSE 87 Km
BATALIK 169 Km
KARGIL 222 Km
THANKS
VISIT AGAIN
PROJECT HIMANK
WE WISH YOU A SAFE AND HAPPY JOURNEY
KUMBATHANG 252 Km
DRASS 278 Km
SRINAGAR 425 Km
JAMMU 716 Km
BRO
HQ 16 BRTF

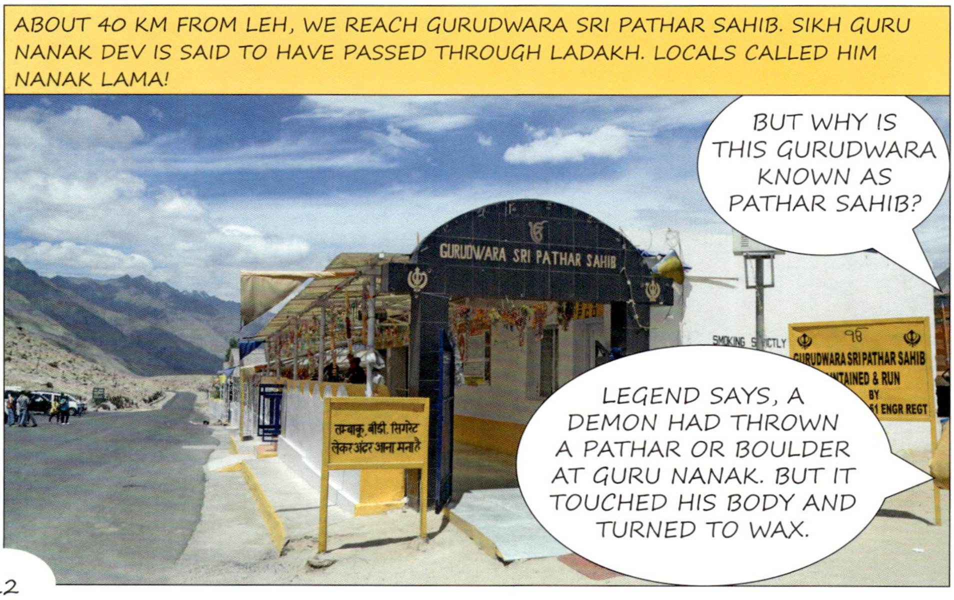

ABOUT 40 KM FROM LEH, WE REACH GURUDWARA SRI PATHAR SAHIB. SIKH GURU NANAK DEV IS SAID TO HAVE PASSED THROUGH LADAKH. LOCALS CALLED HIM NANAK LAMA!
BUT WHY IS THIS GURUDWARA KNOWN AS PATHAR SAHIB?
GURUDWARA SRI PATHAR SAHIB
तम्बाकू, बीड़ी, सिगरेट
लेकर अंदर आना मना है
LEGEND SAYS, A DEMON HAD THROWN A PATHAR OR BOULDER AT GURU NANAK. BUT IT TOUCHED HIS BODY AND TURNED TO WAX.

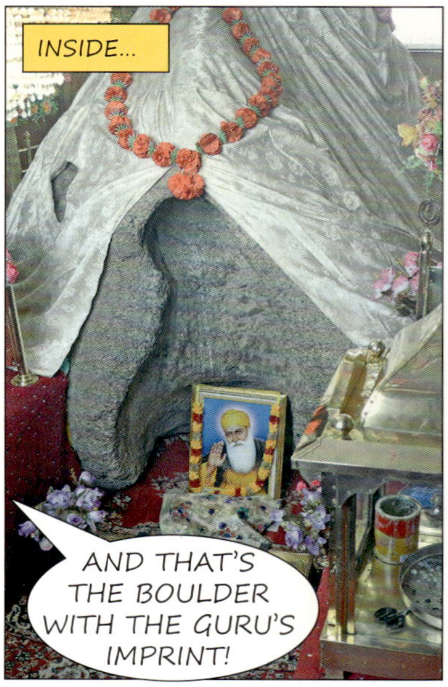

INSIDE...
AND THAT'S THE BOULDER WITH THE GURU'S IMPRINT!

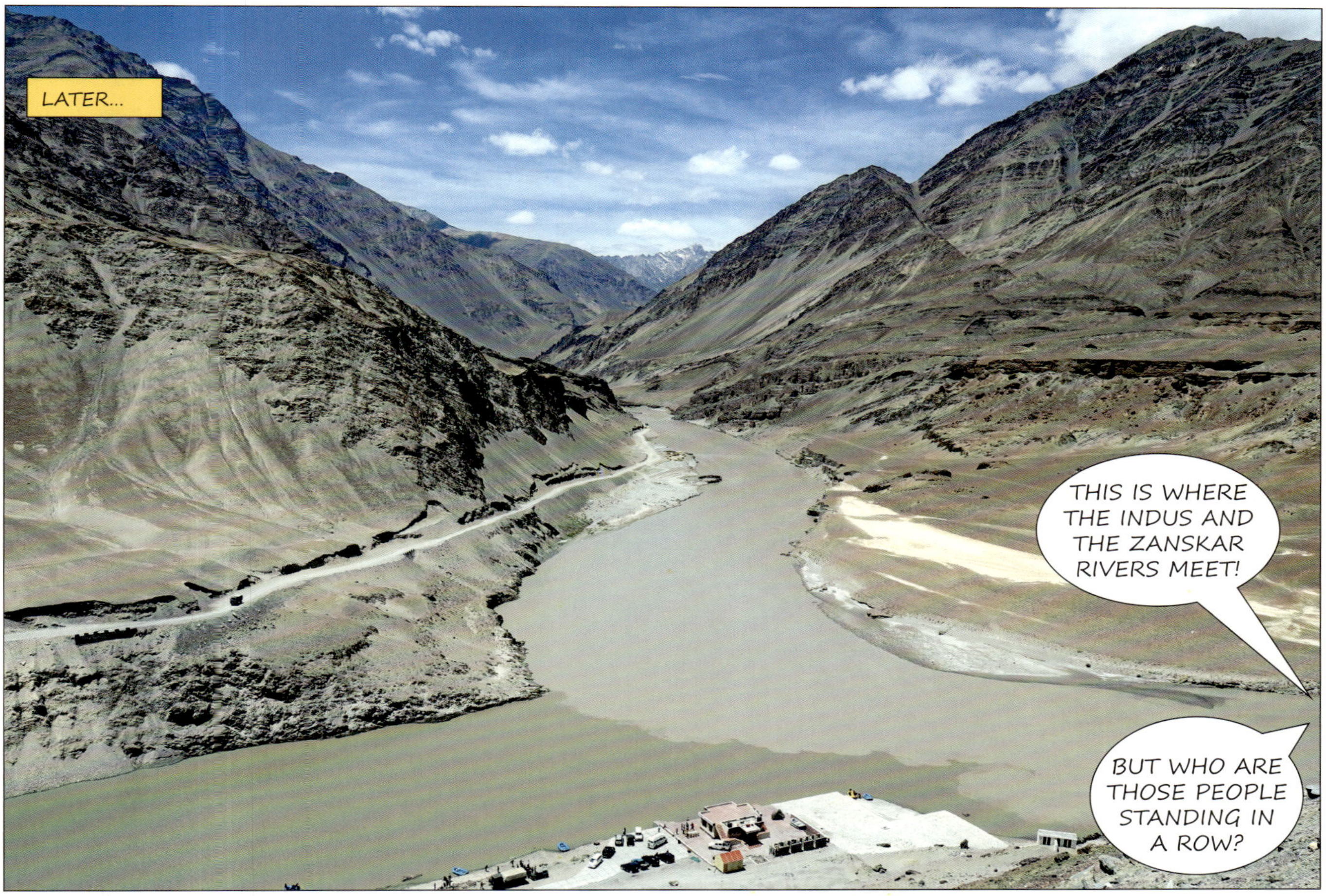
LATER...
THIS IS WHERE THE INDUS AND THE ZANSKAR RIVERS MEET!
BUT WHO ARE THOSE PEOPLE STANDING IN A ROW?

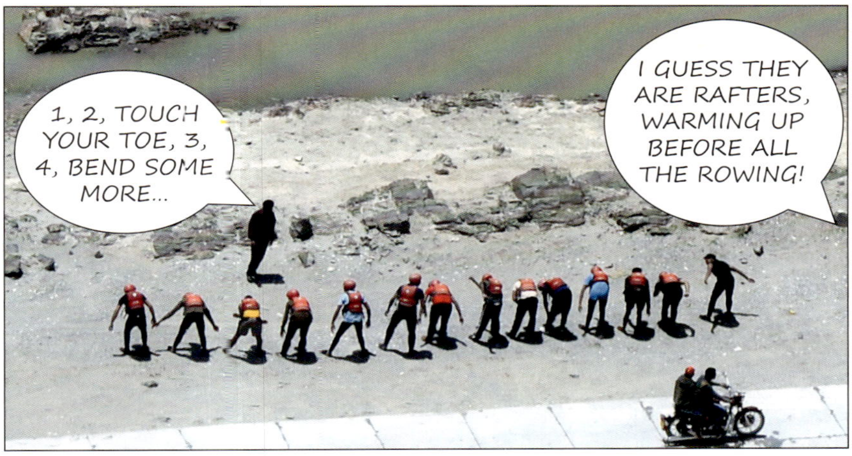
1, 2, TOUCH YOUR TOE, 3, 4, BEND SOME MORE...
I GUESS THEY ARE RAFTERS, WARMING UP BEFORE ALL THE ROWING!

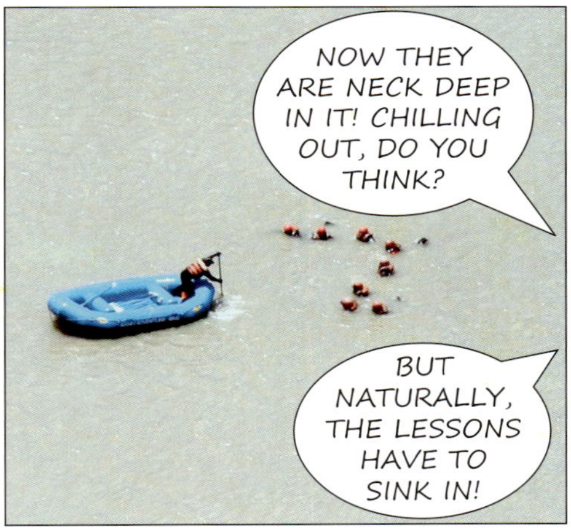
NOW THEY ARE NECK DEEP IN IT! CHILLING OUT, DO YOU THINK?
BUT NATURALLY, THE LESSONS HAVE TO SINK IN!

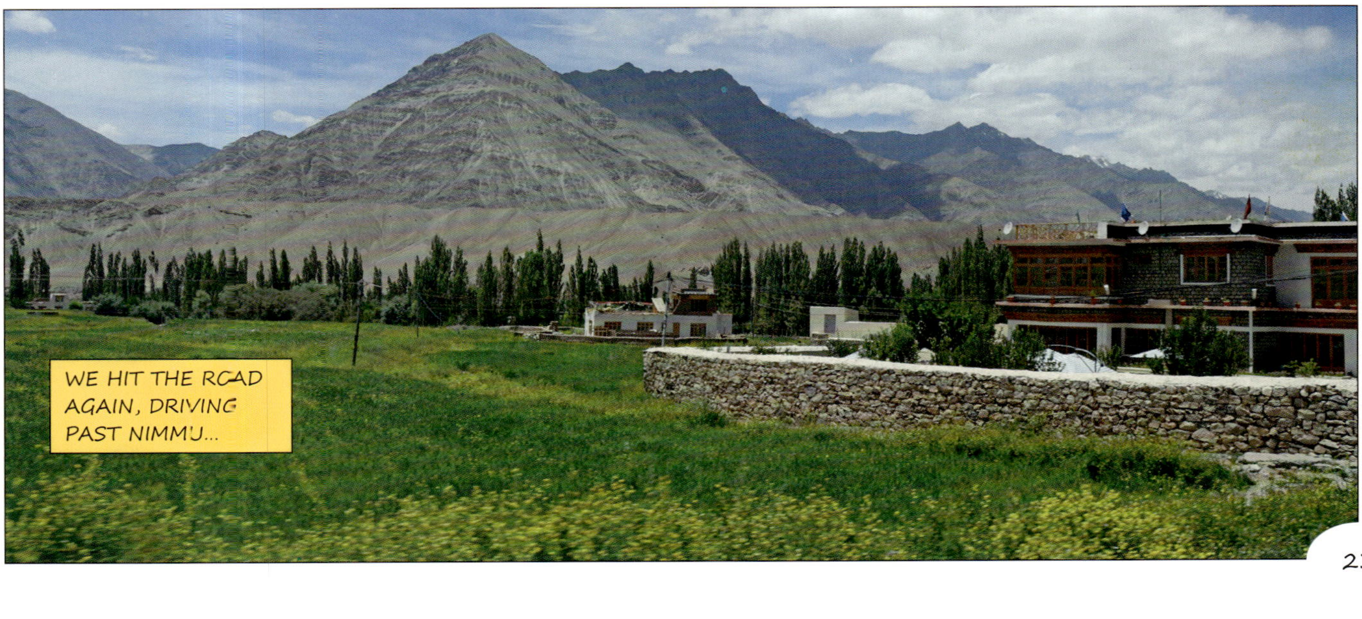
WE HIT THE ROAD AGAIN, DRIVING PAST NIMMU...

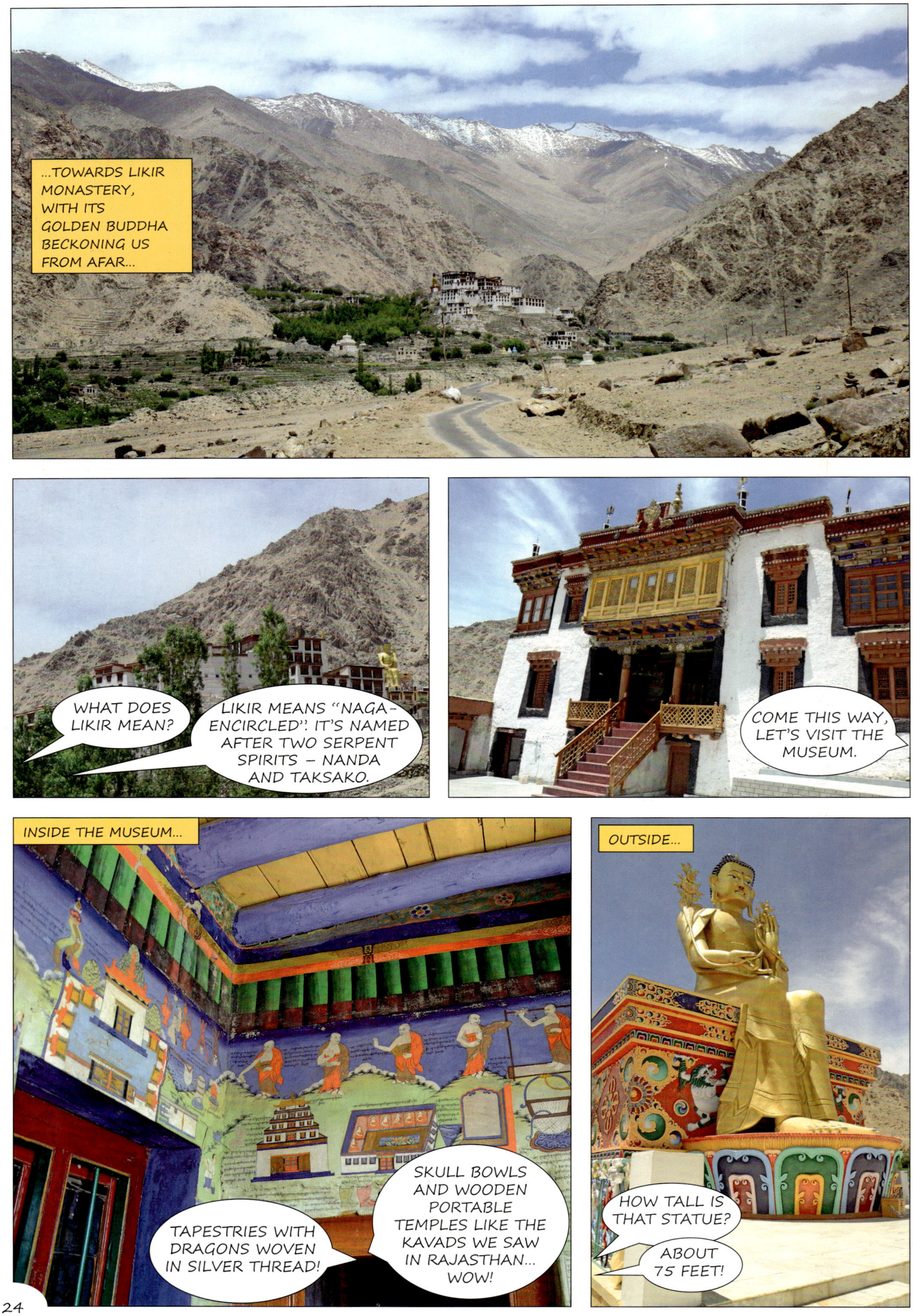
...TOWARDS LIKIR MONASTERY, WITH ITS GOLDEN BUDDHA BECKONING US FROM AFAR...
WHAT DOES LIKIR MEAN?
LIKIR MEANS "NAGA-ENCIRCLED": IT'S NAMED AFTER TWO SERPENT SPIRITS – NANDA AND TAKSAKO.
COME THIS WAY, LET'S VISIT THE MUSEUM.
INSIDE THE MUSEUM...
TAPESTRIES WITH DRAGONS WOVEN IN SILVER THREAD!
SKULL BOWLS AND WOODEN PORTABLE TEMPLES LIKE THE KAVADS WE SAW IN RAJASTHAN... WOW!
OUTSIDE...
HOW TALL IS THAT STATUE?
ABOUT 75 FEET!

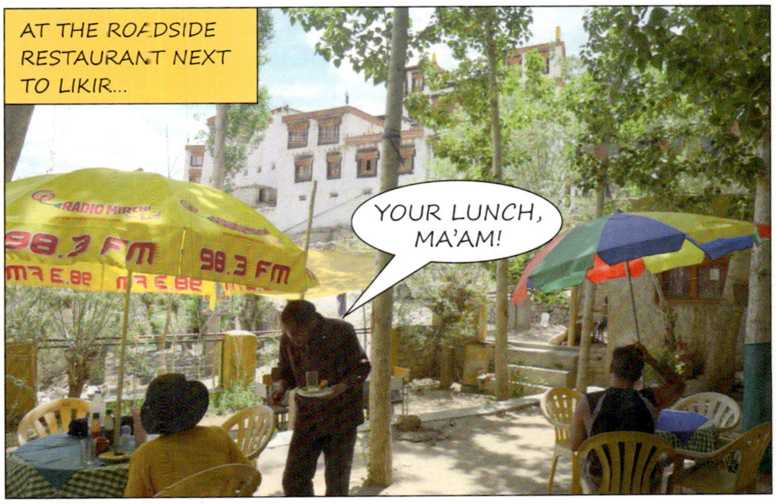
AT THE ROADSIDE RESTAURANT NEXT TO LIKIR...
YOUR LUNCH, MA'AM!

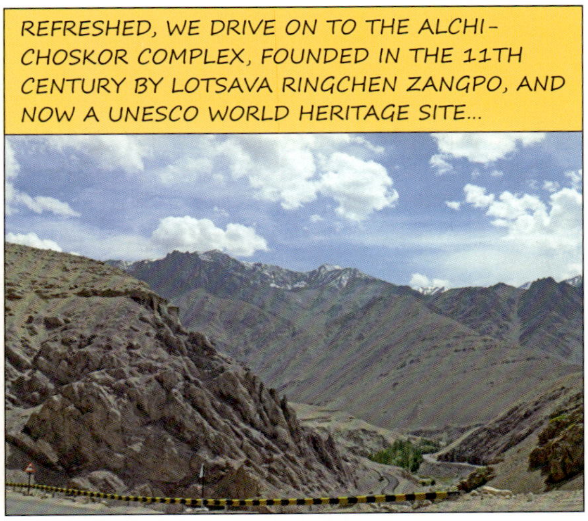
REFRESHED, WE DRIVE ON TO THE ALCHI-CHOSKOR COMPLEX, FOUNDED IN THE 11TH CENTURY BY LOTSAVA RINGCHEN ZANGPO, AND NOW A UNESCO WORLD HERITAGE SITE...

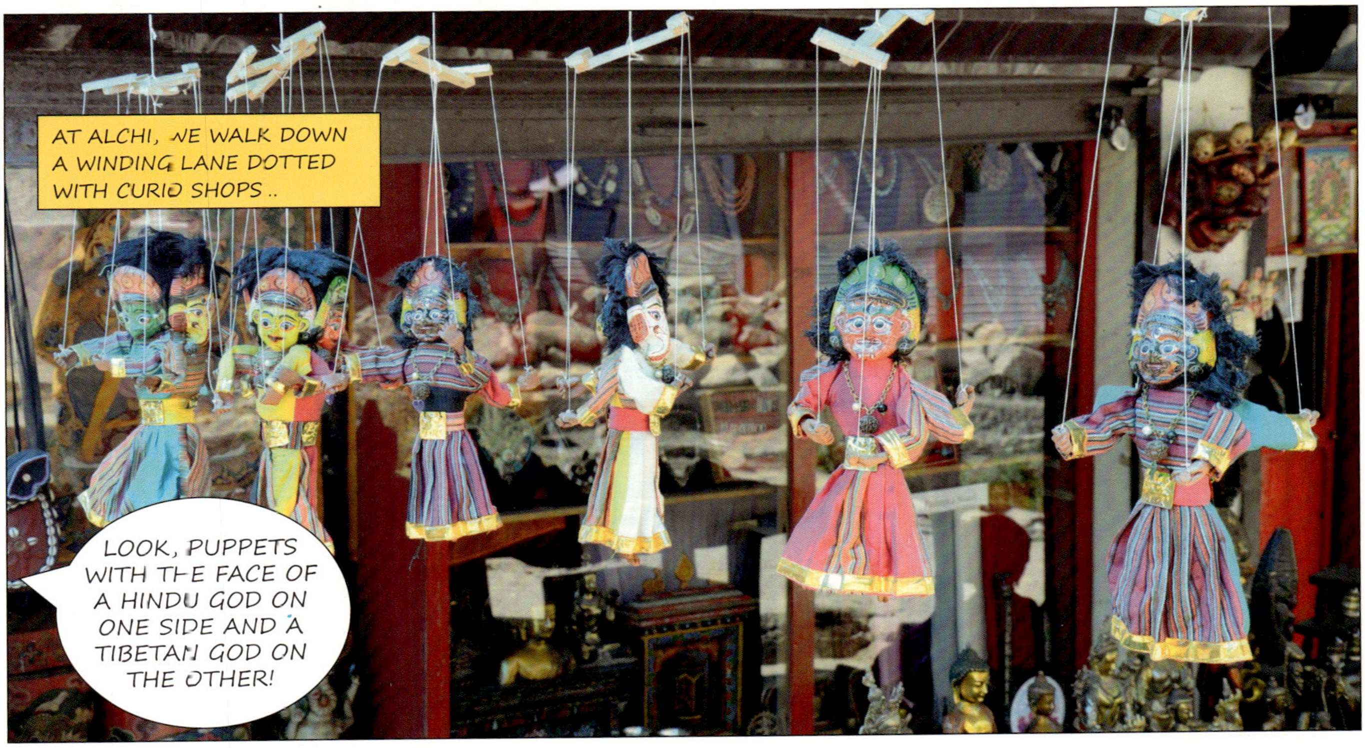
AT ALCHI, WE WALK DOWN A WINDING LANE DOTTED WITH CURIO SHOPS ..
LOOK, PUPPETS WITH THE FACE OF A HINDU GOD ON ONE SIDE AND A TIBETAN GOD ON THE OTHER!

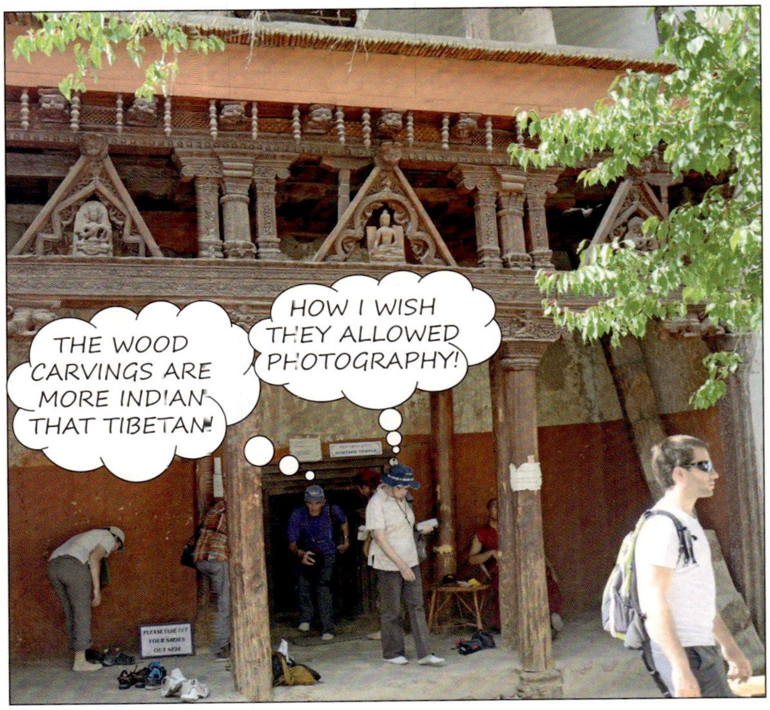
THE WOOD CARVINGS ARE MORE INDIAN THAT TIBETAN!
HOW I WISH THEY ALLOWED PHOTOGRAPHY!

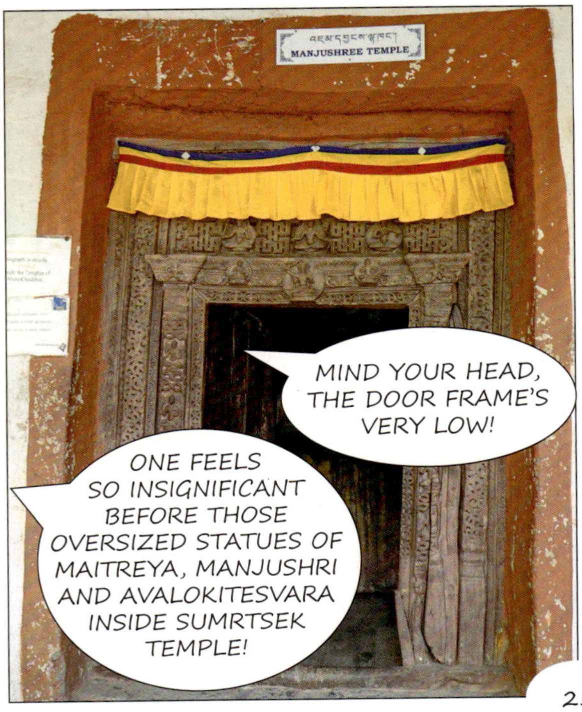
MANJUSHREE TEMPLE
MIND YOUR HEAD, THE DOOR FRAME'S VERY LOW!
ONE FEELS SO INSIGNIFICANT BEFORE THOSE OVERSIZED STATUES OF MAITREYA, MANJUSHRI AND AVALOKITESVARA INSIDE SUMRTSEK TEMPLE!

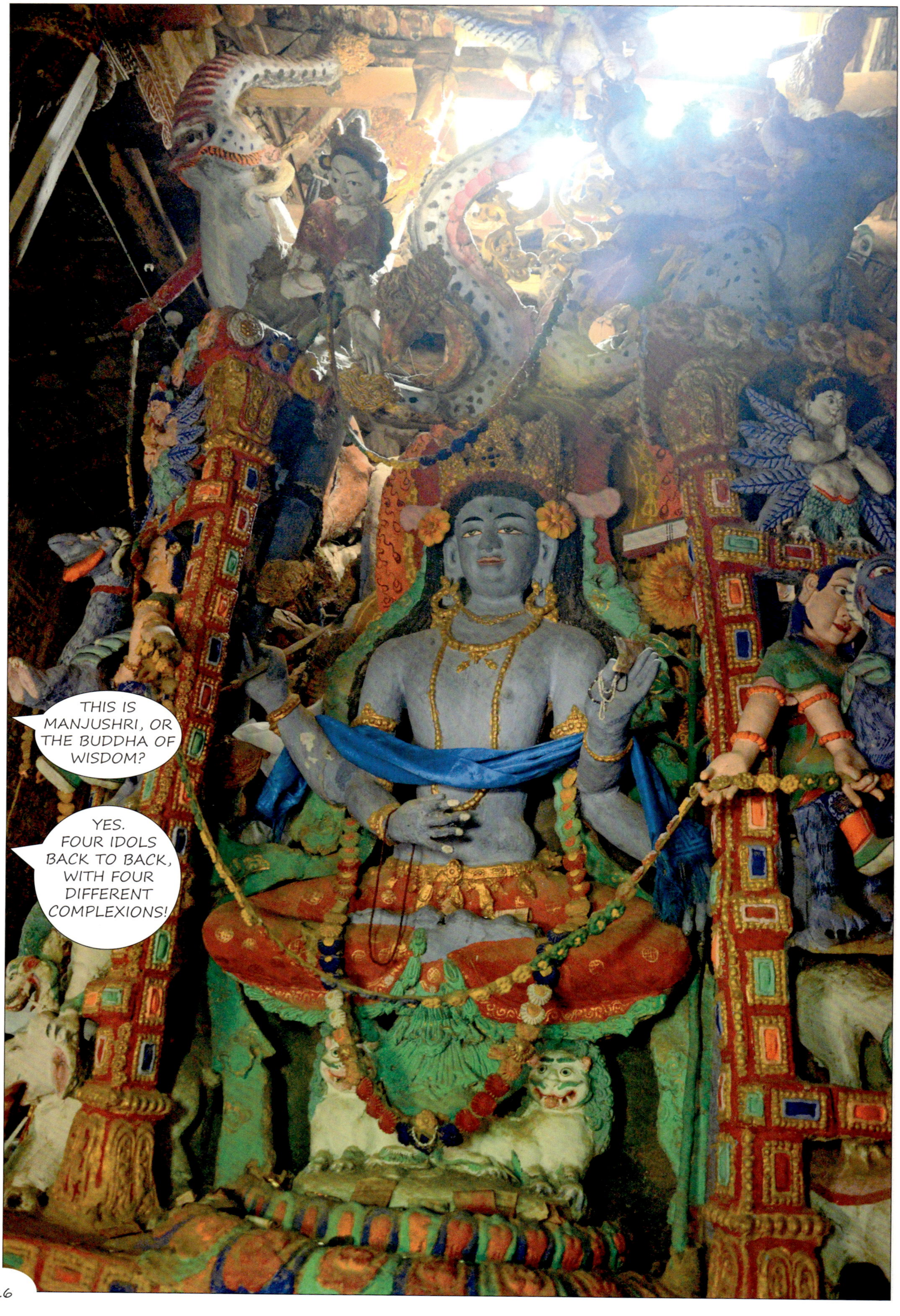
THIS IS MANJUSHRI, OR THE BUDDHA OF WISDOM?
YES. FOUR IDOLS BACK TO BACK, WITH FOUR DIFFERENT COMPLEXIONS!

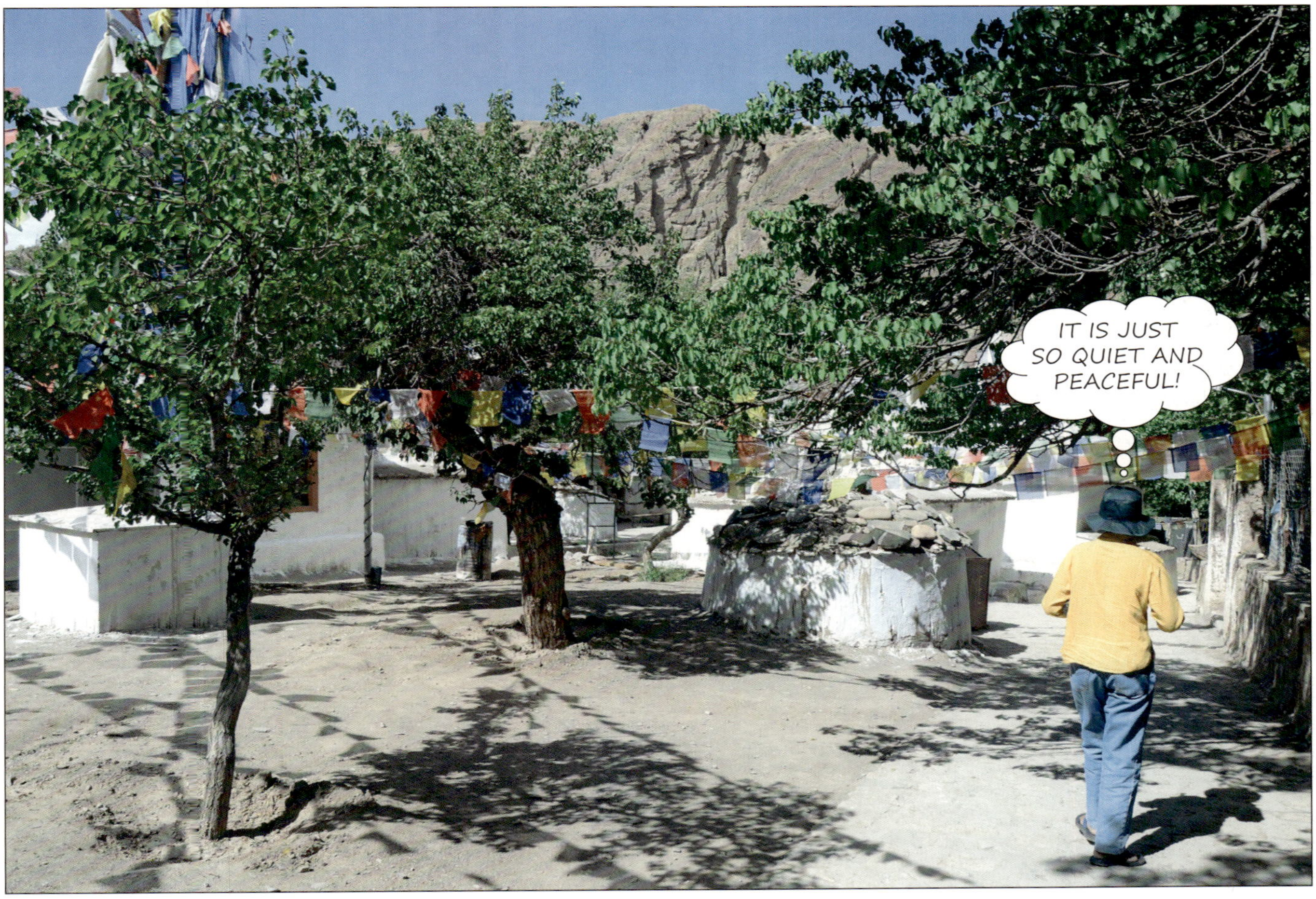
IT IS JUST
SO QUIET AND
PEACEFUL!

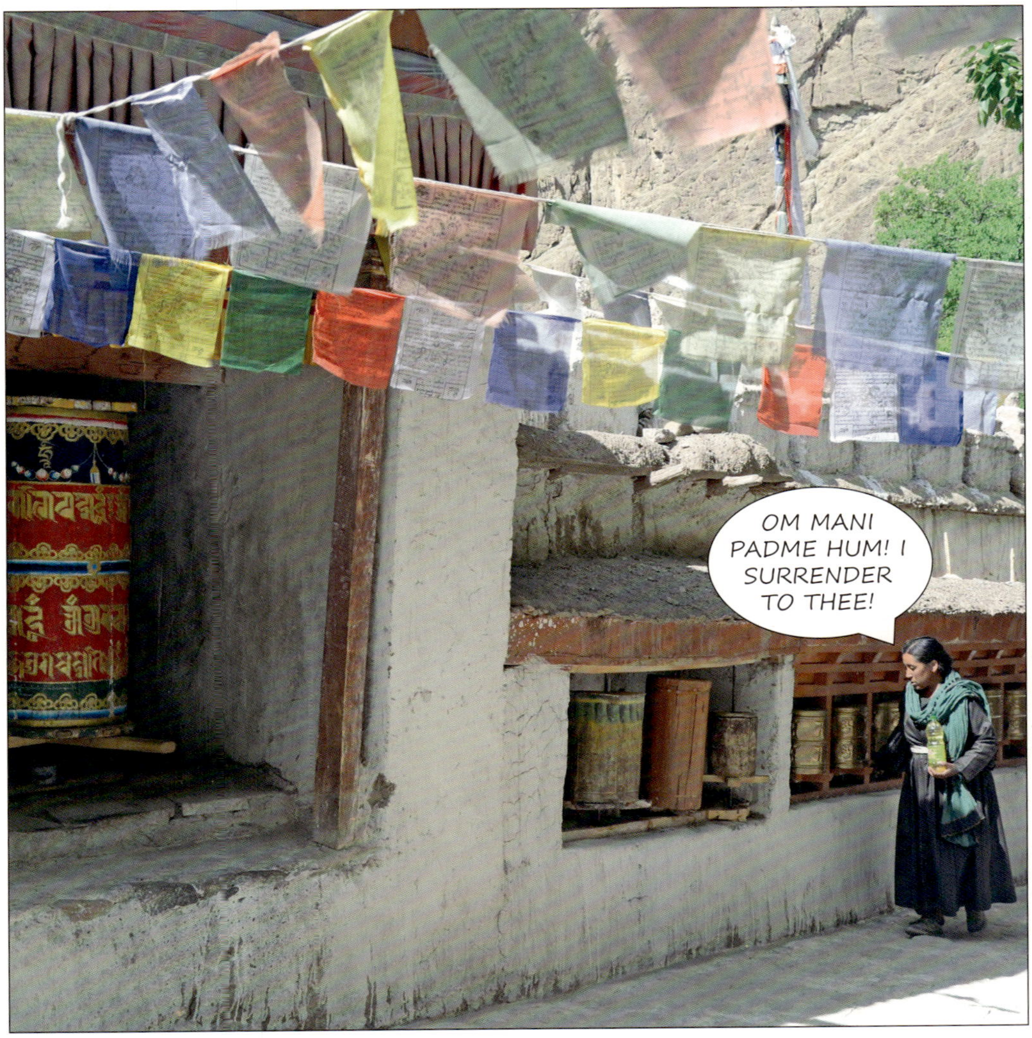
OM MANI
PADME HUM! I
SURRENDER
TO THEE!

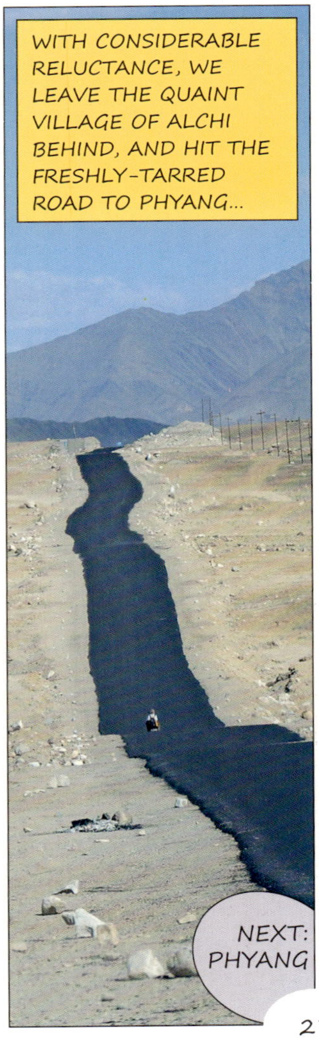
WITH CONSIDERABLE
RELUCTANCE, WE
LEAVE THE QUAINT
VILLAGE OF ALCHI
BEHIND, AND HIT THE
FRESHLY-TARRED
ROAD TO PHYANG...
NEXT:
PHYANG

Chapter II: Phyang

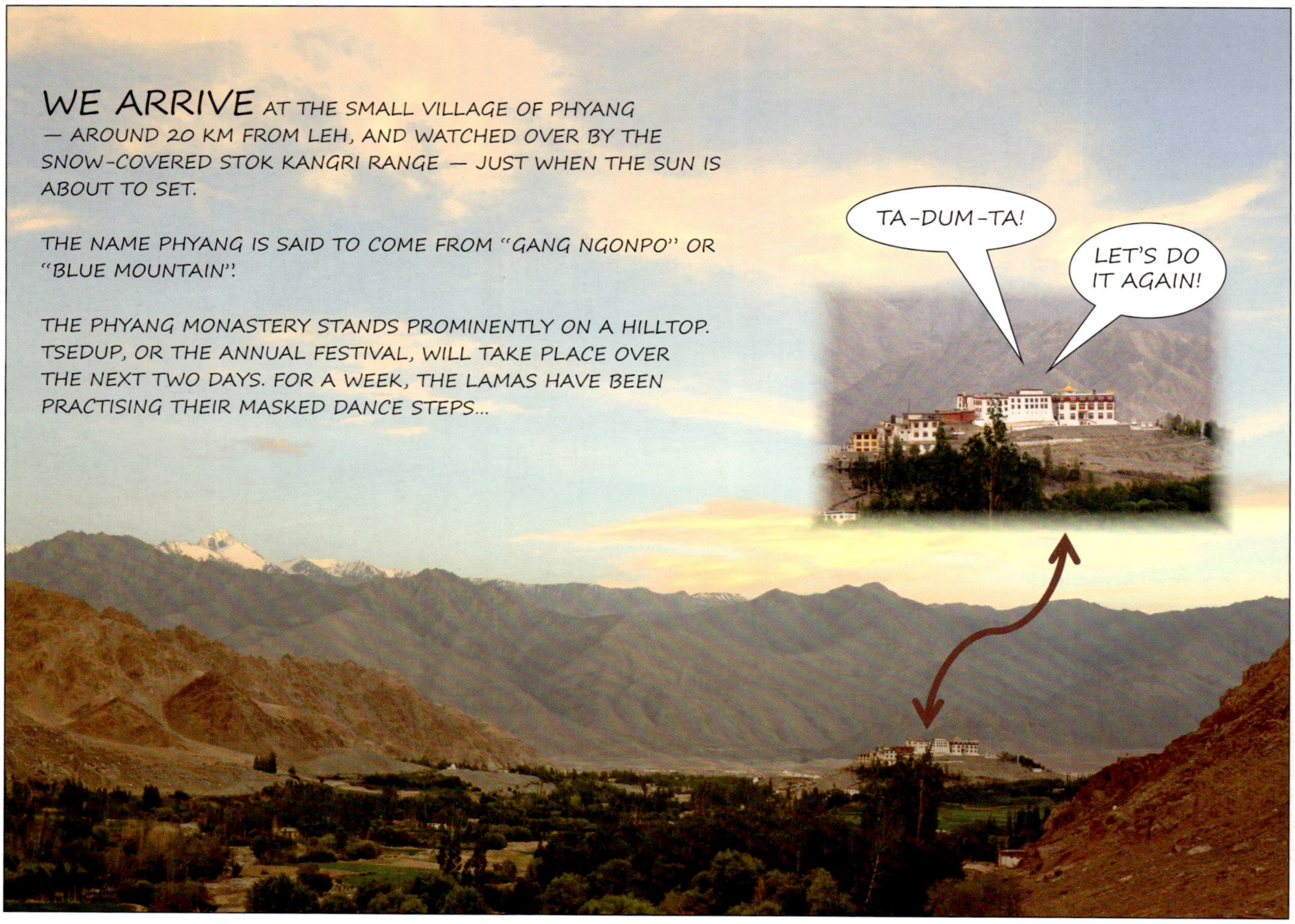

THE HIDDEN NORTH GUEST HOUSE, RUN BY A LADAKHI-ITALIAN FAMILY, IS THE ONLY ACCOMMODATION FOR TOURISTS AT PHYANG.

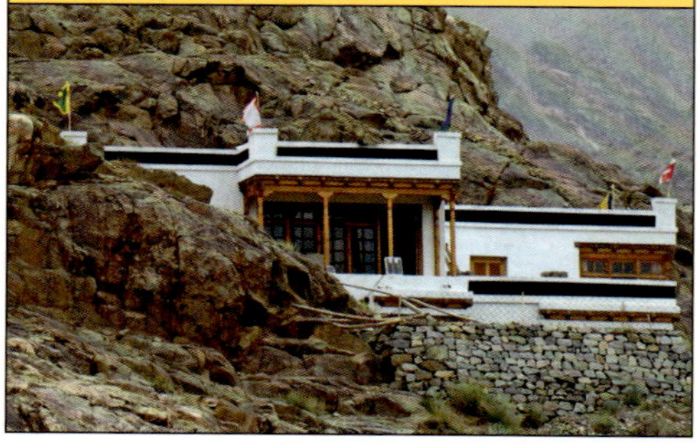

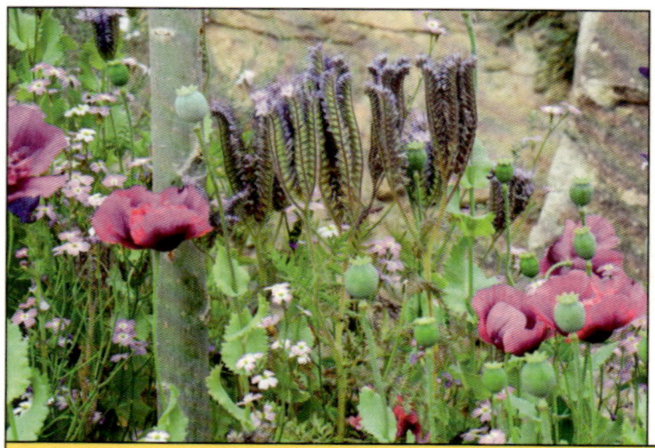

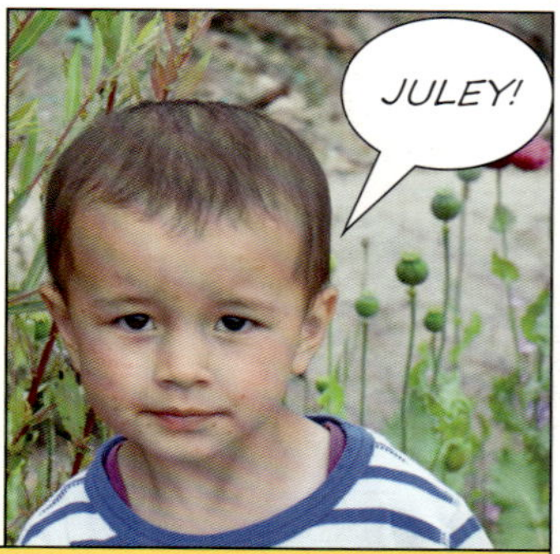

LOVELY FLOWERS BLOOM ON THE GROUNDS OF THE HIDDEN NORTH GUEST HOUSE. THE GARDENER, TASHI NAMGYAL, SAYS "HI" TO US HERE, IN LADAKHI.

SOMETIMES, TASHI NAMGYAL IS BUSY WASHING UTENSILS. AFTER ALL, AS THE FUTURE GUEST HOUSE OWNER, HE HAS TO HELP HIS PARENTS, RIGHT?

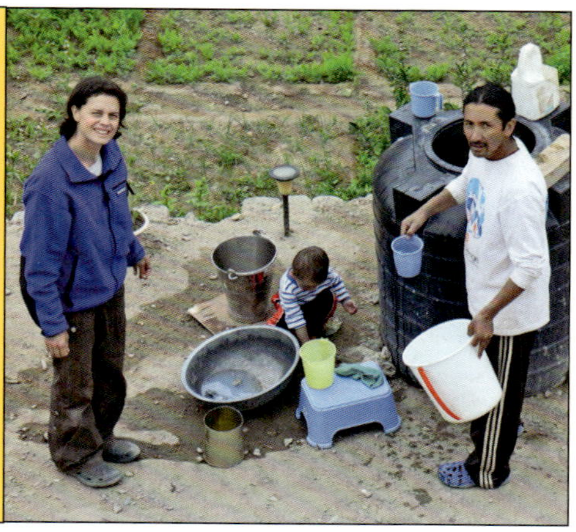

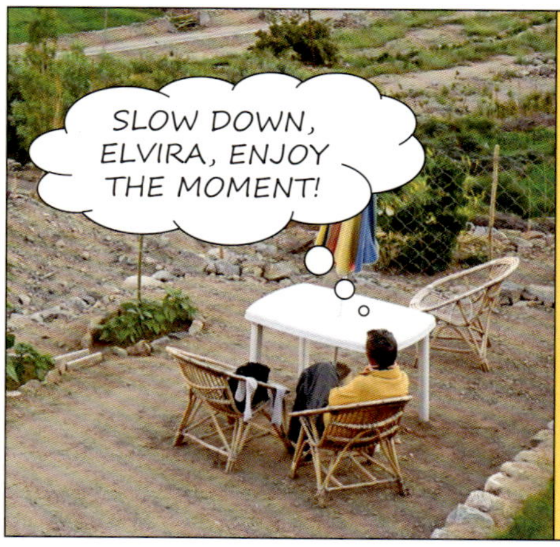

RELAXING IS SERIOUS BUSINESS TOO. THIS GERMAN LADY HAS BEEN TRAVELLING SOLO IN LADAKH, RELYING ON PUBLIC TRANSPORT AND TWO GOOD LEGS.

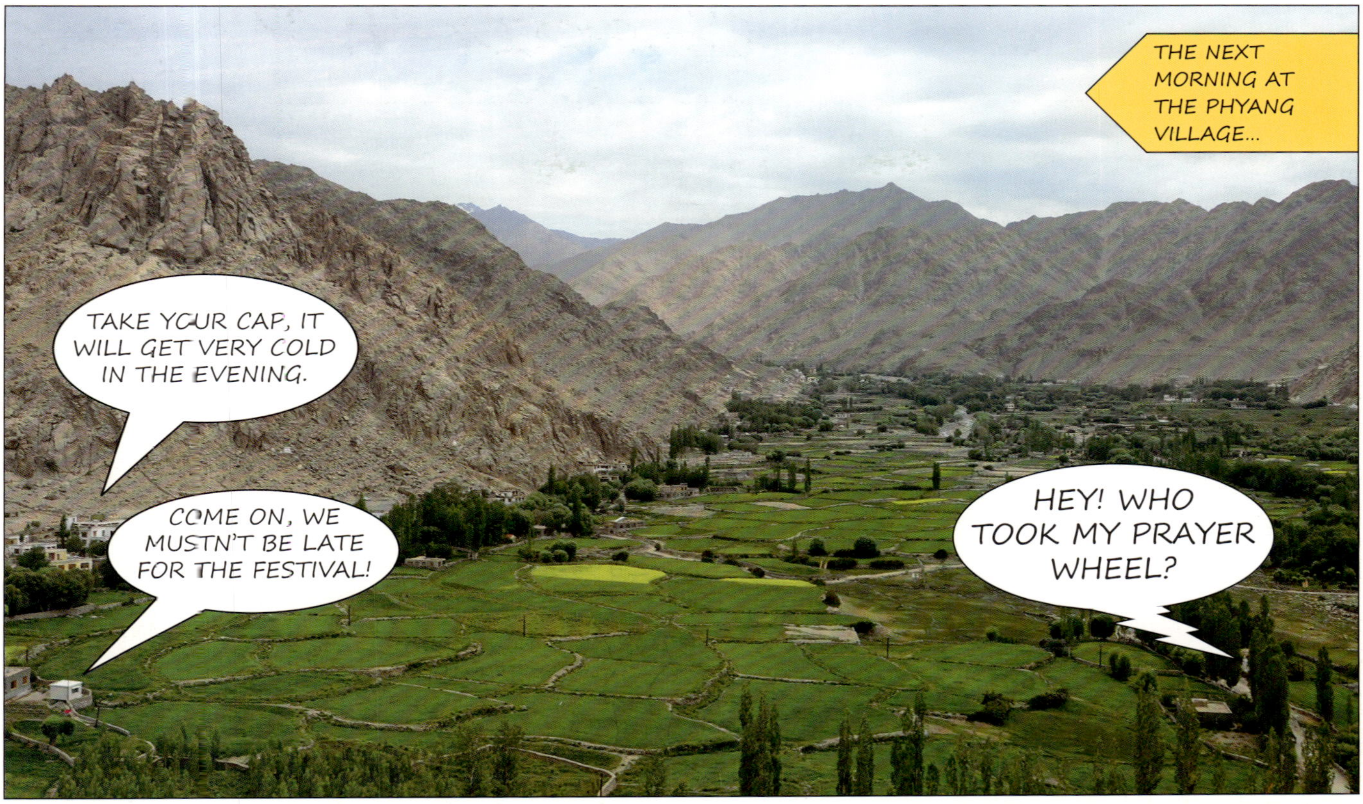
THE NEXT MORNING AT THE PHYANG VILLAGE...
TAKE YOUR CAP, IT WILL GET VERY COLD IN THE EVENING.
COME ON, WE MUSTN'T BE LATE FOR THE FESTIVAL!
HEY! WHO TOOK MY PRAYER WHEEL?

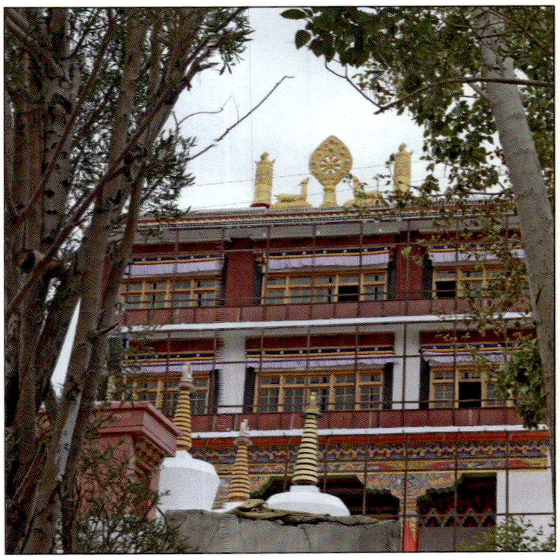

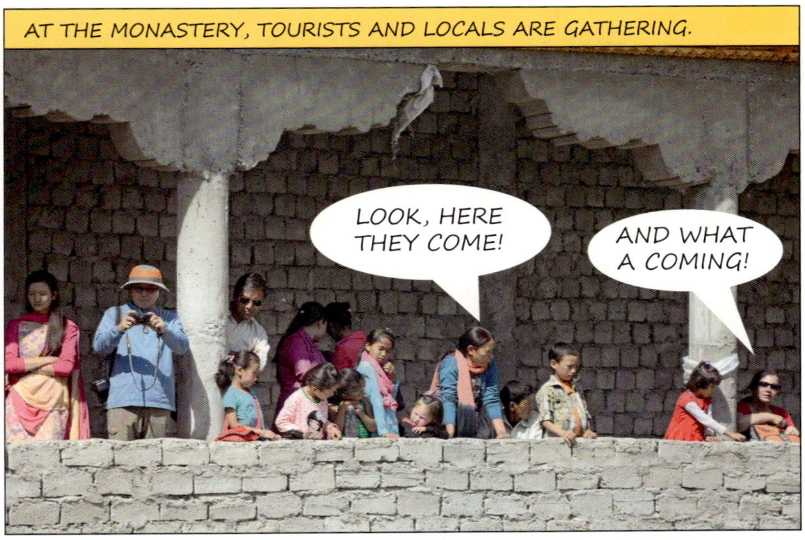
AT THE MONASTERY, TOURISTS AND LOCALS ARE GATHERING.
LOOK, HERE THEY COME!
AND WHAT A COMING!

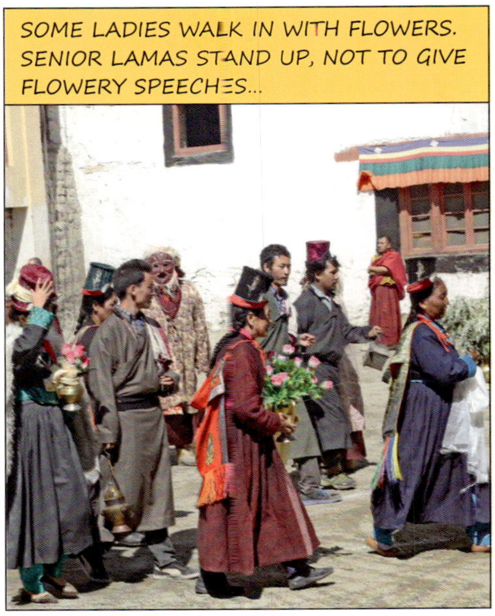
SOME LADIES WALK IN WITH FLOWERS. SENIOR LAMAS STAND UP, NOT TO GIVE FLOWERY SPEECHES...

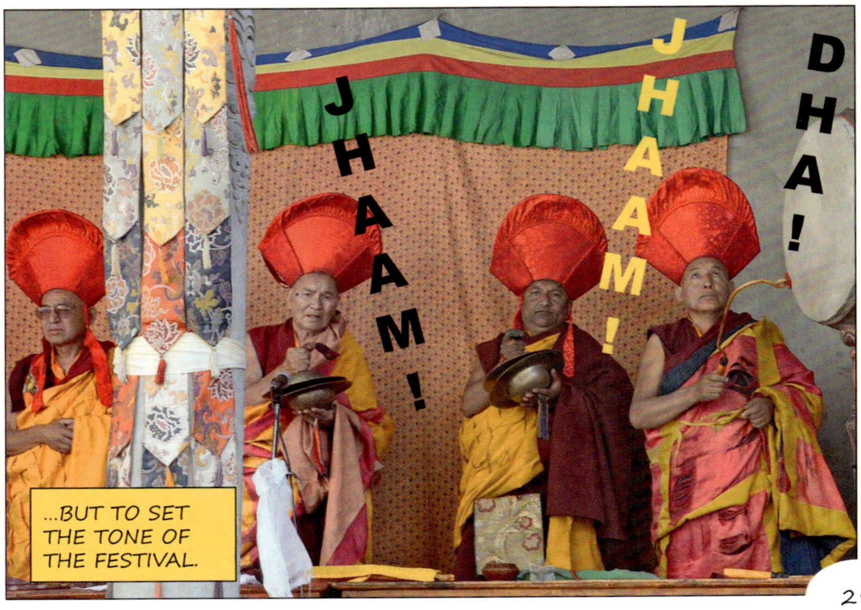
JHAAM!
JHAAM!
DHA!
...BUT TO SET THE TONE OF THE FESTIVAL.

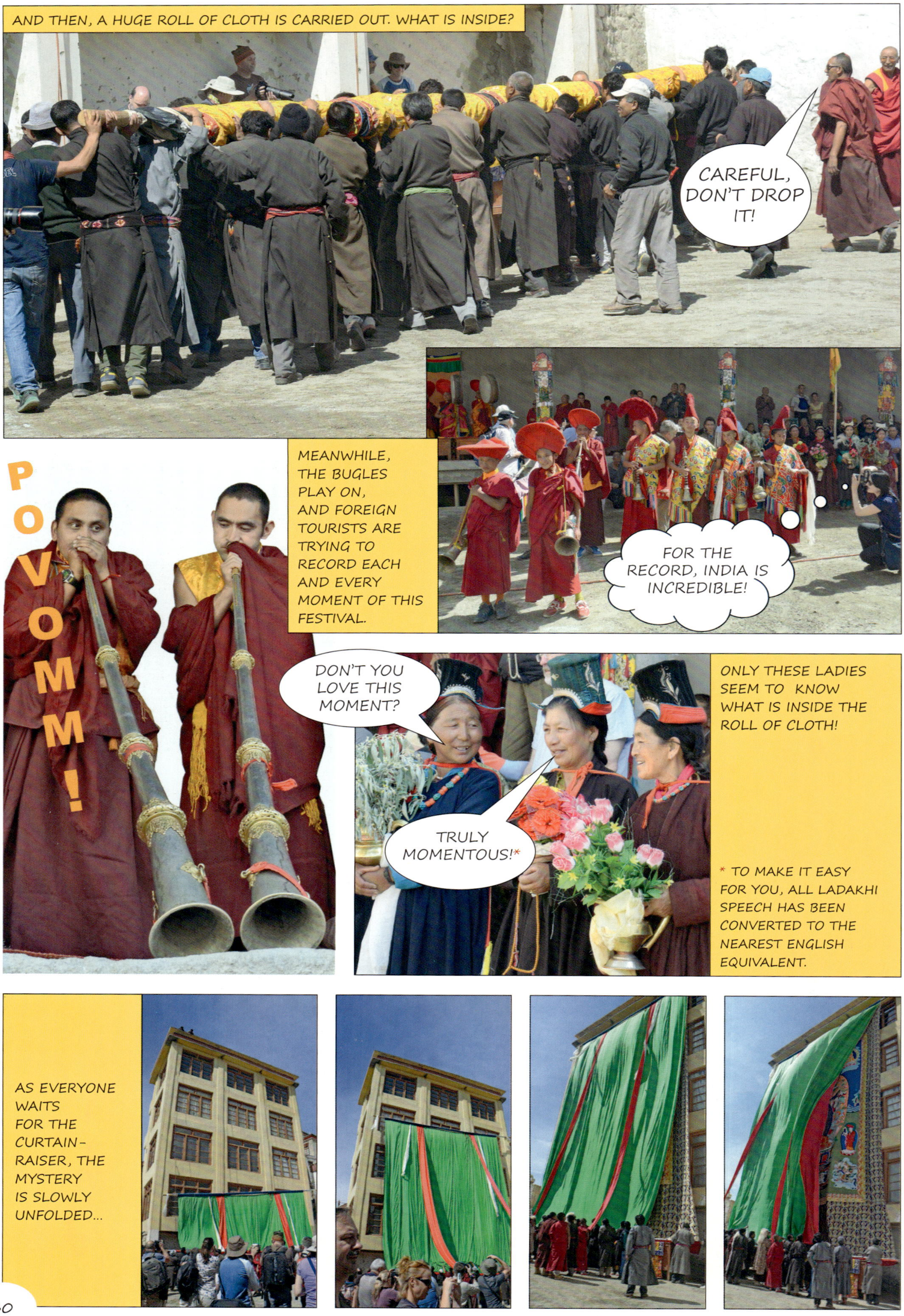
AND THEN, A HUGE ROLL OF CLOTH IS CARRIED OUT. WHAT IS INSIDE?
CAREFUL, DON'T DROP IT!
POVOMM!
MEANWHILE, THE BUGLES PLAY ON, AND FOREIGN TOURISTS ARE TRYING TO RECORD EACH AND EVERY MOMENT OF THIS FESTIVAL.
FOR THE RECORD, INDIA IS INCREDIBLE!
DON'T YOU LOVE THIS MOMENT?
TRULY MOMENTOUS!*
ONLY THESE LADIES SEEM TO KNOW WHAT IS INSIDE THE ROLL OF CLOTH!
* TO MAKE IT EASY FOR YOU, ALL LADAKHI SPEECH HAS BEEN CONVERTED TO THE NEAREST ENGLISH EQUIVALENT.
AS EVERYONE WAITS FOR THE CURTAIN-RAISER, THE MYSTERY IS SLOWLY UNFOLDED...

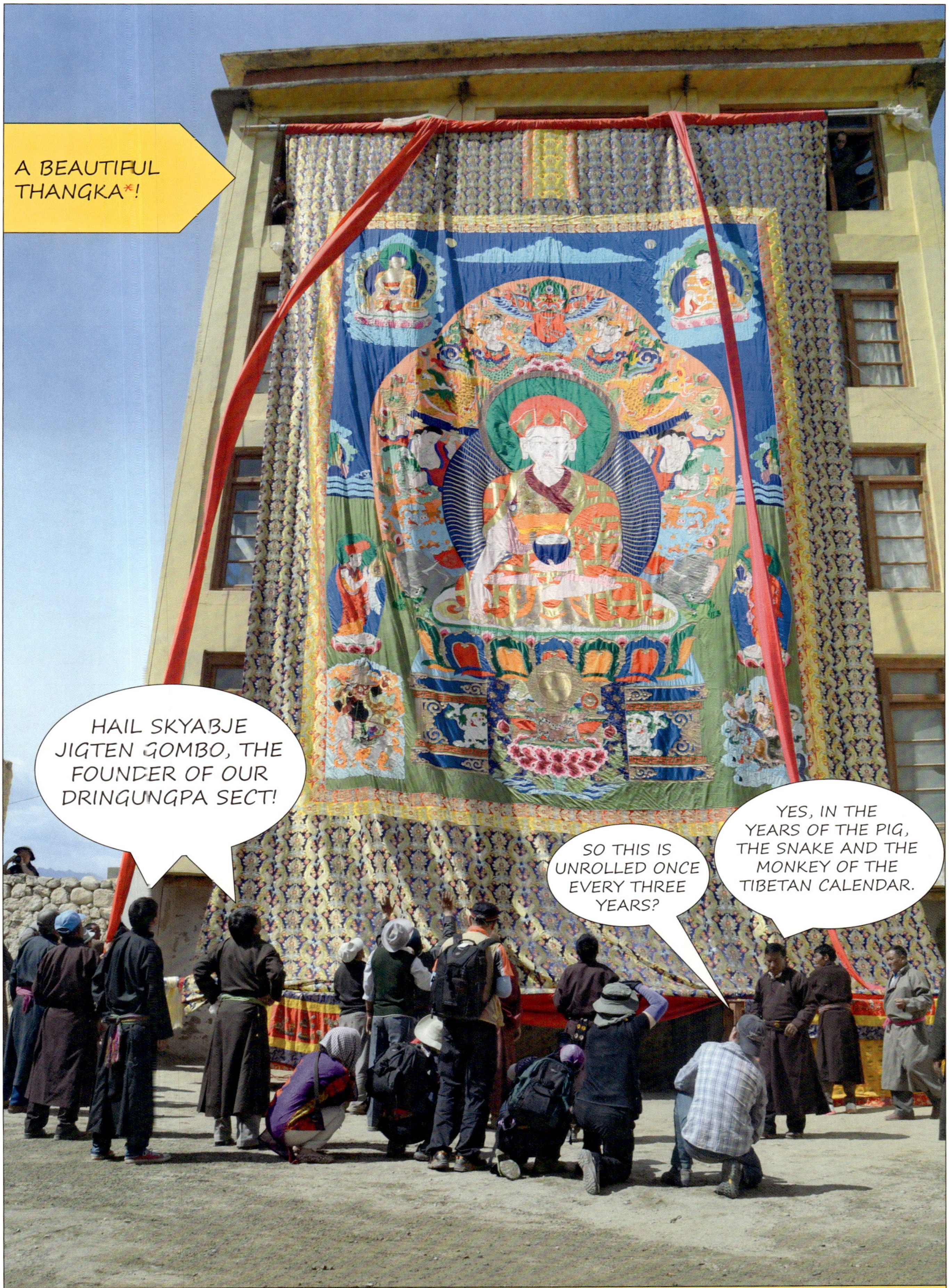

*THE TIBETAN WORDS 'THANG KA' MEAN 'RECORDED MESSAGE'. THANGKAS, PAINTED ON SILK WITH EMBROIDERY OR APPLIQUÉ, DISPLAY A BUDDHIST DEITY OR A SCENE. A LAMA WOULD EASILY CARRY A THANGKA, GO TO A NOMADIC VILLAGE, UNROLL IT AND USE IT TO ILLUSTRATE THE TALES ON BUDDHIST PHILOSOPHY HE WAS NARRATING. ONE ASSUMES THAT THE THANGKA SHOWN HERE WAS NEVER PART OF A TRAVEL KIT!

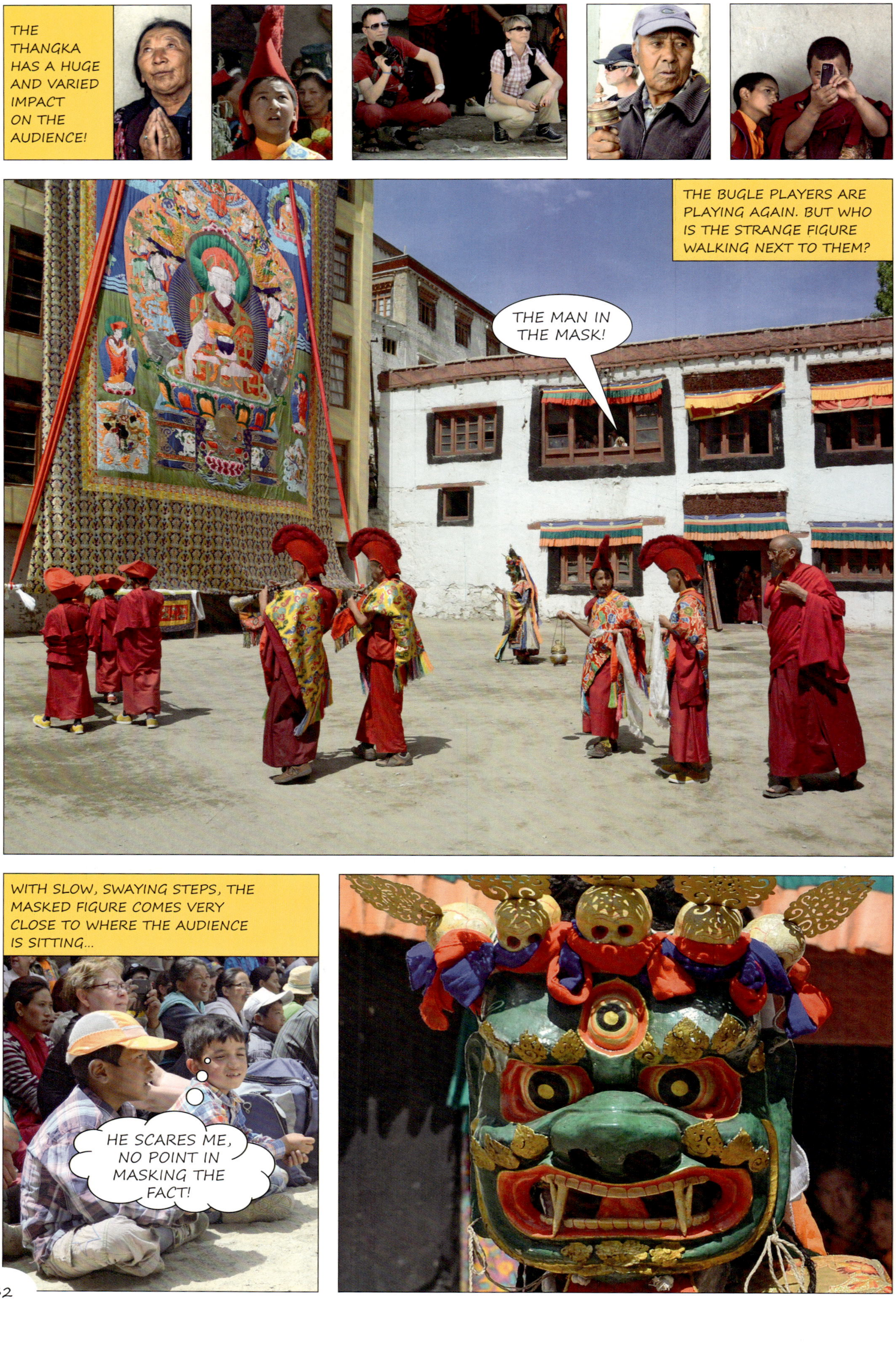
THE THANGKA HAS A HUGE AND VARIED IMPACT ON THE AUDIENCE!
THE BUGLE PLAYERS ARE PLAYING AGAIN. BUT WHO IS THE STRANGE FIGURE WALKING NEXT TO THEM?
THE MAN IN THE MASK!
WITH SLOW, SWAYING STEPS, THE MASKED FIGURE COMES VERY CLOSE TO WHERE THE AUDIENCE IS SITTING...
HE SCARES ME, NO POINT IN MASKING THE FACT!

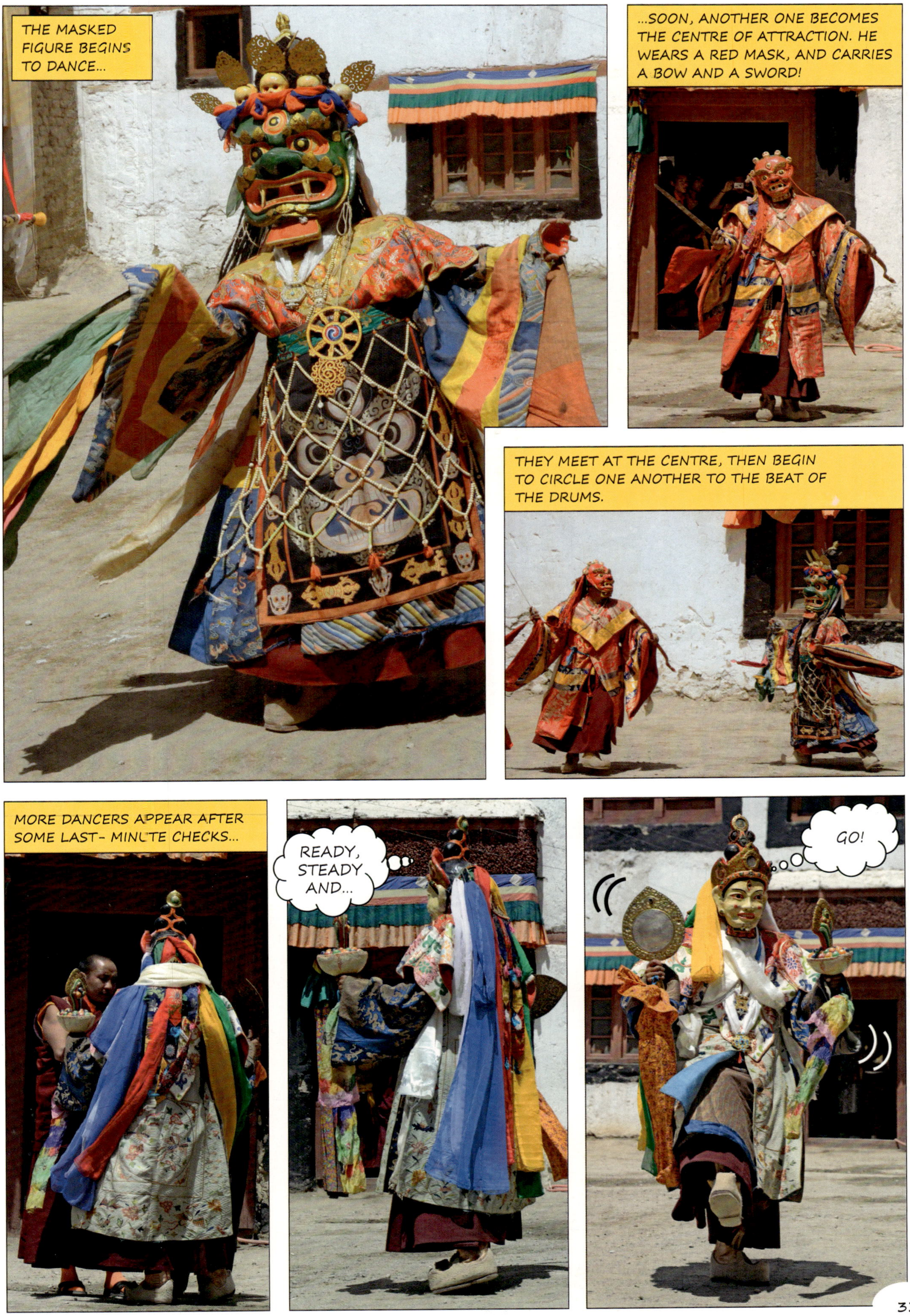
THE MASKED FIGURE BEGINS TO DANCE...
...SOON, ANOTHER ONE BECOMES THE CENTRE OF ATTRACTION. HE WEARS A RED MASK, AND CARRIES A BOW AND A SWORD!
THEY MEET AT THE CENTRE, THEN BEGIN TO CIRCLE ONE ANOTHER TO THE BEAT OF THE DRUMS.
MORE DANCERS APPEAR AFTER SOME LAST- MINUTE CHECKS...
READY, STEADY AND...
GO!

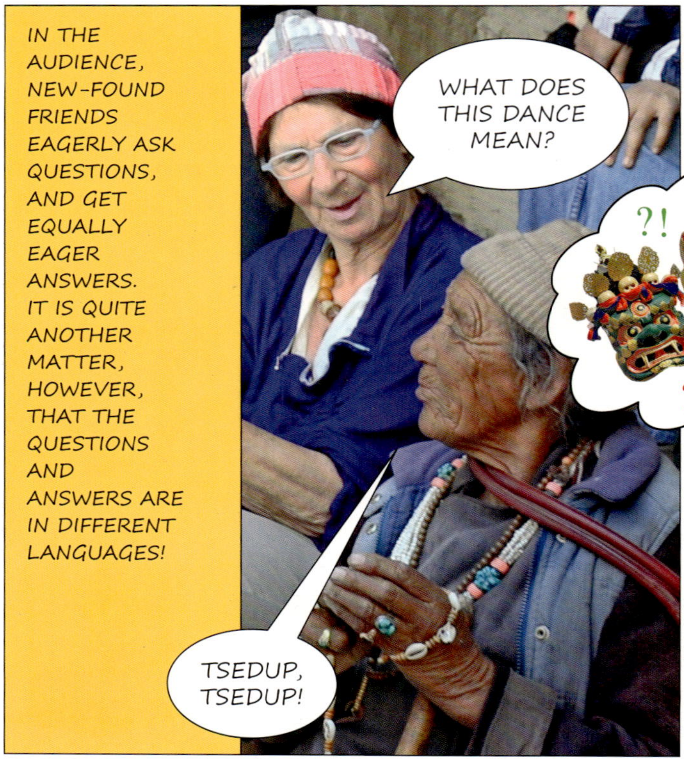
IN THE AUDIENCE, NEW-FOUND FRIENDS EAGERLY ASK QUESTIONS, AND GET EQUALLY EAGER ANSWERS. IT IS QUITE ANOTHER MATTER, HOWEVER, THAT THE QUESTIONS AND ANSWERS ARE IN DIFFERENT LANGUAGES!
WHAT DOES THIS DANCE MEAN?
TSEDUP, TSEDUP!

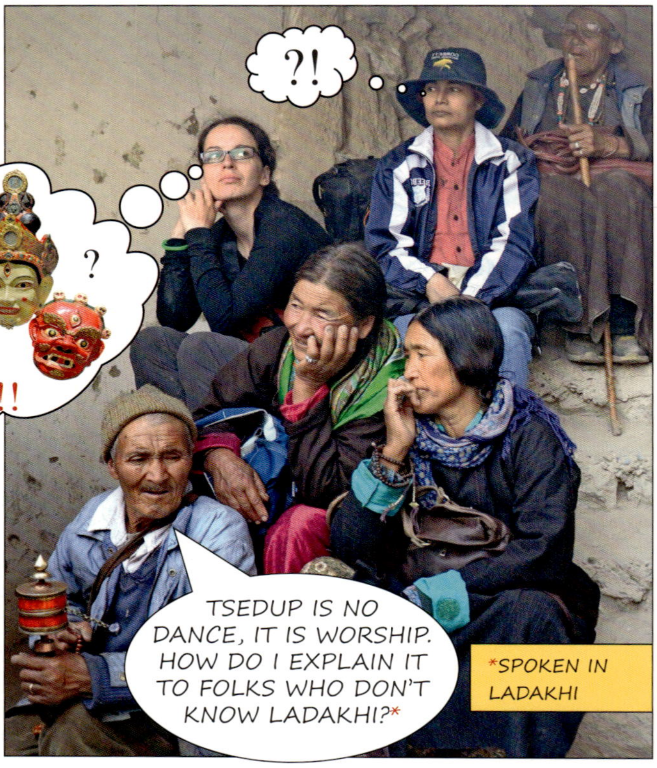
?!
?!
?
?!!
TSEDUP IS NO DANCE, IT IS WORSHIP. HOW DO I EXPLAIN IT TO FOLKS WHO DON'T KNOW LADAKHI?*
*SPOKEN IN LADAKHI

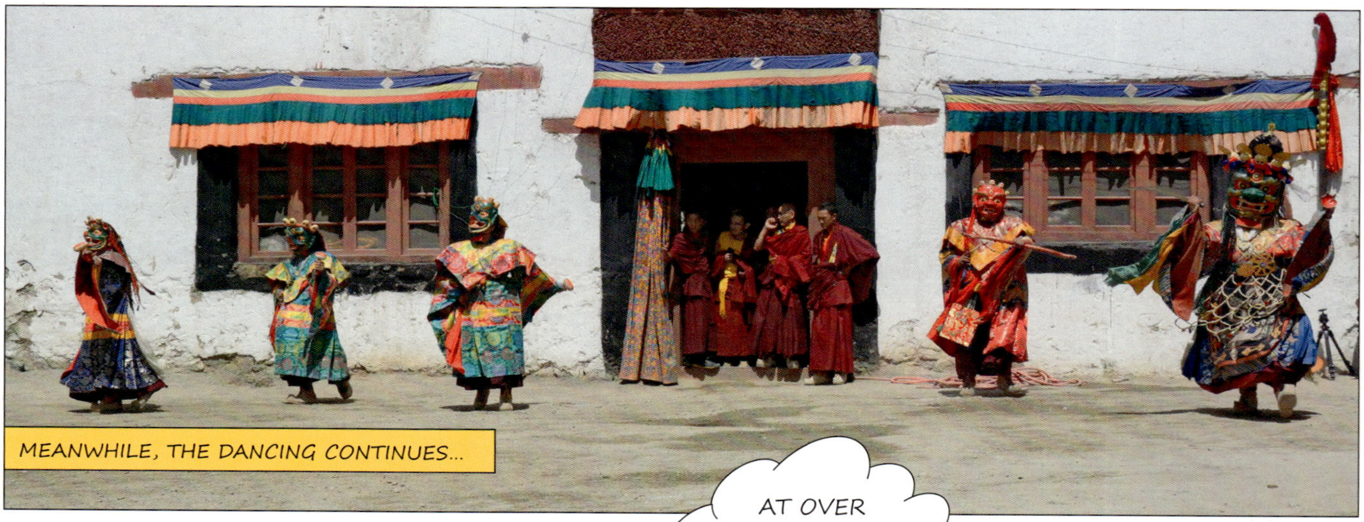
MEANWHILE, THE DANCING CONTINUES...

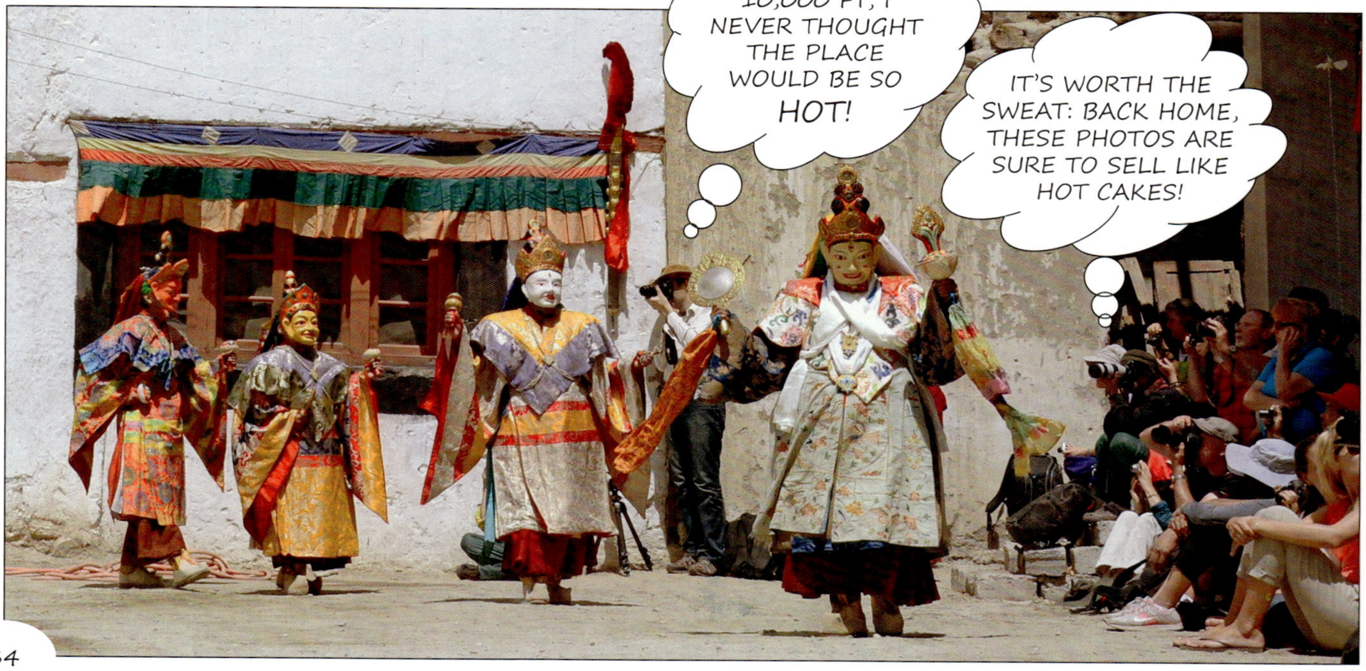
AT OVER 10,000 FT, I NEVER THOUGHT THE PLACE WOULD BE SO HOT!
IT'S WORTH THE SWEAT: BACK HOME, THESE PHOTOS ARE SURE TO SELL LIKE HOT CAKES!

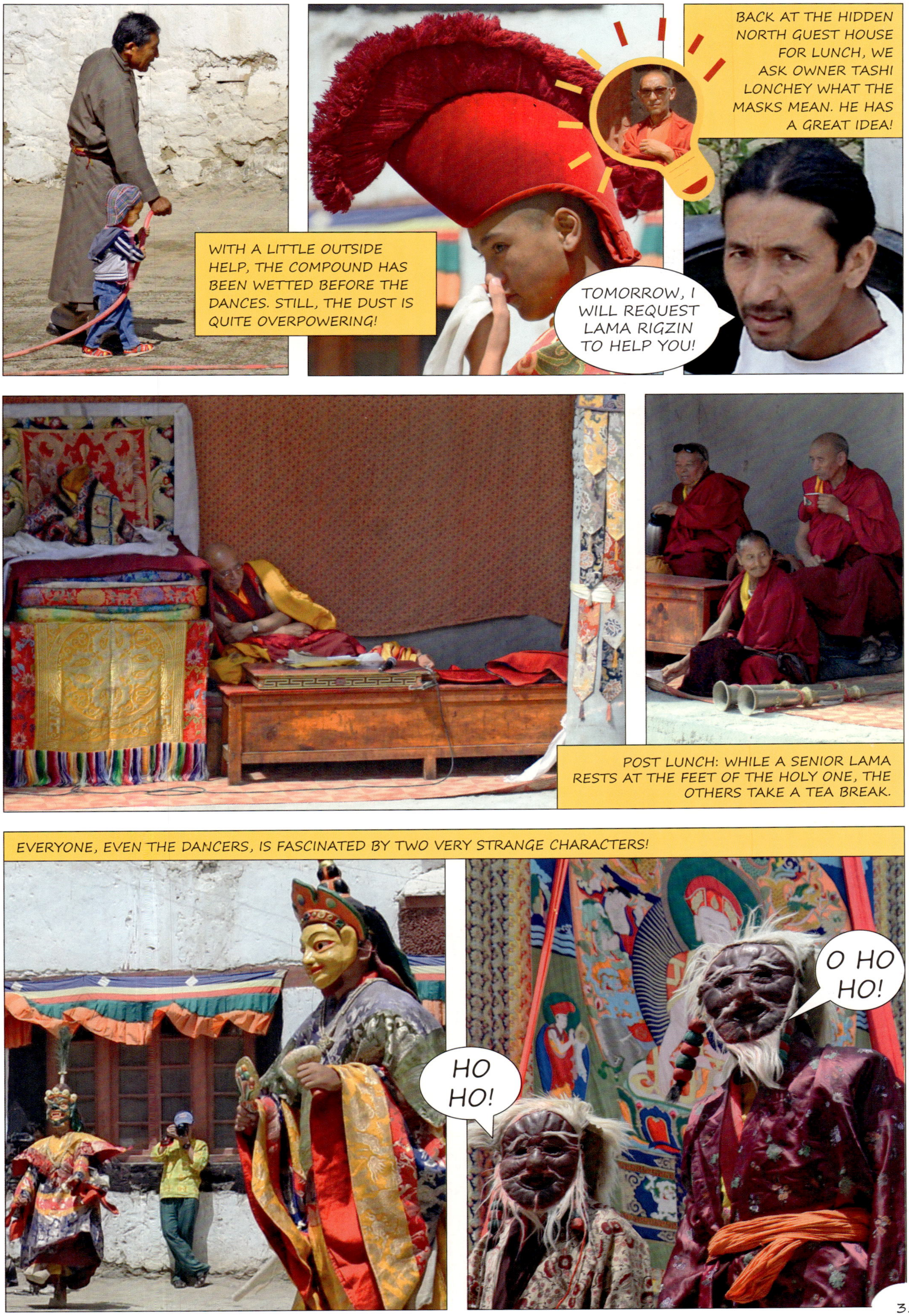
WITH A LITTLE OUTSIDE HELP, THE COMPOUND HAS BEEN WETTED BEFORE THE DANCES. STILL, THE DUST IS QUITE OVERPOWERING!
BACK AT THE HIDDEN NORTH GUEST HOUSE FOR LUNCH, WE ASK OWNER TASHI LONCHEY WHAT THE MASKS MEAN. HE HAS A GREAT IDEA!
TOMORROW, I WILL REQUEST LAMA RIGZIN TO HELP YOU!
POST LUNCH: WHILE A SENIOR LAMA RESTS AT THE FEET OF THE HOLY ONE, THE OTHERS TAKE A TEA BREAK.
EVERYONE, EVEN THE DANCERS, IS FASCINATED BY TWO VERY STRANGE CHARACTERS!
HO HO!
O HO HO!

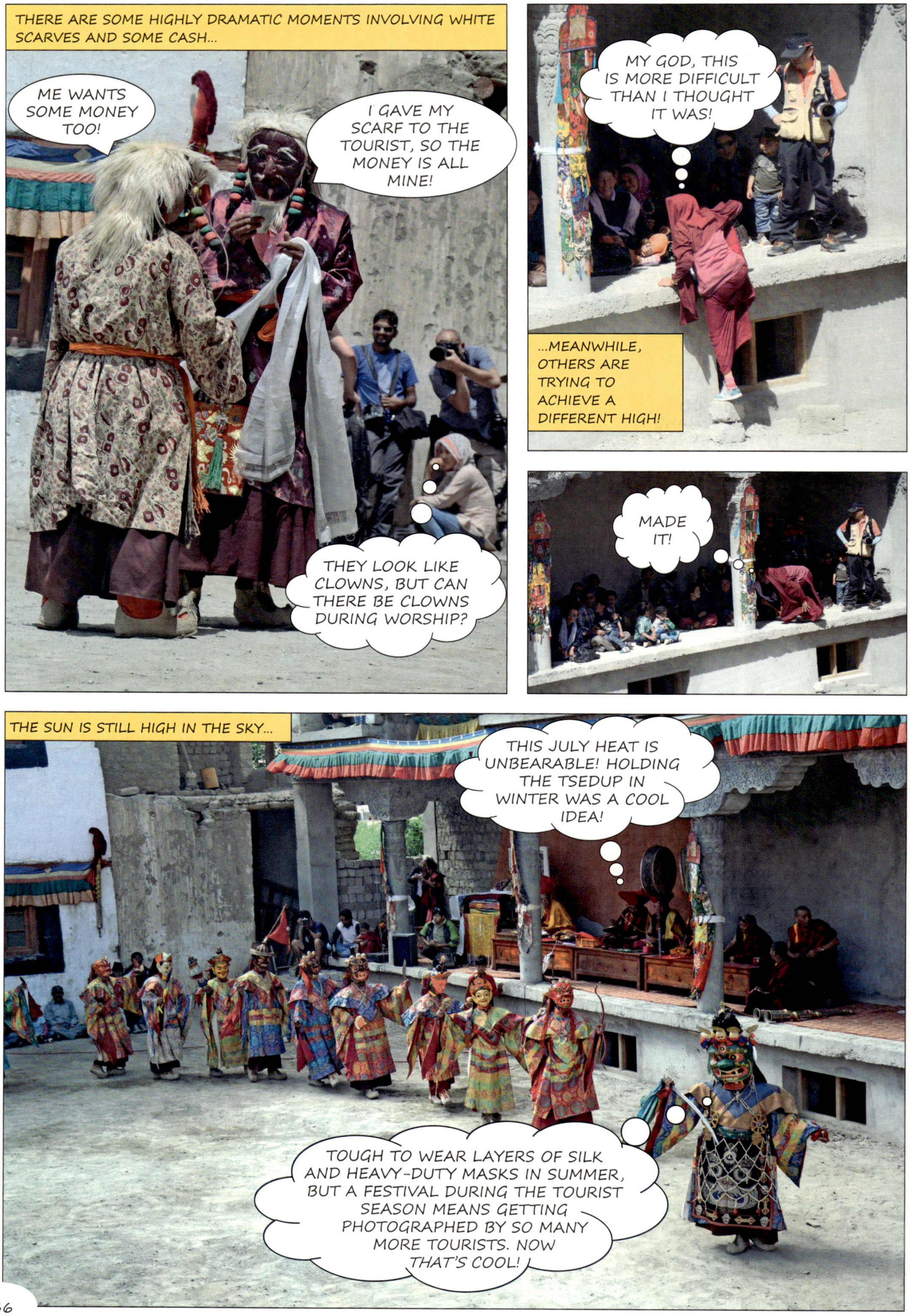
THERE ARE SOME HIGHLY DRAMATIC MOMENTS INVOLVING WHITE SCARVES AND SOME CASH...
ME WANTS SOME MONEY TOO!
I GAVE MY SCARF TO THE TOURIST, SO THE MONEY IS ALL MINE!
THEY LOOK LIKE CLOWNS, BUT CAN THERE BE CLOWNS DURING WORSHIP?
MY GOD, THIS IS MORE DIFFICULT THAN I THOUGHT IT WAS!
...MEANWHILE, OTHERS ARE TRYING TO ACHIEVE A DIFFERENT HIGH!
MADE IT!
THE SUN IS STILL HIGH IN THE SKY...
THIS JULY HEAT IS UNBEARABLE! HOLDING THE TSEDUP IN WINTER WAS A COOL IDEA!
TOUGH TO WEAR LAYERS OF SILK AND HEAVY-DUTY MASKS IN SUMMER, BUT A FESTIVAL DURING THE TOURIST SEASON MEANS GETTING PHOTOGRAPHED BY SO MANY MORE TOURISTS. NOW THAT'S COOL!

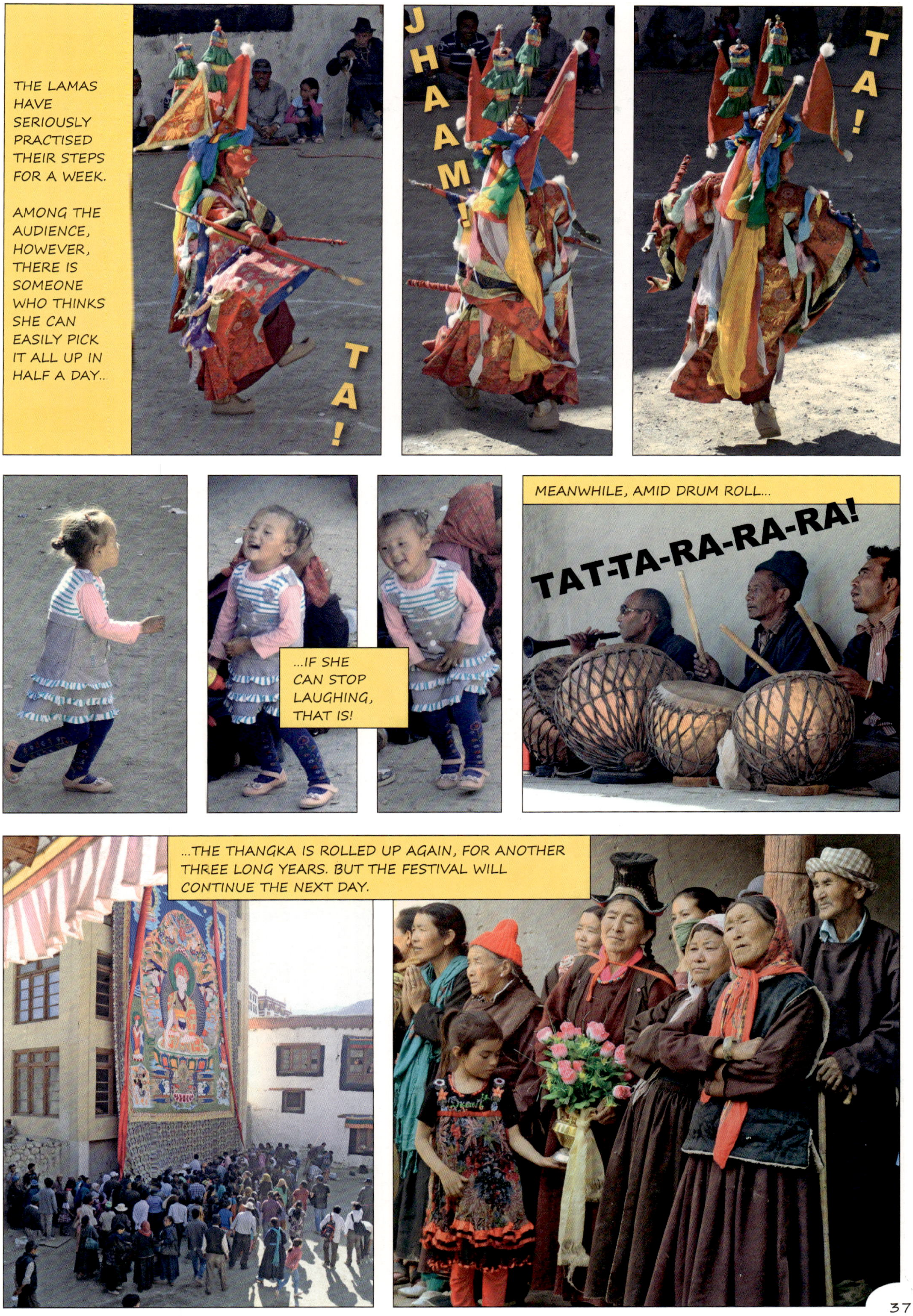
THE LAMAS HAVE SERIOUSLY PRACTISED THEIR STEPS FOR A WEEK.
AMONG THE AUDIENCE, HOWEVER, THERE IS SOMEONE WHO THINKS SHE CAN EASILY PICK IT ALL UP IN HALF A DAY...
TA!
JHAAM!
TA!
...IF SHE CAN STOP LAUGHING, THAT IS!
MEANWHILE, AMID DRUM ROLL...
TAT-TA-RA-RA-RA!
...THE THANGKA IS ROLLED UP AGAIN, FOR ANOTHER THREE LONG YEARS. BUT THE FESTIVAL WILL CONTINUE THE NEXT DAY.

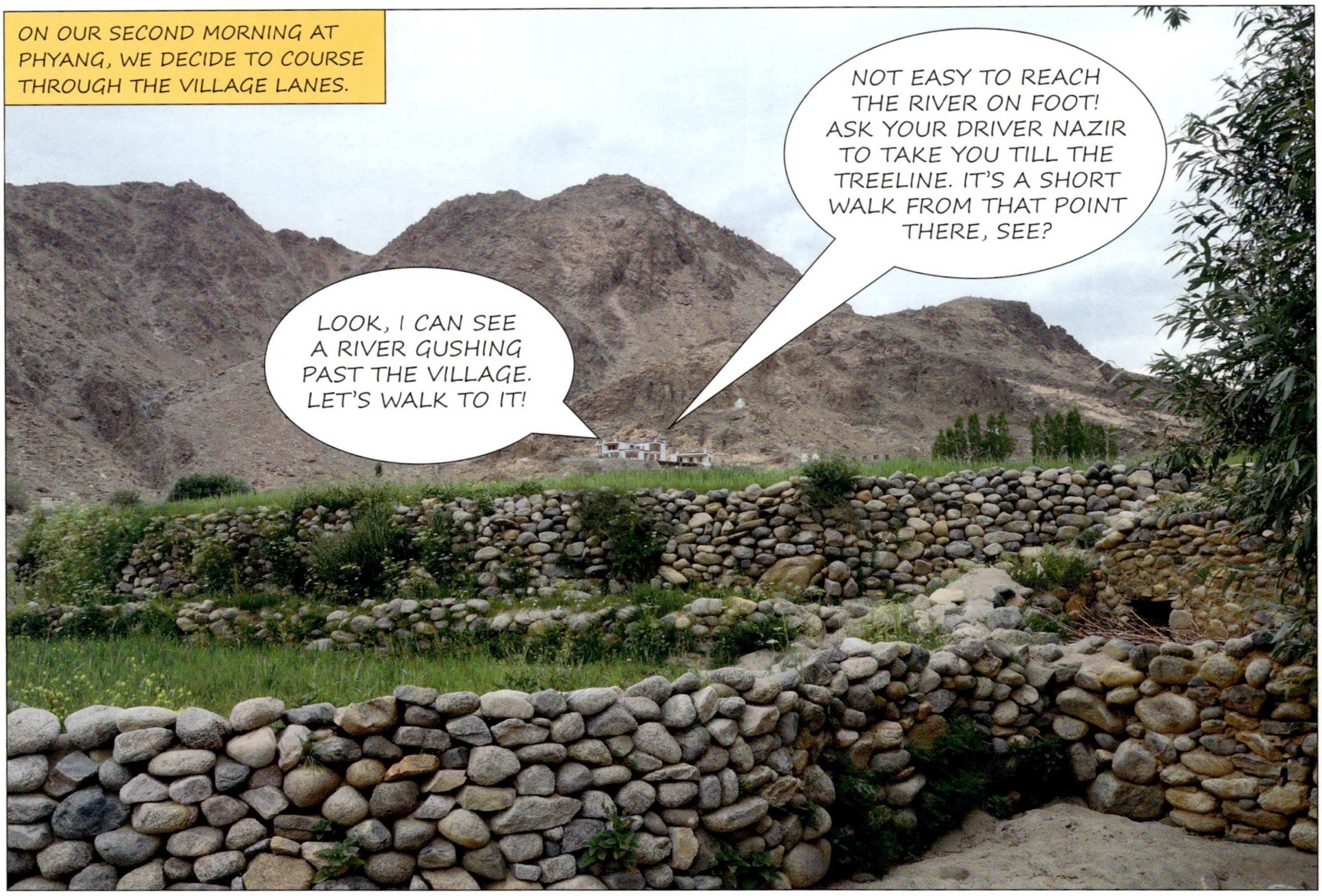

PHYANG TOKPO (TOKPO = RIVER) FLOODED THE VILLAGE SOME YEARS AGO, AND BROUGHT HAVOC. IT COURSES GENTLY PAST US NOW, WITH UPROOTED TREES IN ITS WINDING ROUTE...

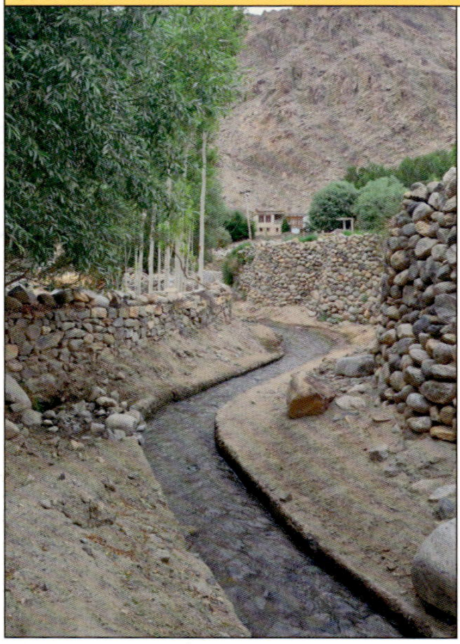

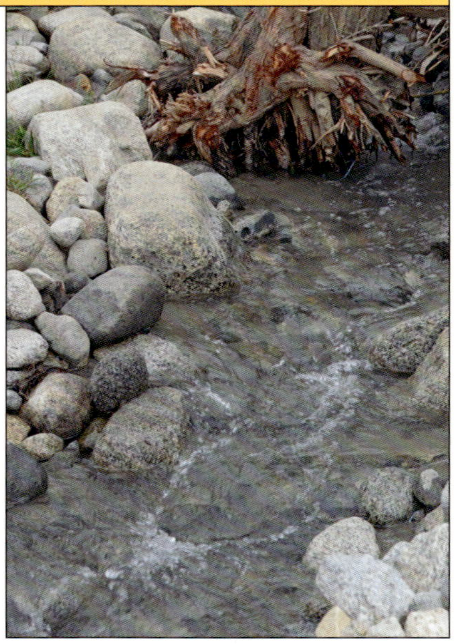

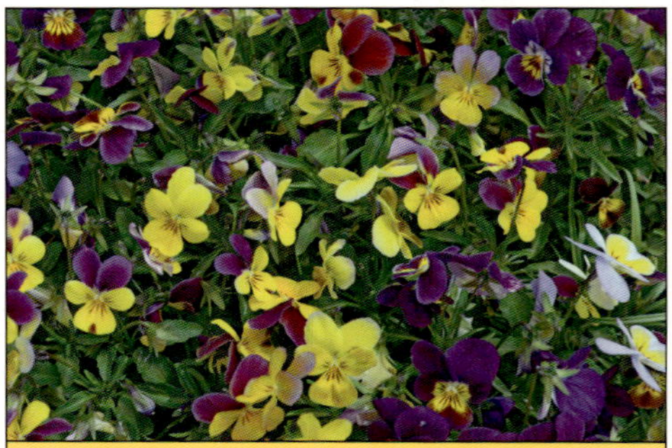

...AND LOVELY FLOWERS TOO!

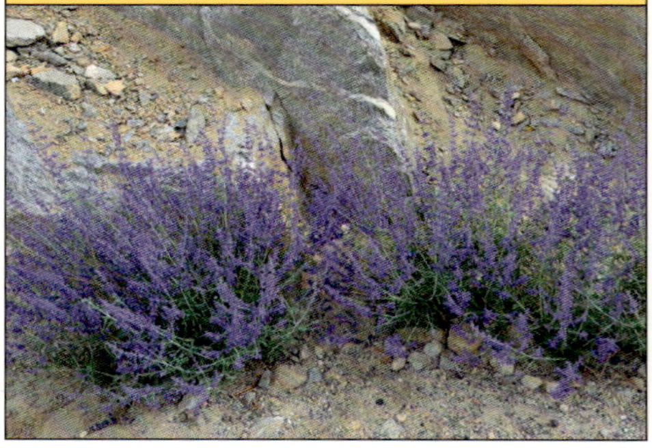

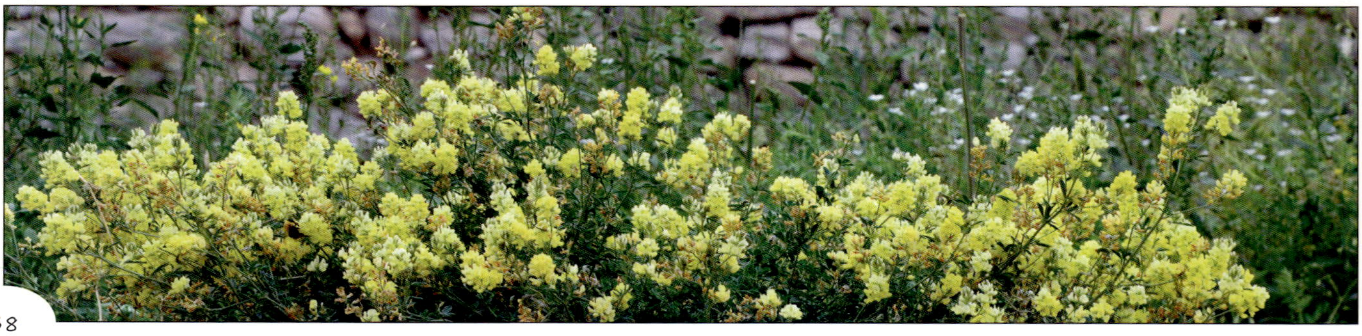

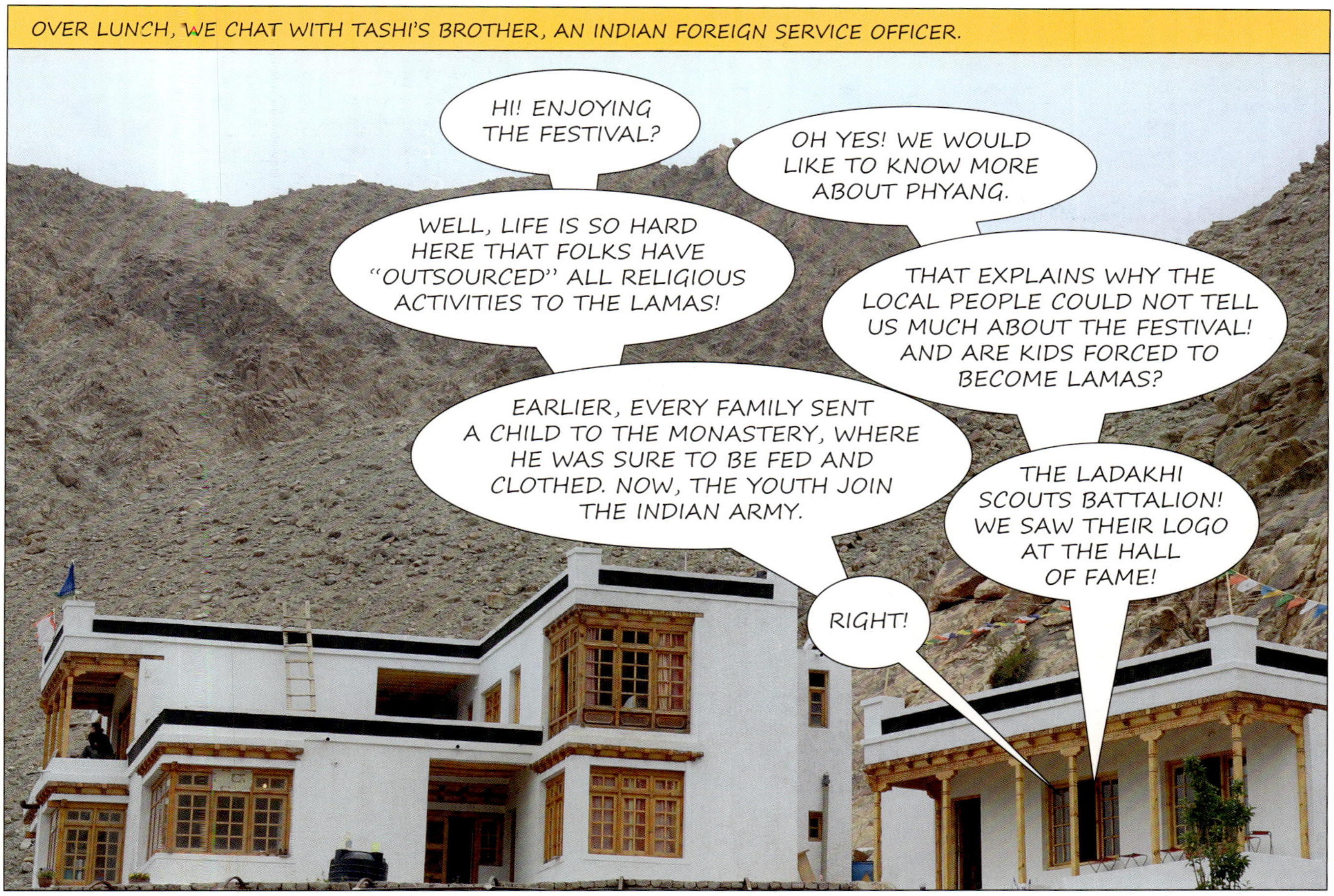
OVER LUNCH, WE CHAT WITH TASHI'S BROTHER, AN INDIAN FOREIGN SERVICE OFFICER.
HI! ENJOYING THE FESTIVAL?
OH YES! WE WOULD LIKE TO KNOW MORE ABOUT PHYANG.
WELL, LIFE IS SO HARD HERE THAT FOLKS HAVE "OUTSOURCED" ALL RELIGIOUS ACTIVITIES TO THE LAMAS!
THAT EXPLAINS WHY THE LOCAL PEOPLE COULD NOT TELL US MUCH ABOUT THE FESTIVAL! AND ARE KIDS FORCED TO BECOME LAMAS?
EARLIER, EVERY FAMILY SENT A CHILD TO THE MONASTERY, WHERE HE WAS SURE TO BE FED AND CLOTHED. NOW, THE YOUTH JOIN THE INDIAN ARMY.
THE LADAKHI SCOUTS BATTALION! WE SAW THEIR LOGO AT THE HALL OF FAME!
RIGHT!

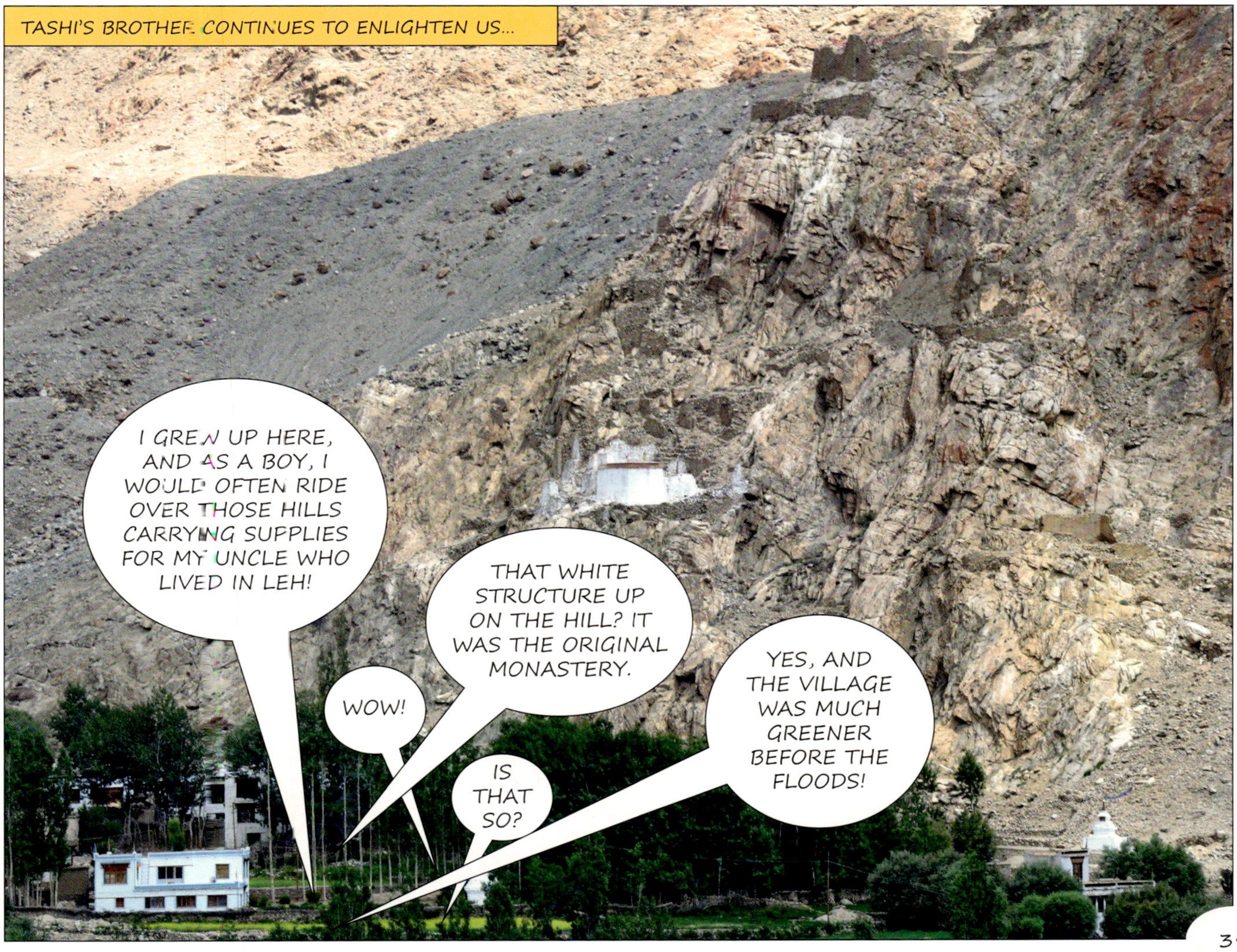
TASHI'S BROTHER CONTINUES TO ENLIGHTEN US...
I GREW UP HERE, AND AS A BOY, I WOULD OFTEN RIDE OVER THOSE HILLS CARRYING SUPPLIES FOR MY UNCLE WHO LIVED IN LEH!
THAT WHITE STRUCTURE UP ON THE HILL? IT WAS THE ORIGINAL MONASTERY.
WOW!
IS THAT SO?
YES, AND THE VILLAGE WAS MUCH GREENER BEFORE THE FLOODS!

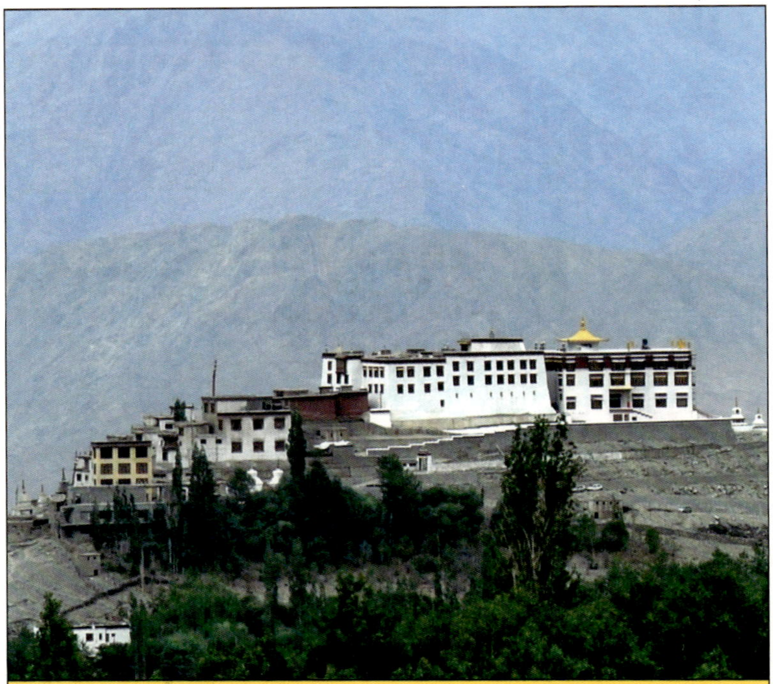

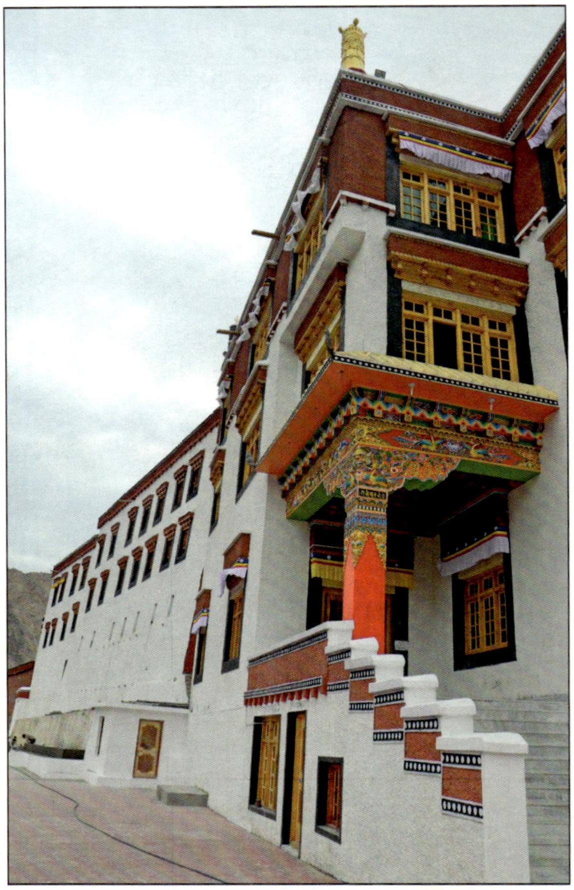

WE RETURN TO THE MONASTERY. A TOUR OF THE PRAYER ROOMS REVEALS RICH FRESCOES AND ANCIENT IDOLS WITH MANY HANDS. BUT THE MOST FAMILIAR OF THEM ALL IS THAT OF ATISH DIPANKAR SRIGYAN, OR ATIŚA DĪPAṂKARA ŚRĪJÑĀNA, WHO HAILED FROM BENGAL IN THE 10TH CENTURY AD. HE WAS A MASTER OF MAHAYANA AND VAJRAYANA BUDDHISM AND HAD TRAVELLED ACROSS THE HIMALAYAS AS A PREACHER.

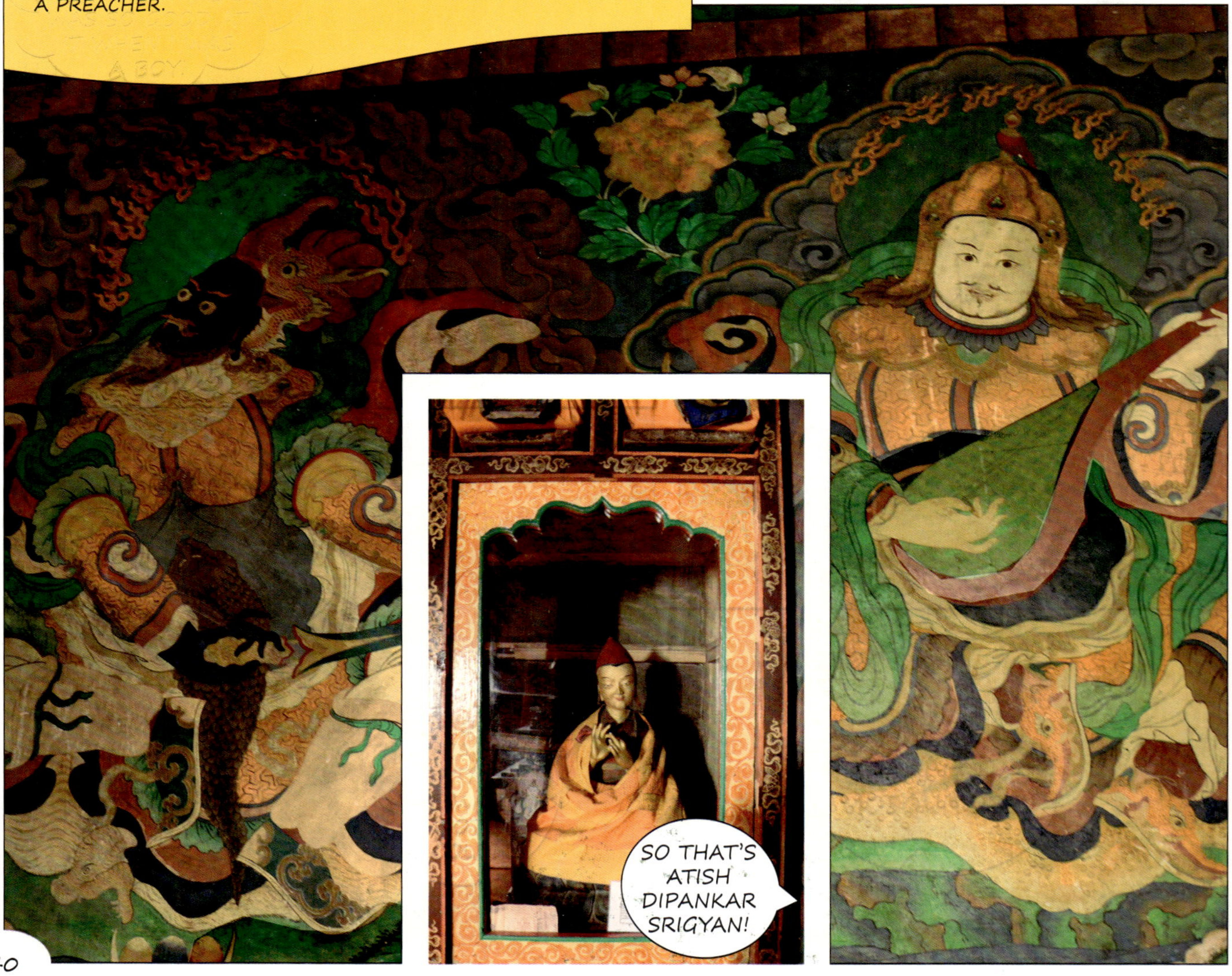

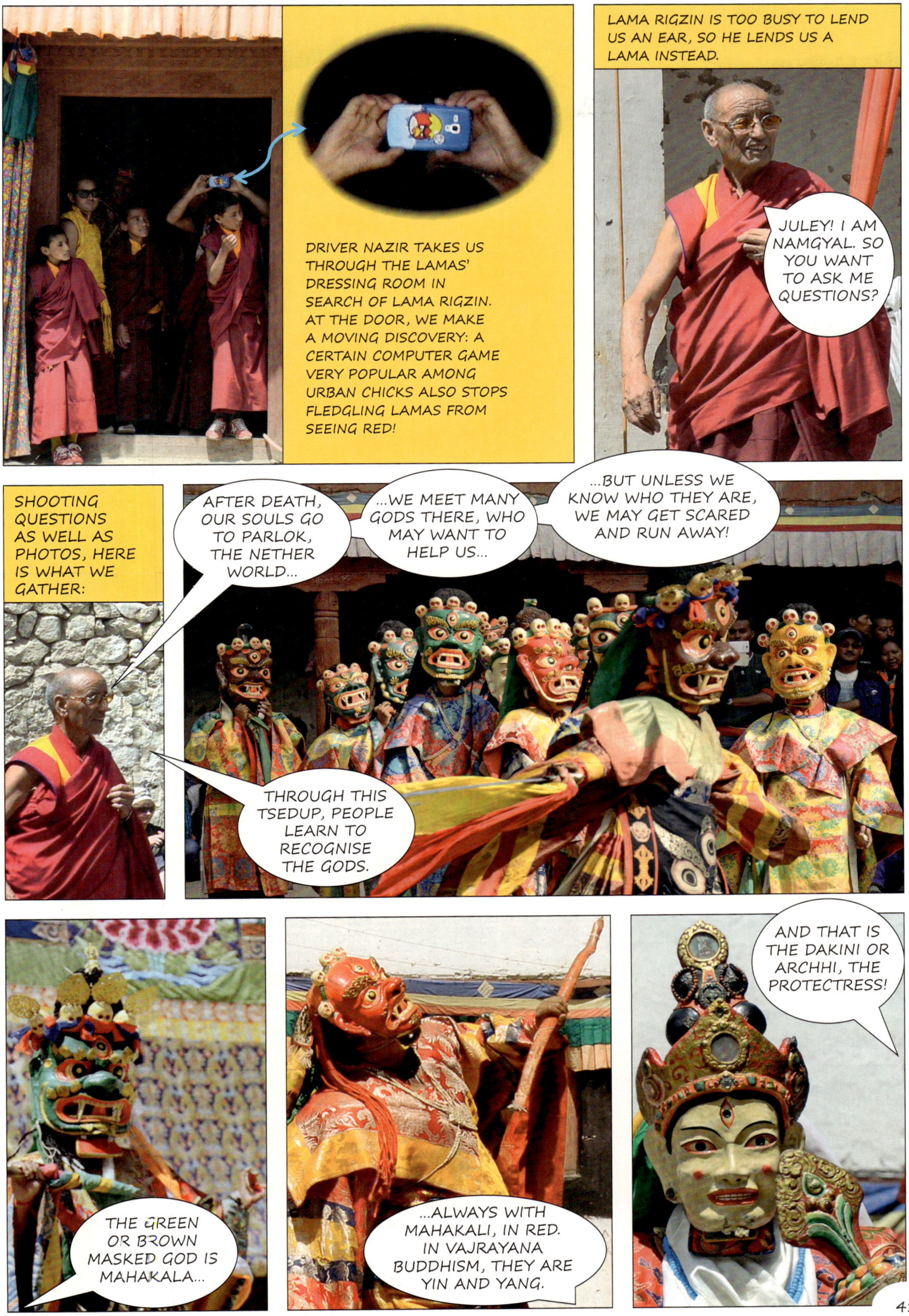
DRIVER NAZIR TAKES US THROUGH THE LAMAS' DRESSING ROOM IN SEARCH OF LAMA RIGZIN. AT THE DOOR, WE MAKE A MOVING DISCOVERY: A CERTAIN COMPUTER GAME VERY POPULAR AMONG URBAN CHICKS ALSO STOPS FLEDGLING LAMAS FROM SEEING RED!
LAMA RIGZIN IS TOO BUSY TO LEND US AN EAR, SO HE LENDS US A LAMA INSTEAD.
JULEY! I AM NAMGYAL. SO YOU WANT TO ASK ME QUESTIONS?
SHOOTING QUESTIONS AS WELL AS PHOTOS, HERE IS WHAT WE GATHER:
AFTER DEATH, OUR SOULS GO TO PARLOK, THE NETHER WORLD...
...WE MEET MANY GODS THERE, WHO MAY WANT TO HELP US...
...BUT UNLESS WE KNOW WHO THEY ARE, WE MAY GET SCARED AND RUN AWAY!
THROUGH THIS TSEDUP, PEOPLE LEARN TO RECOGNISE THE GODS.
THE GREEN OR BROWN MASKED GOD IS MAHAKALA...
...ALWAYS WITH MAHAKALI, IN RED. IN VAJRAYANA BUDDHISM, THEY ARE YIN AND YANG.
AND THAT IS THE DAKINI OR ARCHHI, THE PROTECTRESS!

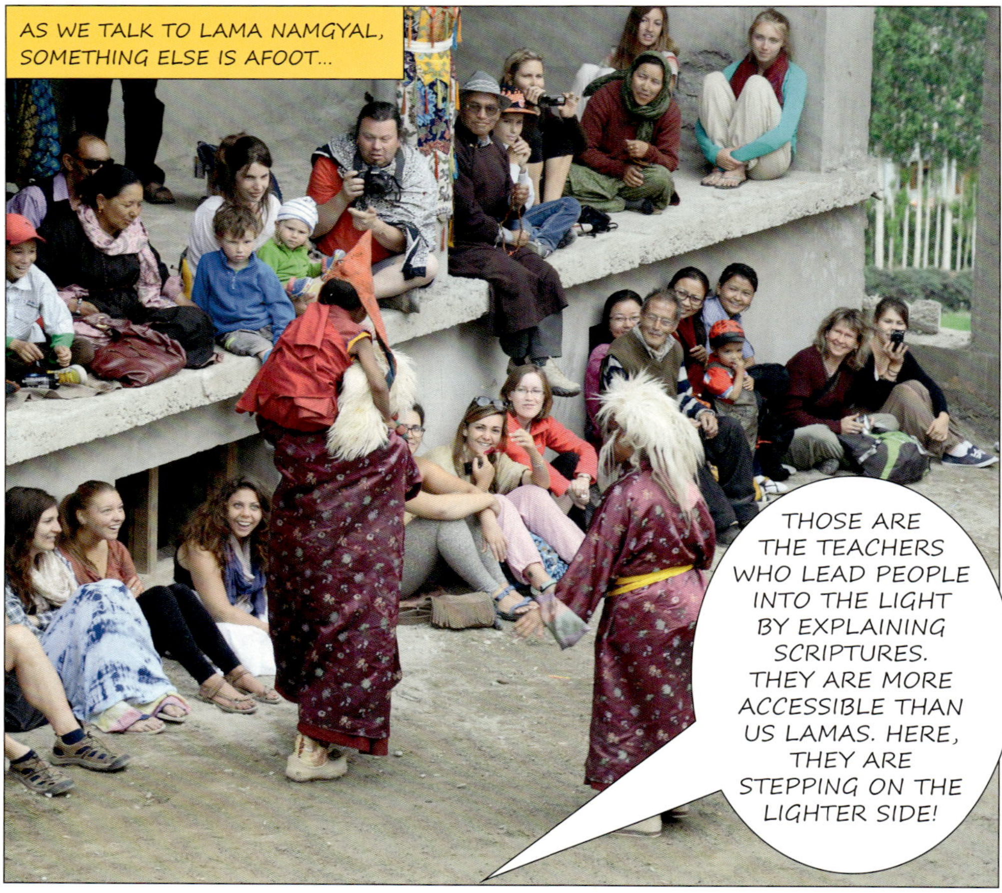
AS WE TALK TO LAMA NAMGYAL, SOMETHING ELSE IS AFOOT...
THOSE ARE THE TEACHERS WHO LEAD PEOPLE INTO THE LIGHT BY EXPLAINING SCRIPTURES. THEY ARE MORE ACCESSIBLE THAN US LAMAS. HERE, THEY ARE STEPPING ON THE LIGHTER SIDE!

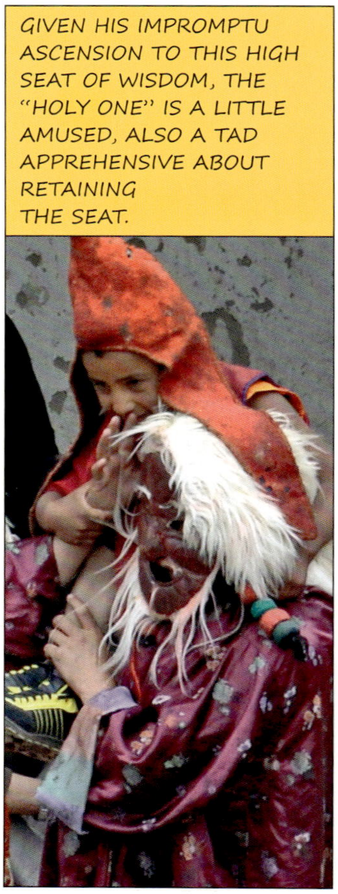
GIVEN HIS IMPROMPTU ASCENSION TO THIS HIGH SEAT OF WISDOM, THE "HOLY ONE" IS A LITTLE AMUSED, ALSO A TAD APPREHENSIVE ABOUT RETAINING THE SEAT.

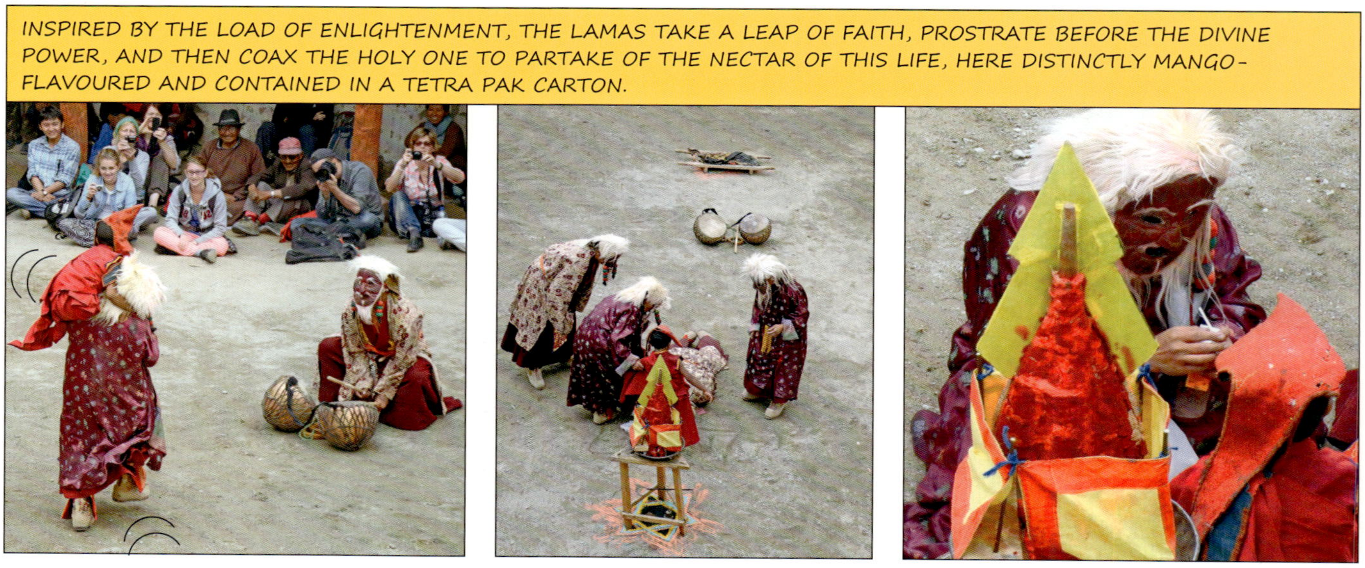
INSPIRED BY THE LOAD OF ENLIGHTENMENT, THE LAMAS TAKE A LEAP OF FAITH, PROSTRATE BEFORE THE DIVINE POWER, AND THEN COAX THE HOLY ONE TO PARTAKE OF THE NECTAR OF THIS LIFE, HERE DISTINCTLY MANGO-FLAVOURED AND CONTAINED IN A TETRA PAK CARTON.

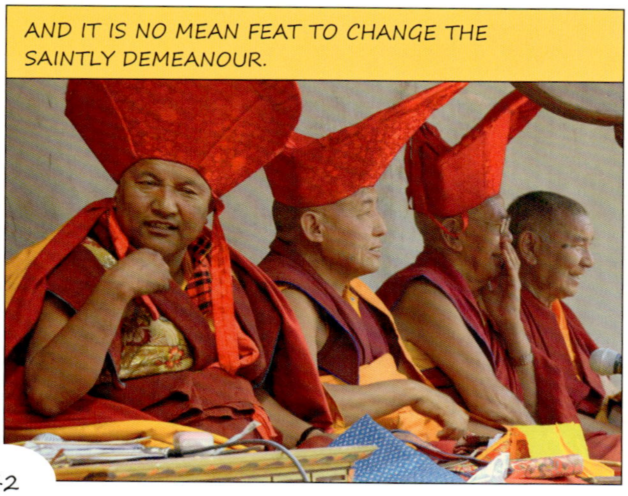
AND IT IS NO MEAN FEAT TO CHANGE THE SAINTLY DEMEANOUR.

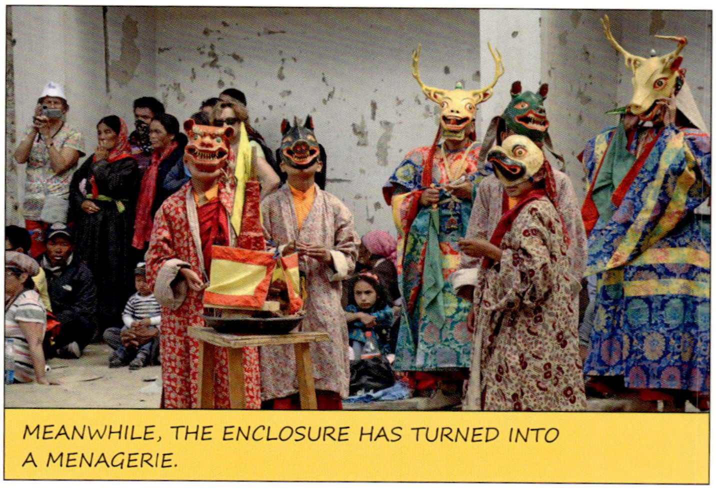
MEANWHILE, THE ENCLOSURE HAS TURNED INTO A MENAGERIE.

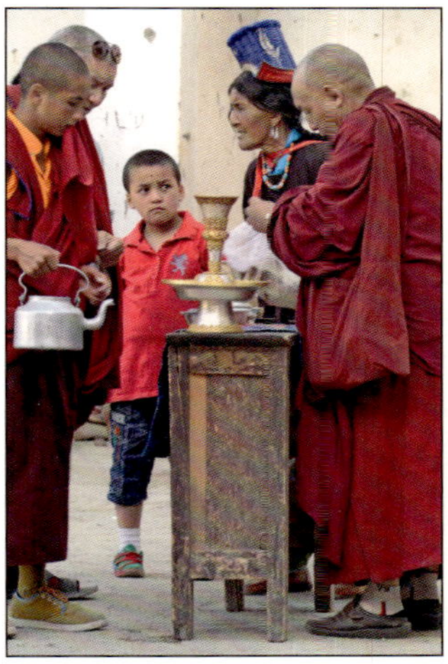

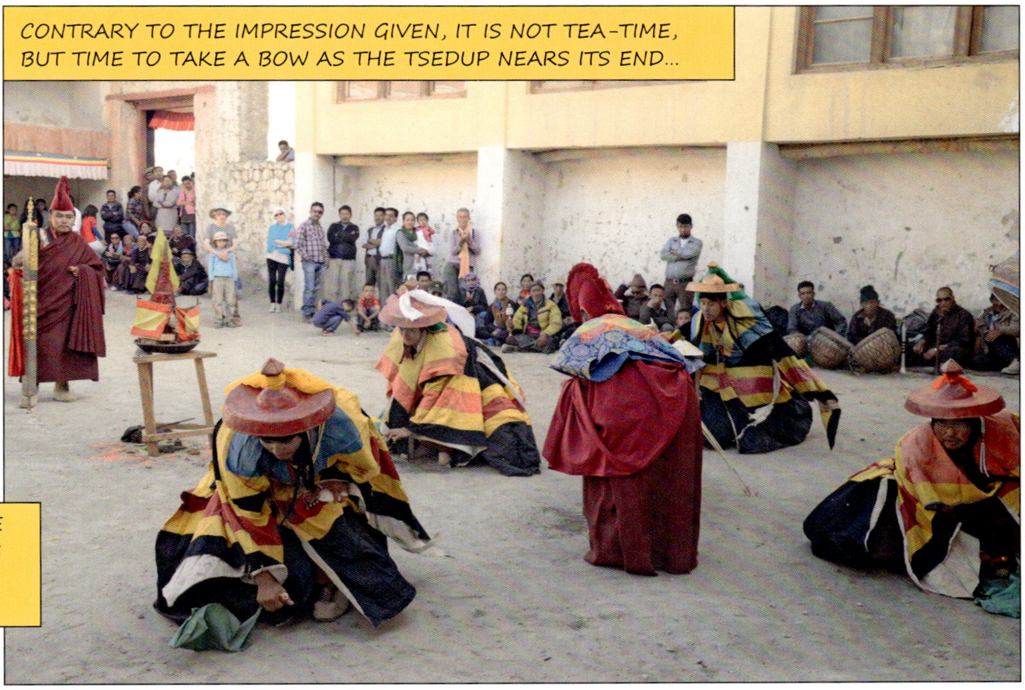
CONTRARY TO THE IMPRESSION GIVEN, IT IS NOT TEA-TIME, BUT TIME TO TAKE A BOW AS THE TSEDUP NEARS ITS END...

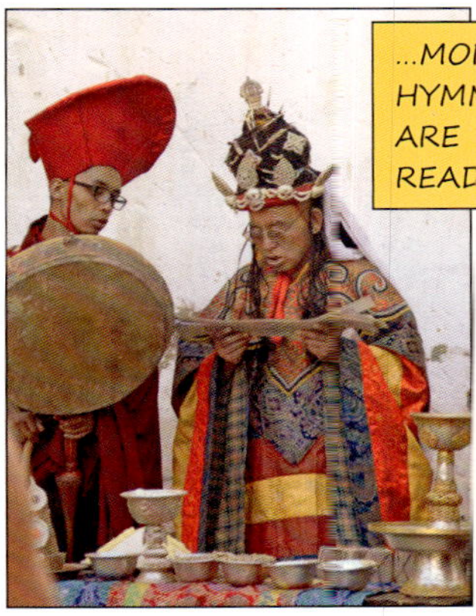
...MORE HYMNS ARE READ...

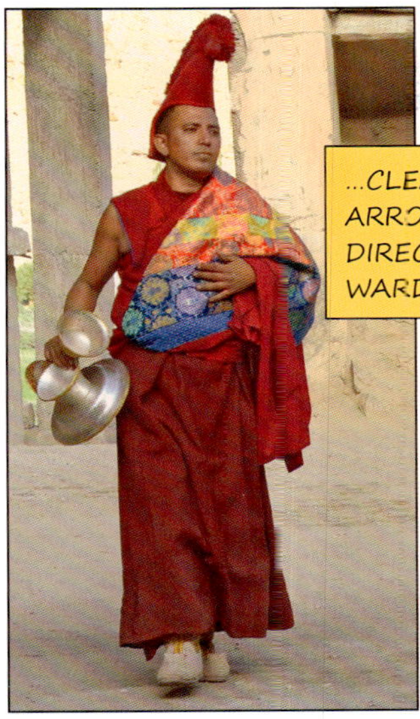

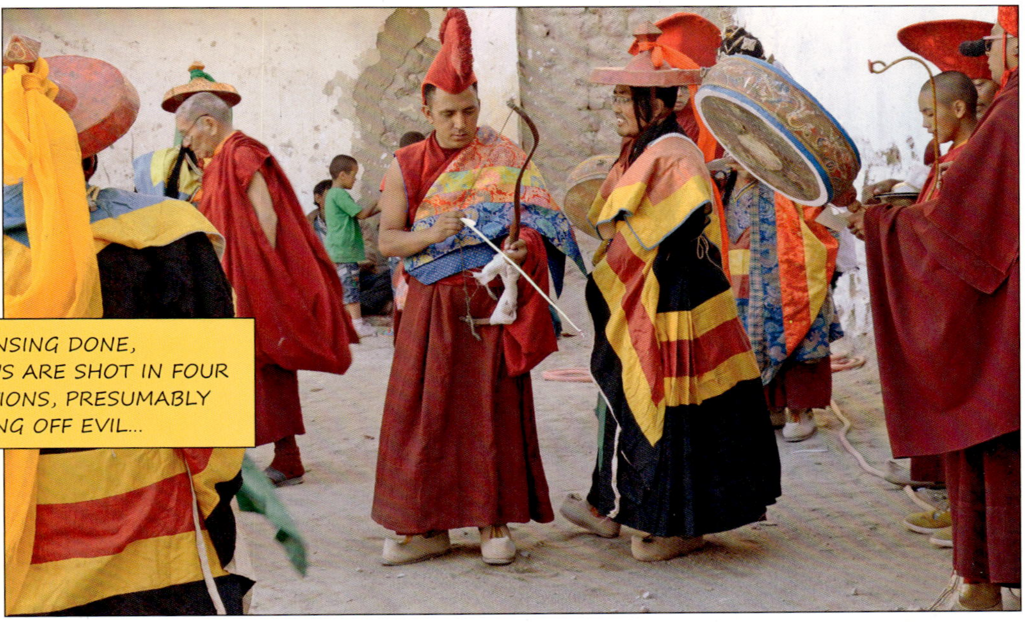
...CLEANSING DONE, ARROWS ARE SHOT IN FOUR DIRECTIONS, PRESUMABLY WARDING OFF EVIL...

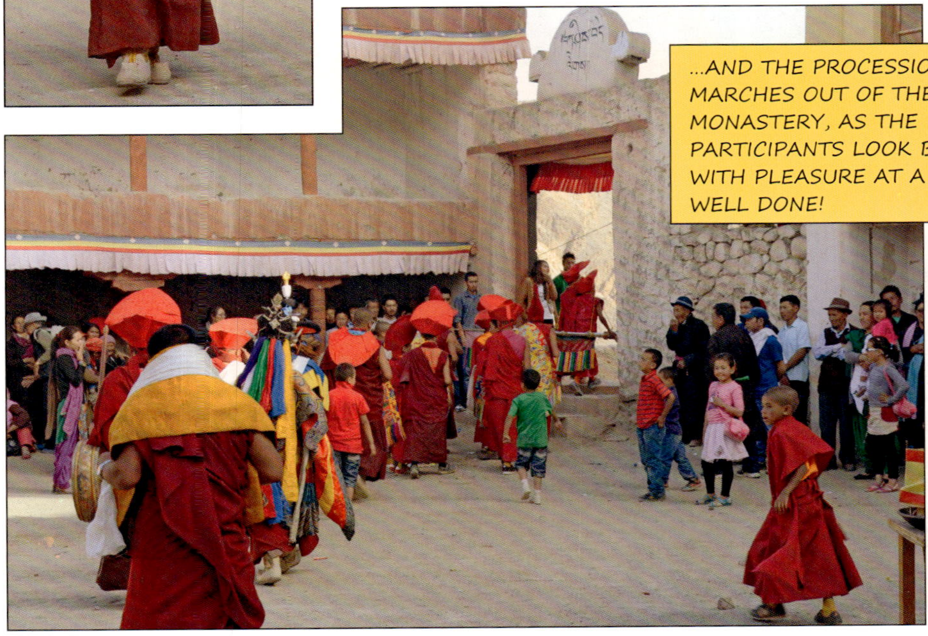
...AND THE PROCESSION MARCHES OUT OF THE MONASTERY, AS THE PARTICIPANTS LOOK BACK WITH PLEASURE AT A JOB WELL DONE!

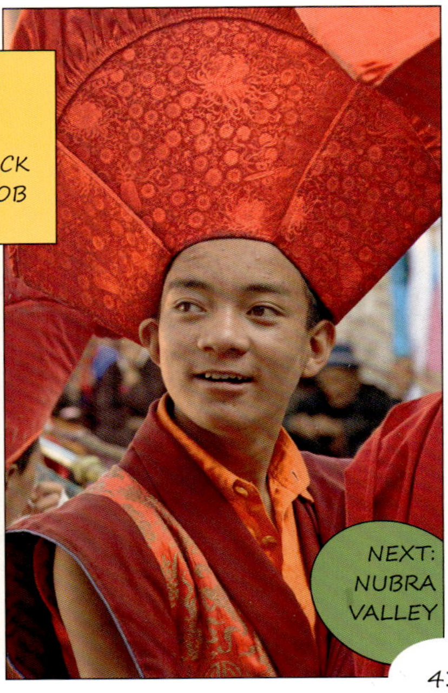
NEXT: NUBRA VALLEY

Chapter III: Nubra Valley

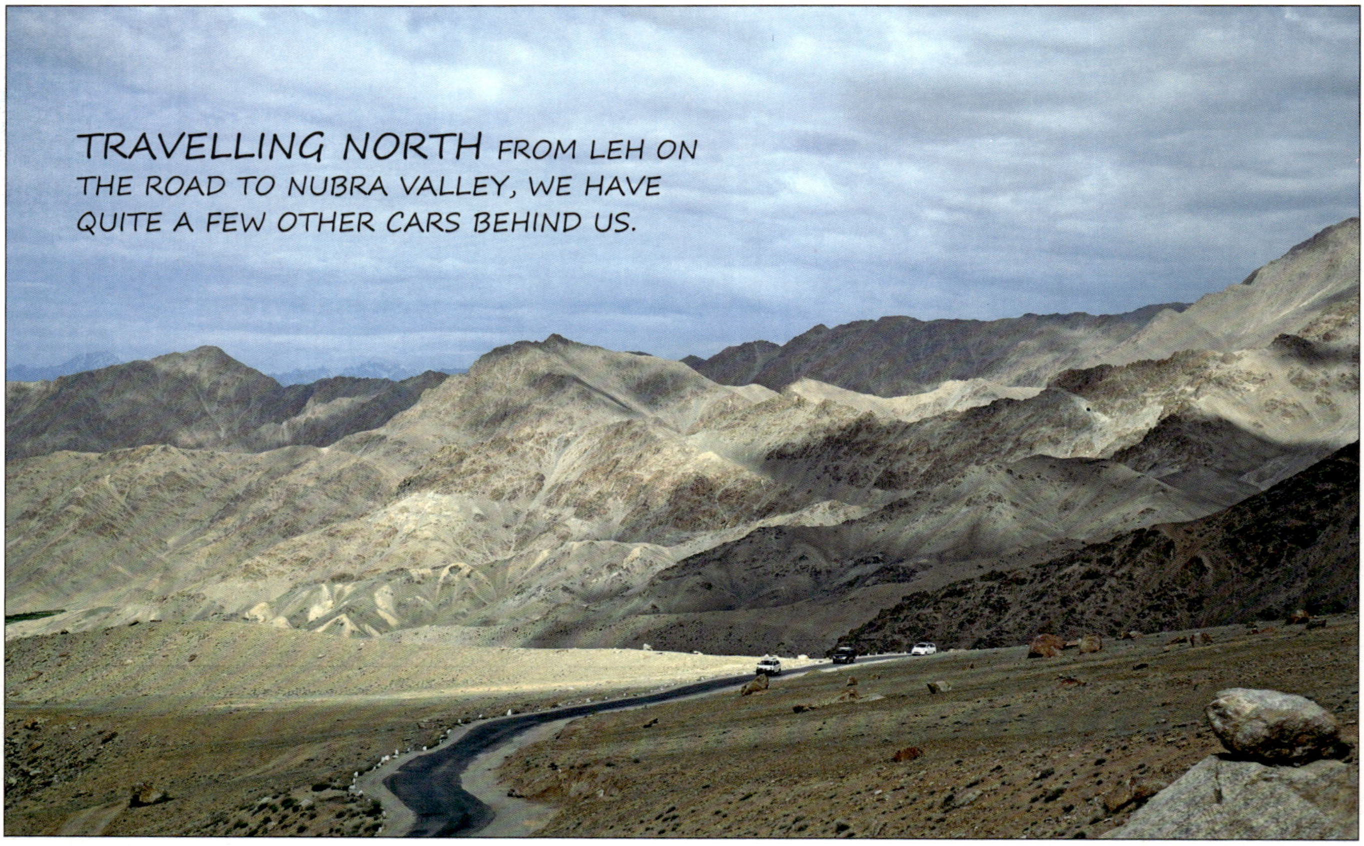

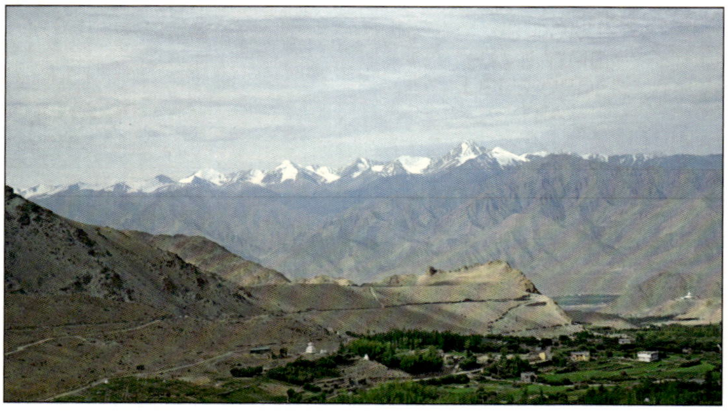

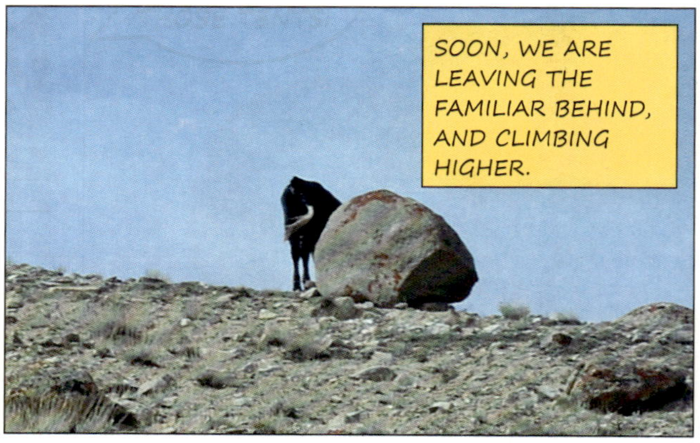

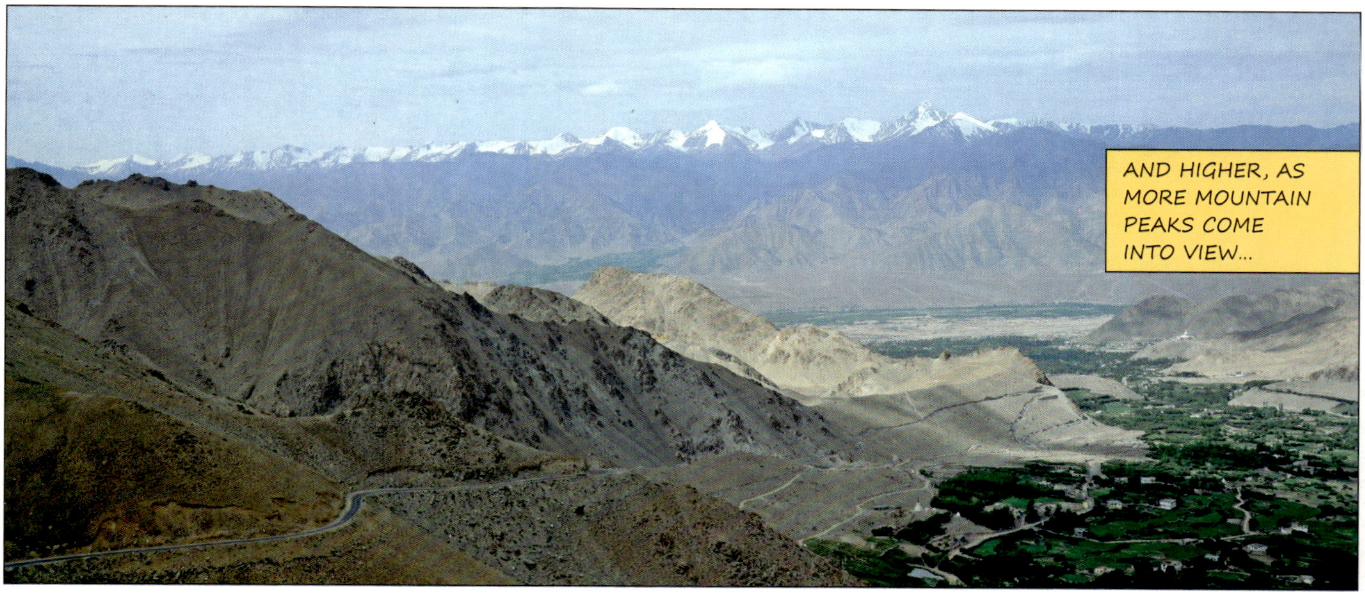

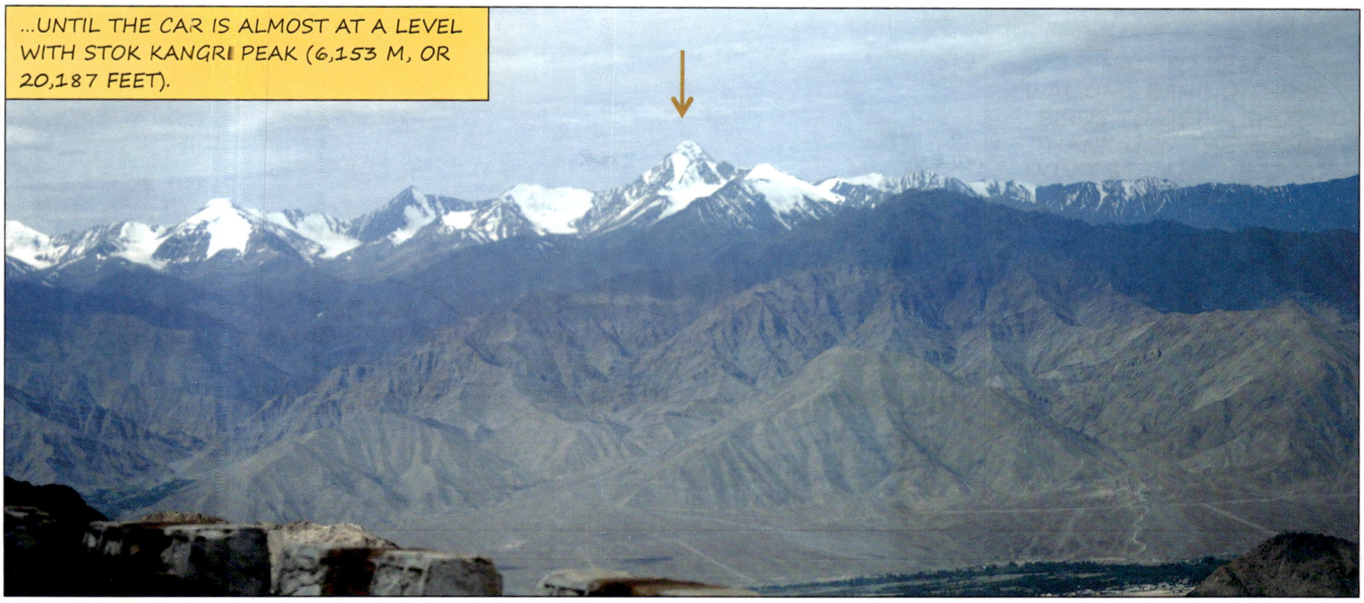
...UNTIL THE CAR IS ALMOST AT A LEVEL WITH STOK KANGRI PEAK (6,153 M, OR 20,187 FEET).

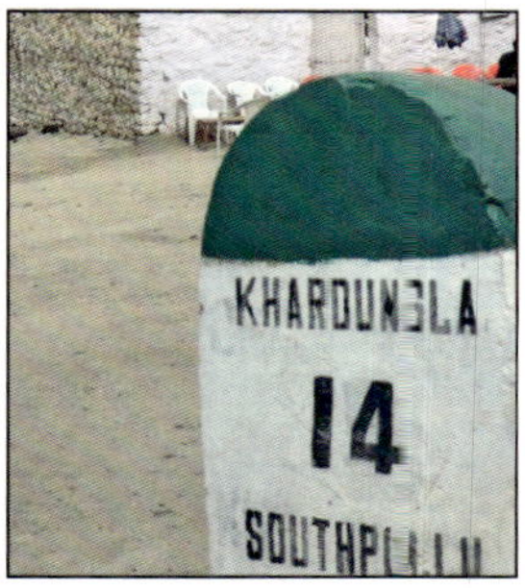
KHARDUNGLA
14

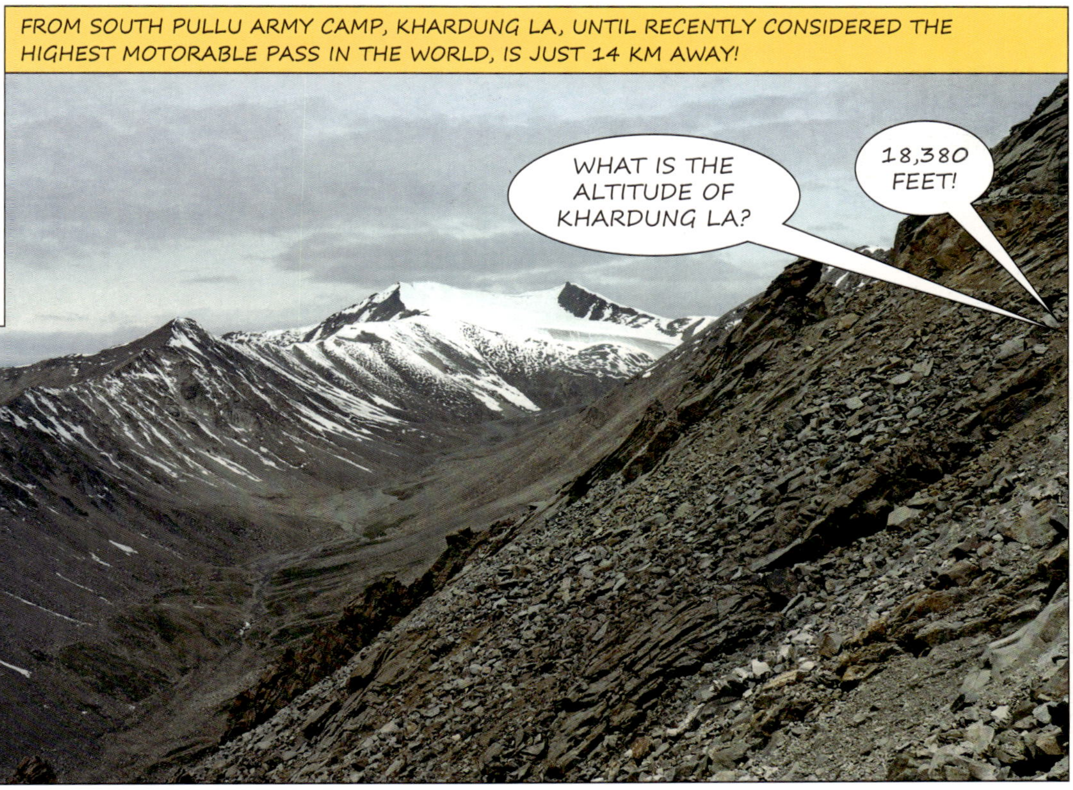
FROM SOUTH PULLU ARMY CAMP, KHARDUNG LA, UNTIL RECENTLY CONSIDERED THE HIGHEST MOTORABLE PASS IN THE WORLD, IS JUST 14 KM AWAY!
WHAT IS THE ALTITUDE OF KHARDUNG LA?
18,380 FEET!

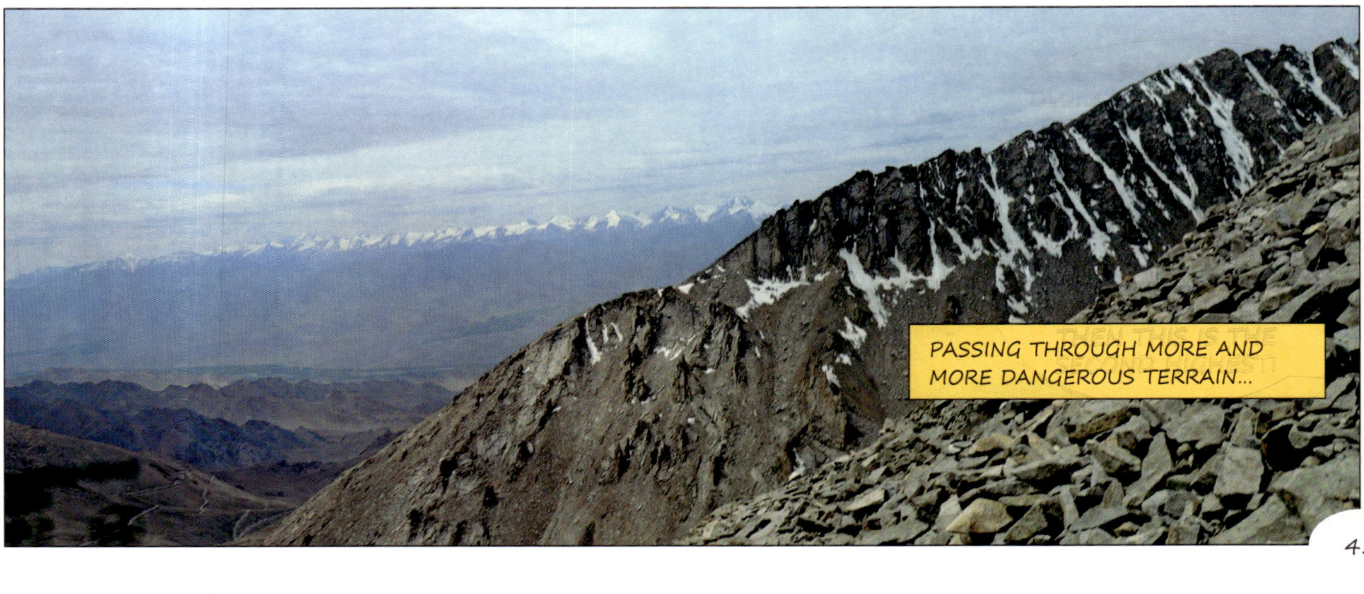
PASSING THROUGH MORE AND MORE DANGEROUS TERRAIN...

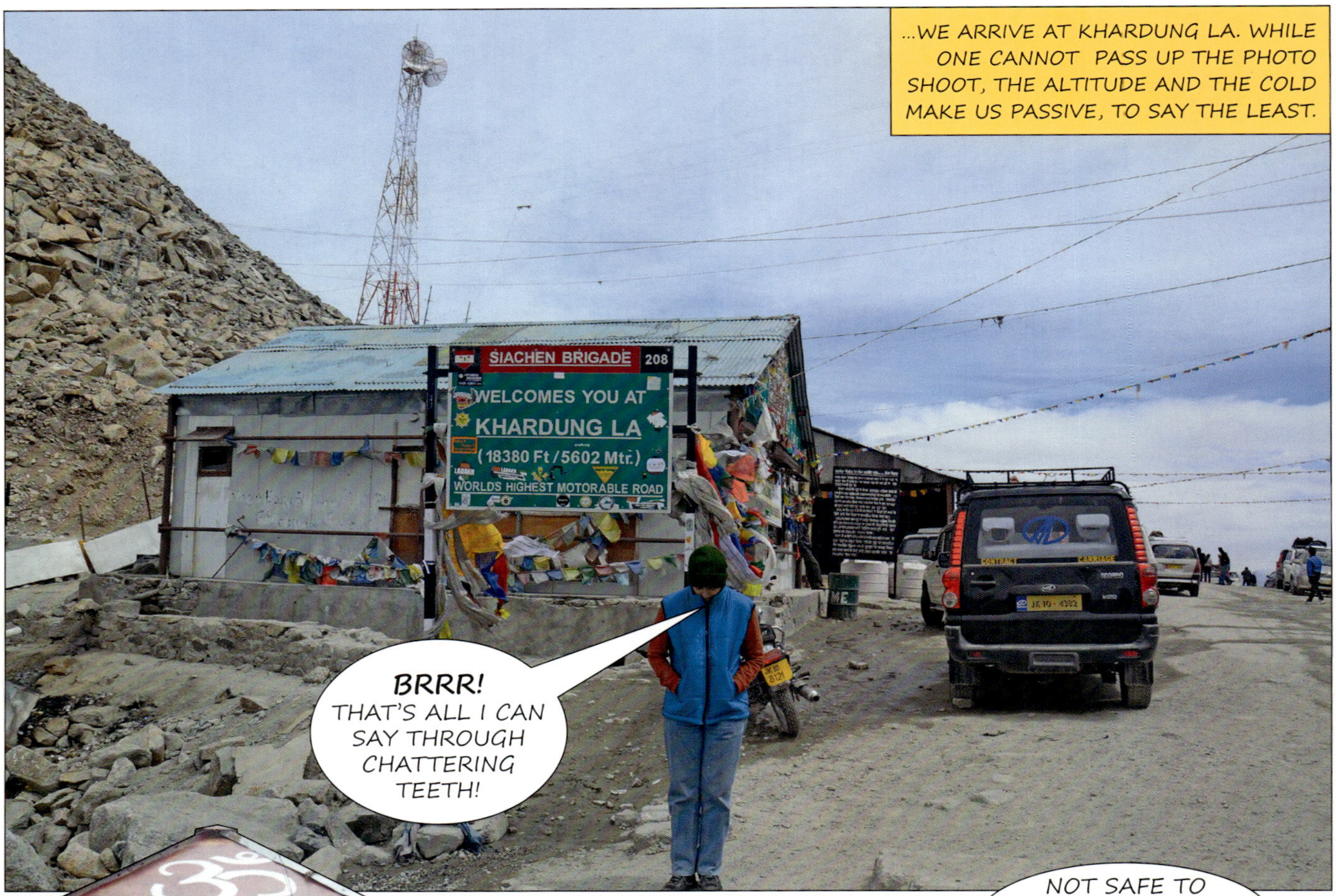
...WE ARRIVE AT KHARDUNG LA. WHILE ONE CANNOT PASS UP THE PHOTO SHOOT, THE ALTITUDE AND THE COLD MAKE US PASSIVE, TO SAY THE LEAST.
SIACHEN BRIGADE 208
WELCOMES YOU AT
KHARDUNG LA
(18380 Ft / 5602 Mtr.)
WORLDS HIGHEST MOTORABLE ROAD
BRRR! THAT'S ALL I CAN SAY THROUGH CHATTERING TEETH!

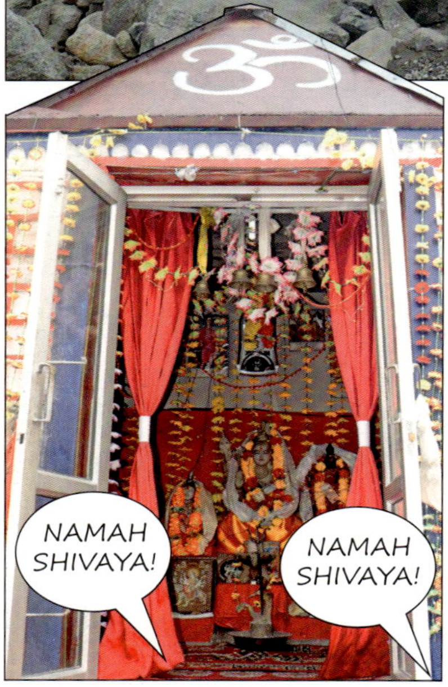
NAMAH SHIVAYA!
NAMAH SHIVAYA!

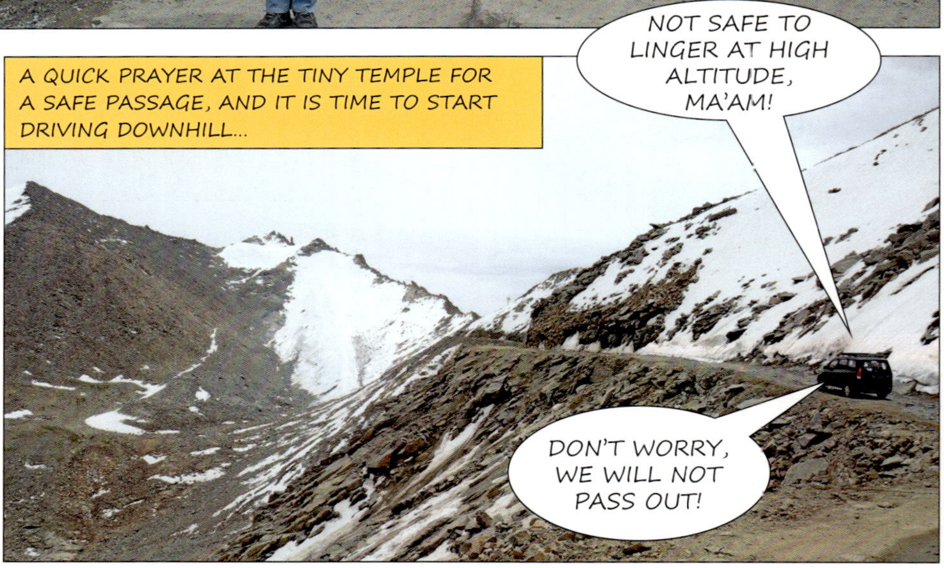
A QUICK PRAYER AT THE TINY TEMPLE FOR A SAFE PASSAGE, AND IT IS TIME TO START DRIVING DOWNHILL...
NOT SAFE TO LINGER AT HIGH ALTITUDE, MA'AM!
DON'T WORRY, WE WILL NOT PASS OUT!

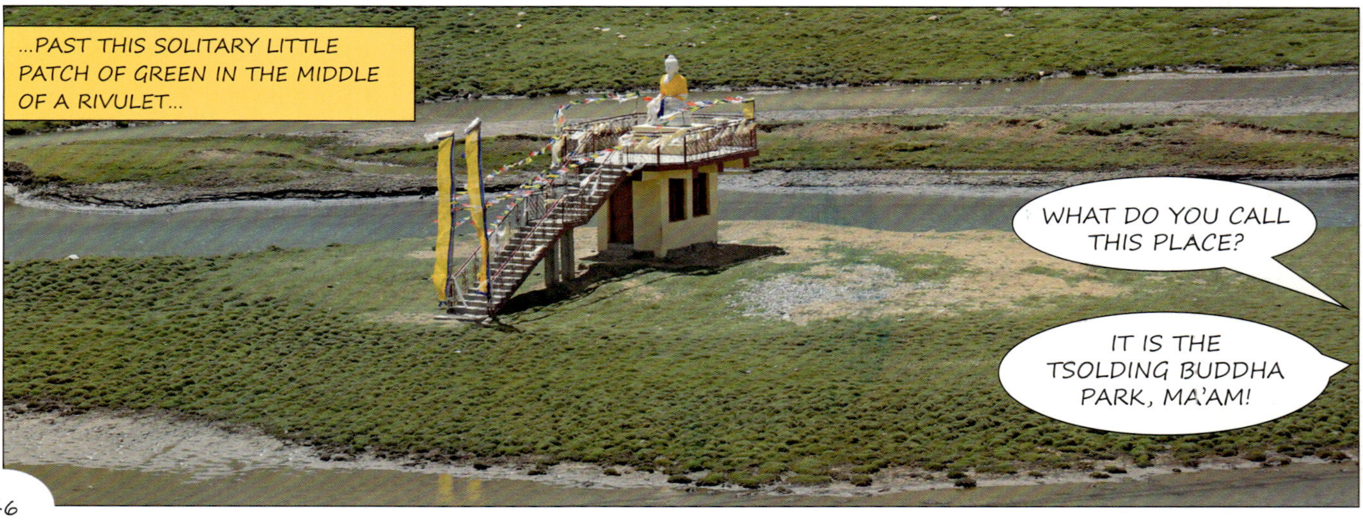
...PAST THIS SOLITARY LITTLE PATCH OF GREEN IN THE MIDDLE OF A RIVULET...
WHAT DO YOU CALL THIS PLACE?
IT IS THE TSOLDING BUDDHA PARK, MA'AM!

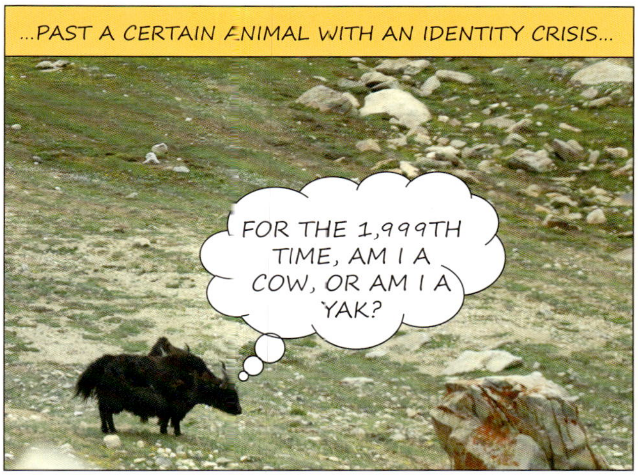
...PAST A CERTAIN ANIMAL WITH AN IDENTITY CRISIS...
FOR THE 1,999TH TIME, AM I A COW, OR AM I A YAK?

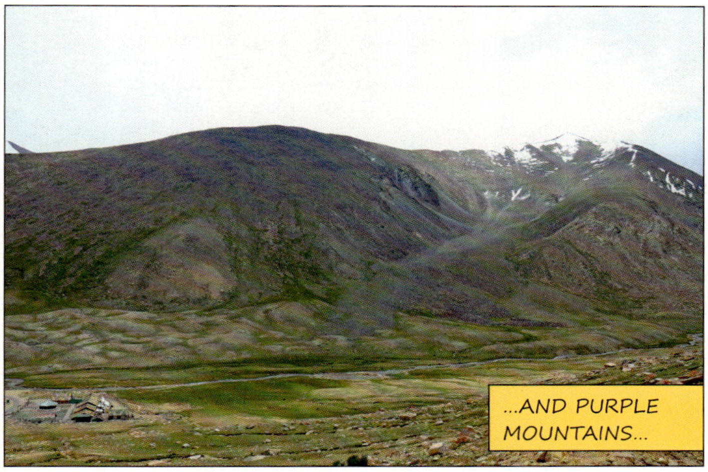
...AND PURPLE MOUNTAINS...

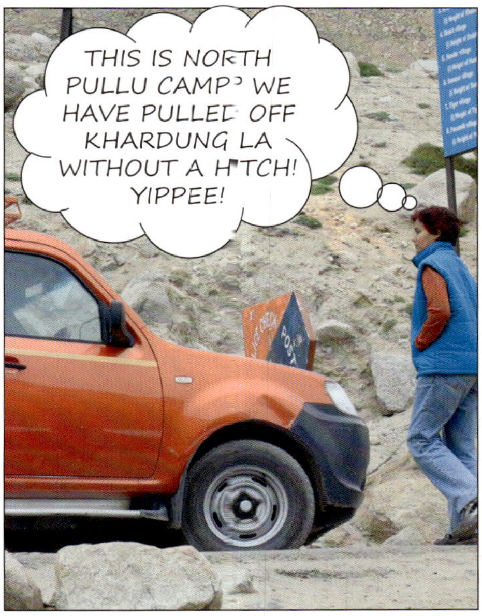
THIS IS NORTH PULLU CAMP! WE HAVE PULLED OFF KHARDUNG LA WITHOUT A HITCH! YIPPEE!

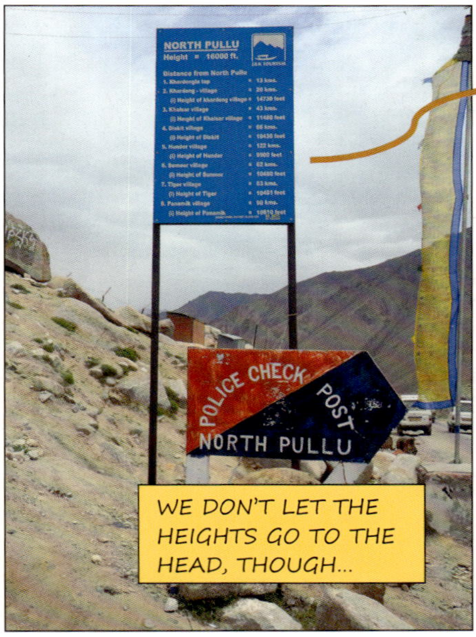
POLICE CHECK POST
NORTH PULLU
WE DON'T LET THE HEIGHTS GO TO THE HEAD, THOUGH...

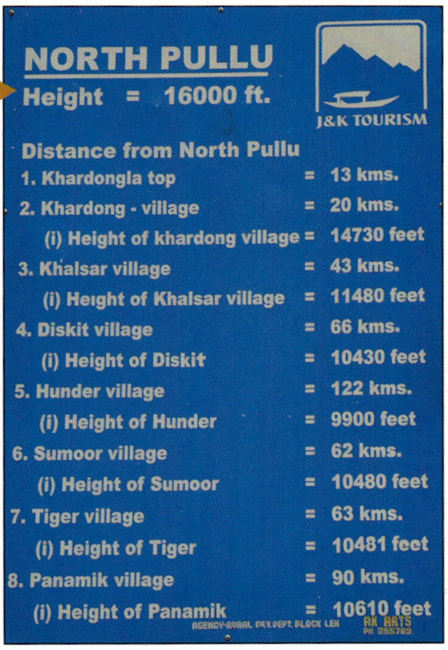
NORTH PULLU
Height = 16000 ft.
J&K TOURISM
Distance from North Pullu
1. Khardongla top = 13 kms.
2. Khardong - village = 20 kms.
(i) Height of khardong village = 14730 feet
3. Khalsar village = 43 kms.
(i) Height of Khalsar village = 11480 feet
4. Diskit village = 66 kms.
(i) Height of Diskit = 10430 feet
5. Hunder village = 122 kms.
(i) Height of Hunder = 9900 feet
6. Sumoor village = 62 kms.
(i) Height of Sumoor = 10480 feet
7. Tiger village = 63 kms.
(i) Height of Tiger = 10481 feet
8. Panamik village = 90 kms.
(i) Height of Panamik = 10610 feet
AK ARTS

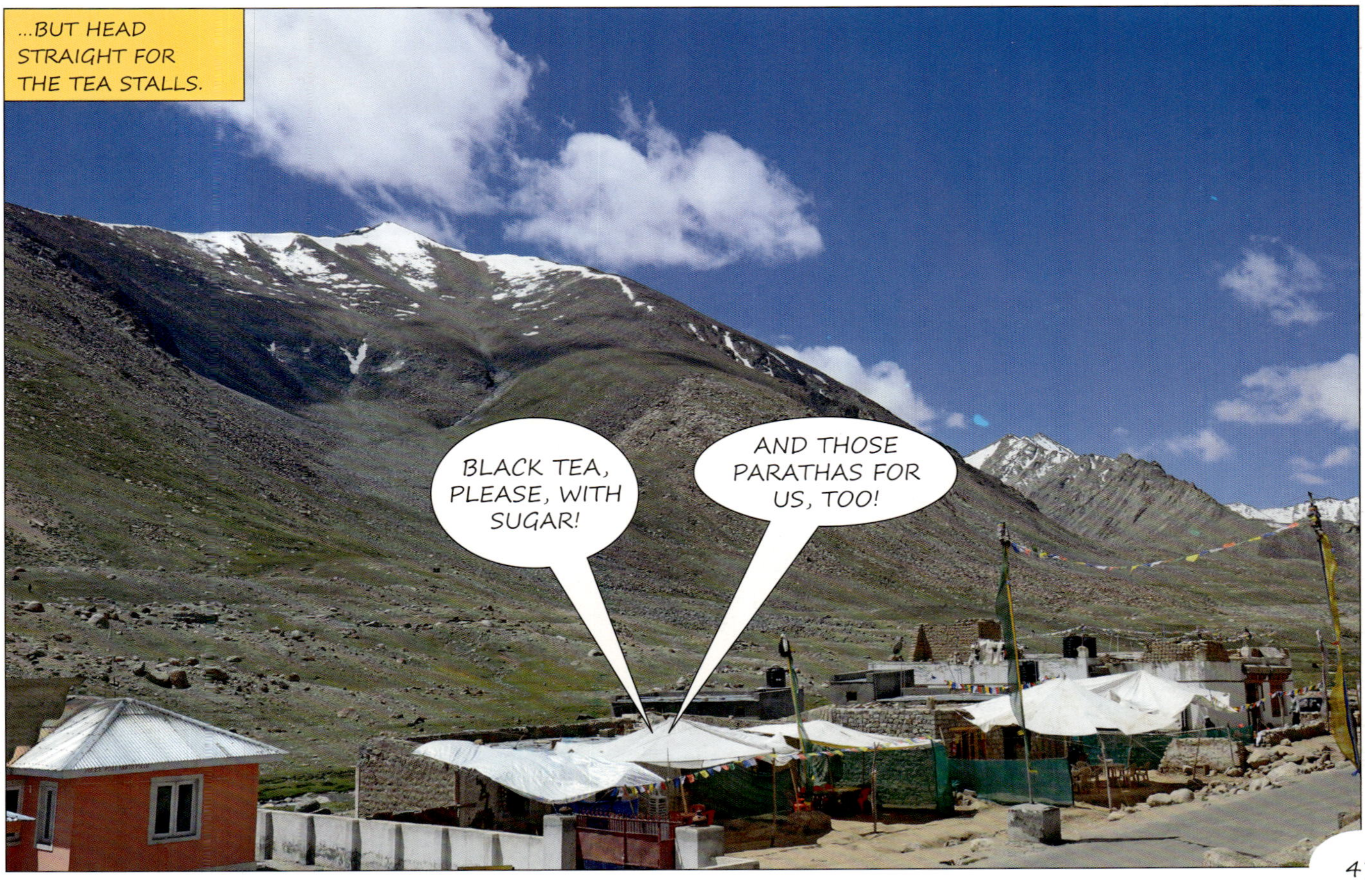
...BUT HEAD STRAIGHT FOR THE TEA STALLS.
BLACK TEA, PLEASE, WITH SUGAR!
AND THOSE PARATHAS FOR US, TOO!

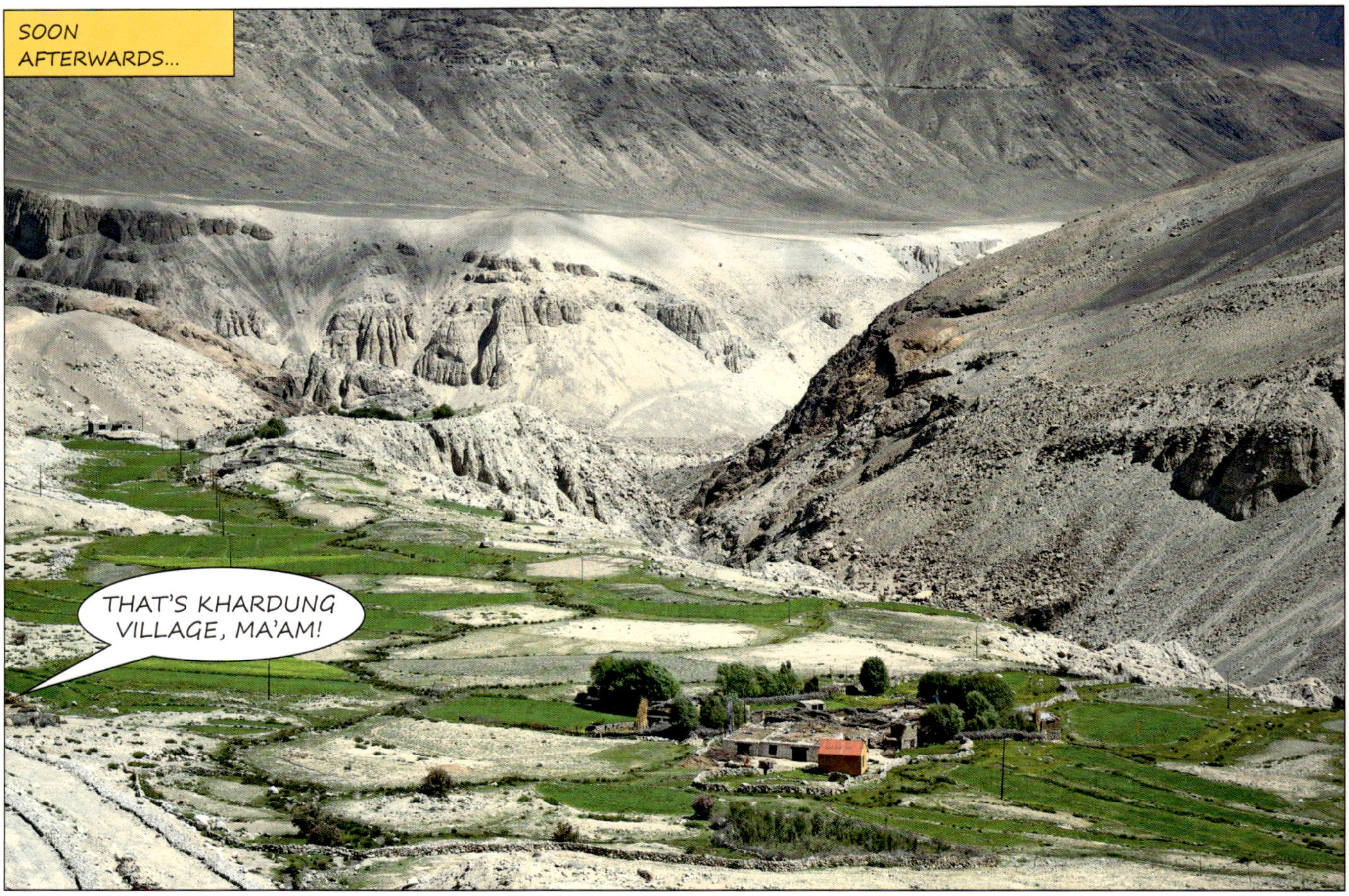
SOON AFTERWARDS...
THAT'S KHARDUNG VILLAGE, MA'AM!

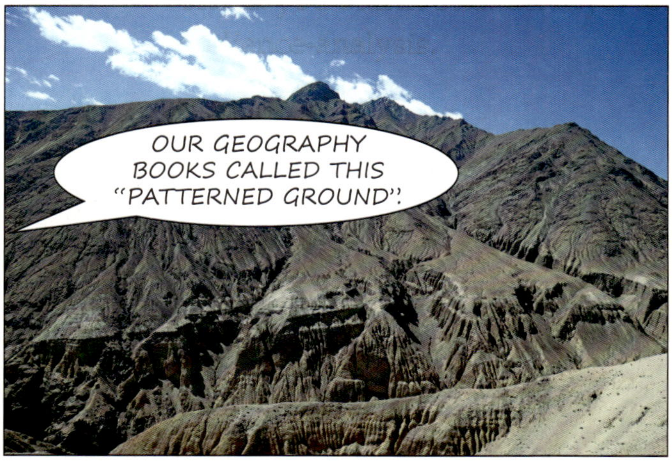
OUR GEOGRAPHY BOOKS CALLED THIS "PATTERNED GROUND".

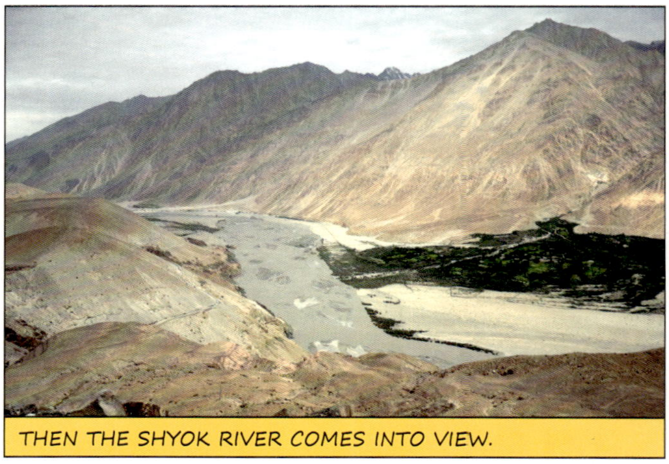
THEN THE SHYOK RIVER COMES INTO VIEW.

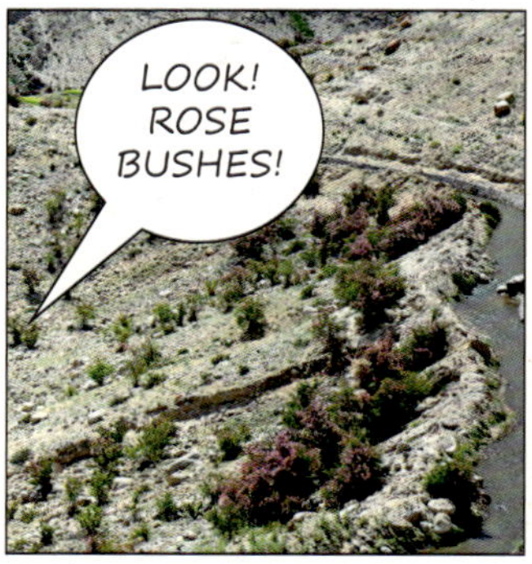
LOOK! ROSE BUSHES!

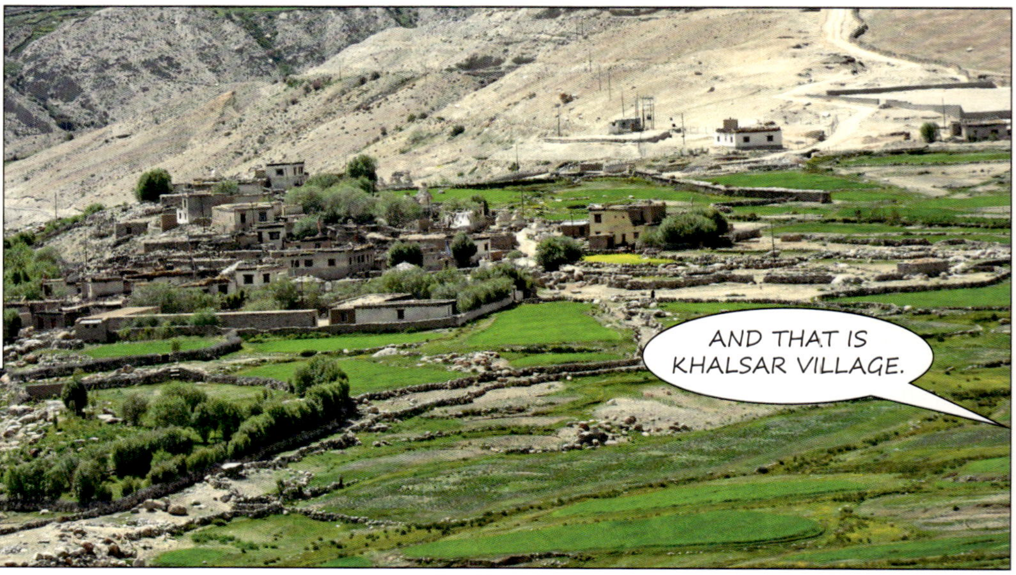
AND THAT IS KHALSAR VILLAGE.

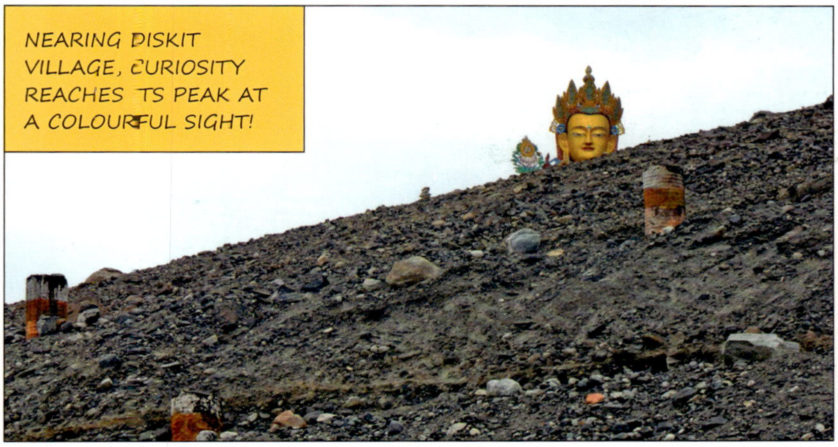
NEARING DISKIT VILLAGE, CURIOSITY REACHES ITS PEAK AT A COLOURFUL SIGHT!

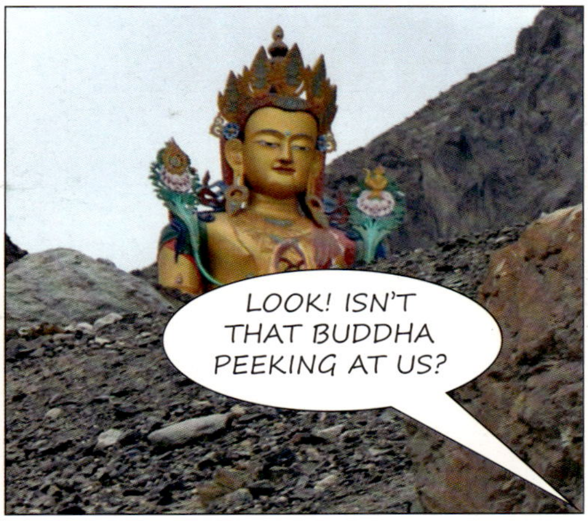
LOOK! ISN'T THAT BUDDHA PEEKING AT US?

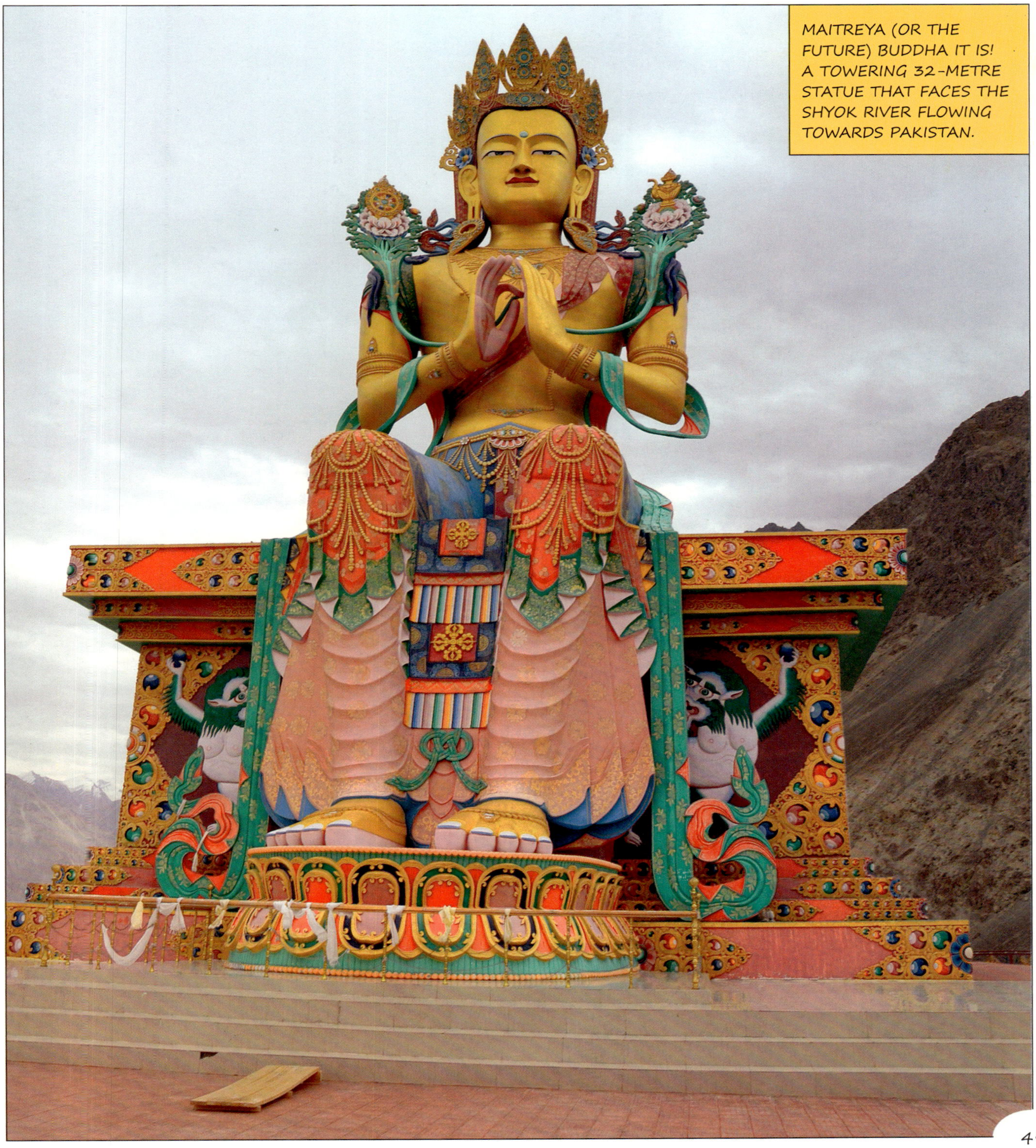
MAITREYA (OR THE FUTURE) BUDDHA IT IS! A TOWERING 32-METRE STATUE THAT FACES THE SHYOK RIVER FLOWING TOWARDS PAKISTAN.

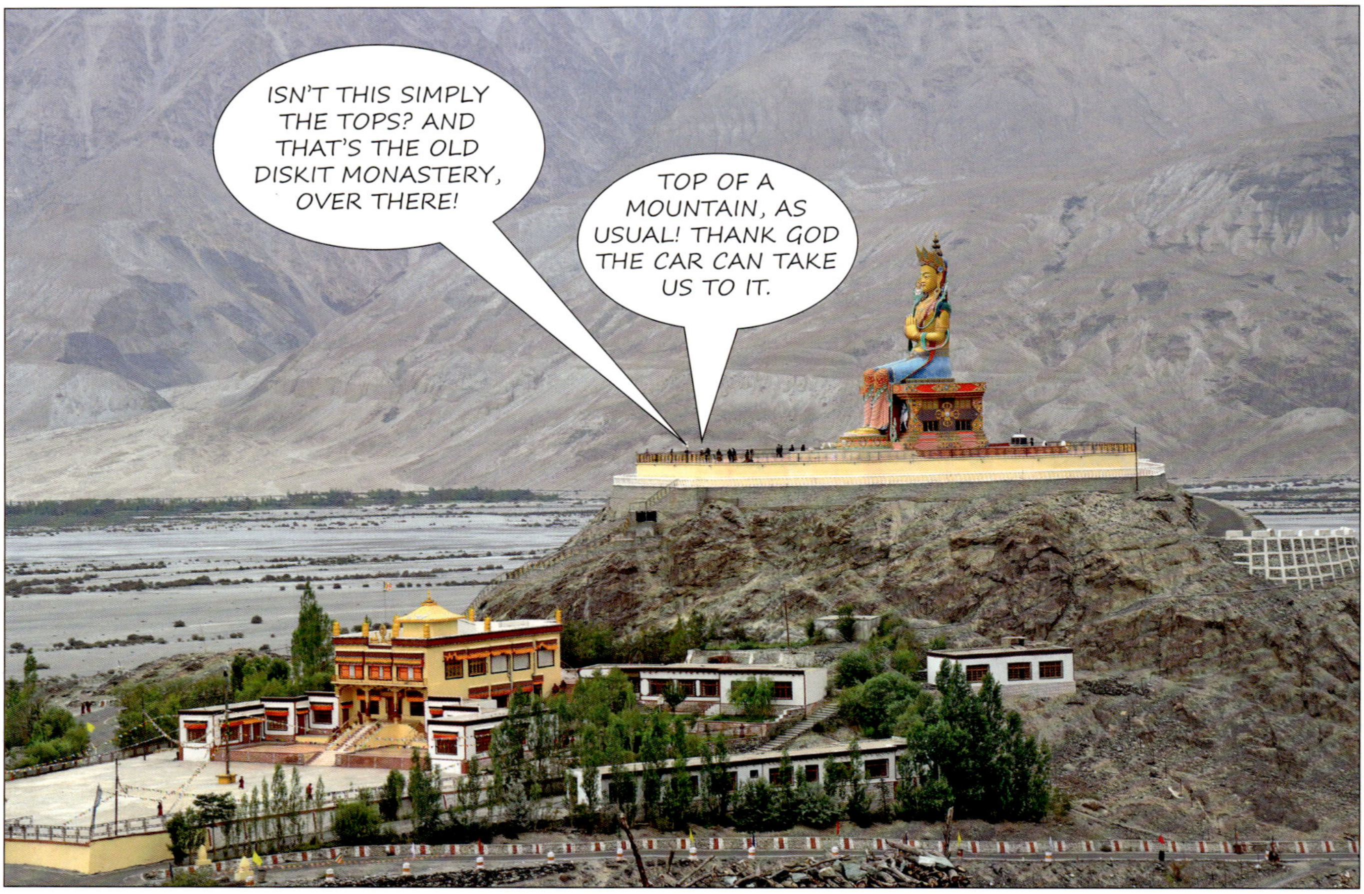

DISKIT MONASTERY, THE LARGEST AND THE OLDEST SURVIVING MONASTERY OF NUBRA VALLEY, IS SAID TO HAVE BEEN FOUNDED BY CHANGZEM TSERAB ZANGPO, A DISCIPLE OF TSONG-KHA-PA, IN THE 14TH CENTURY. DISKIT IS ALSO THE ADMINISTRATIVE HEADQUARTERS OF THIS AREA.

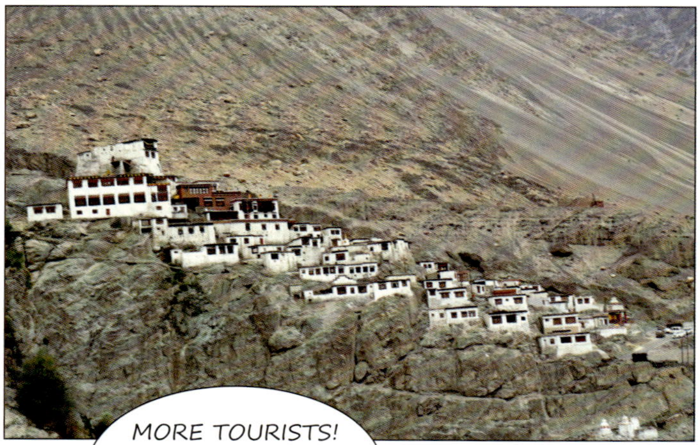

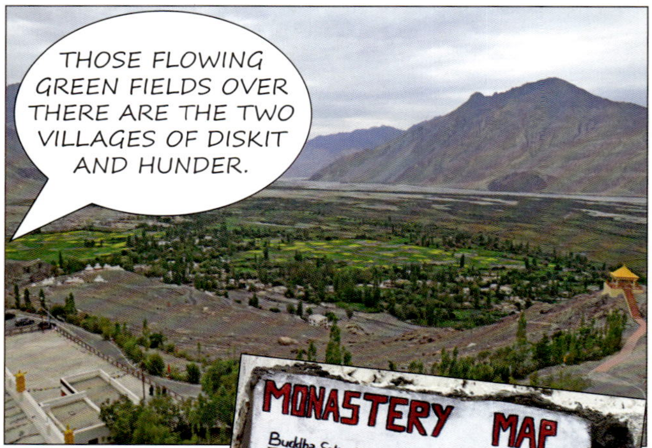

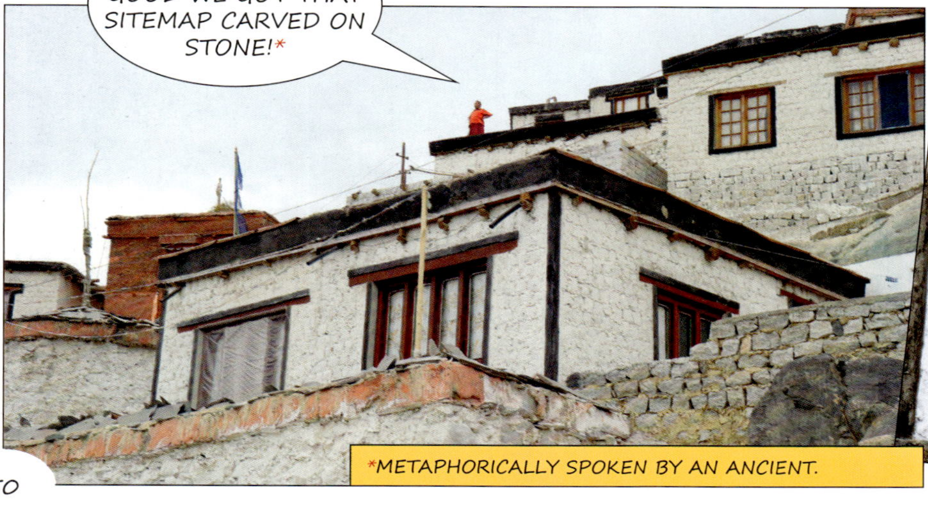

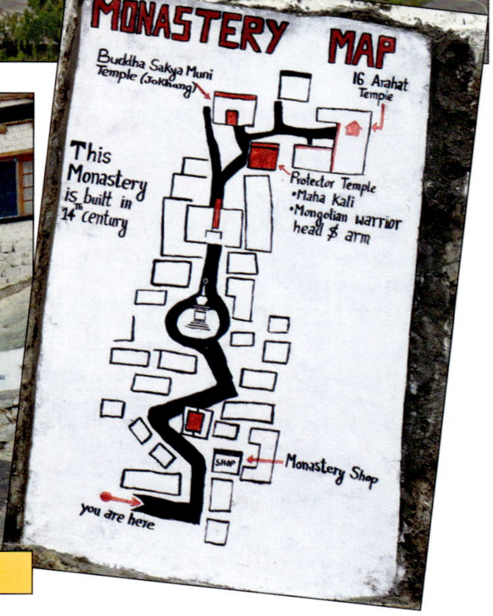

*METAPHORICALLY SPOKEN BY AN ANCIENT.

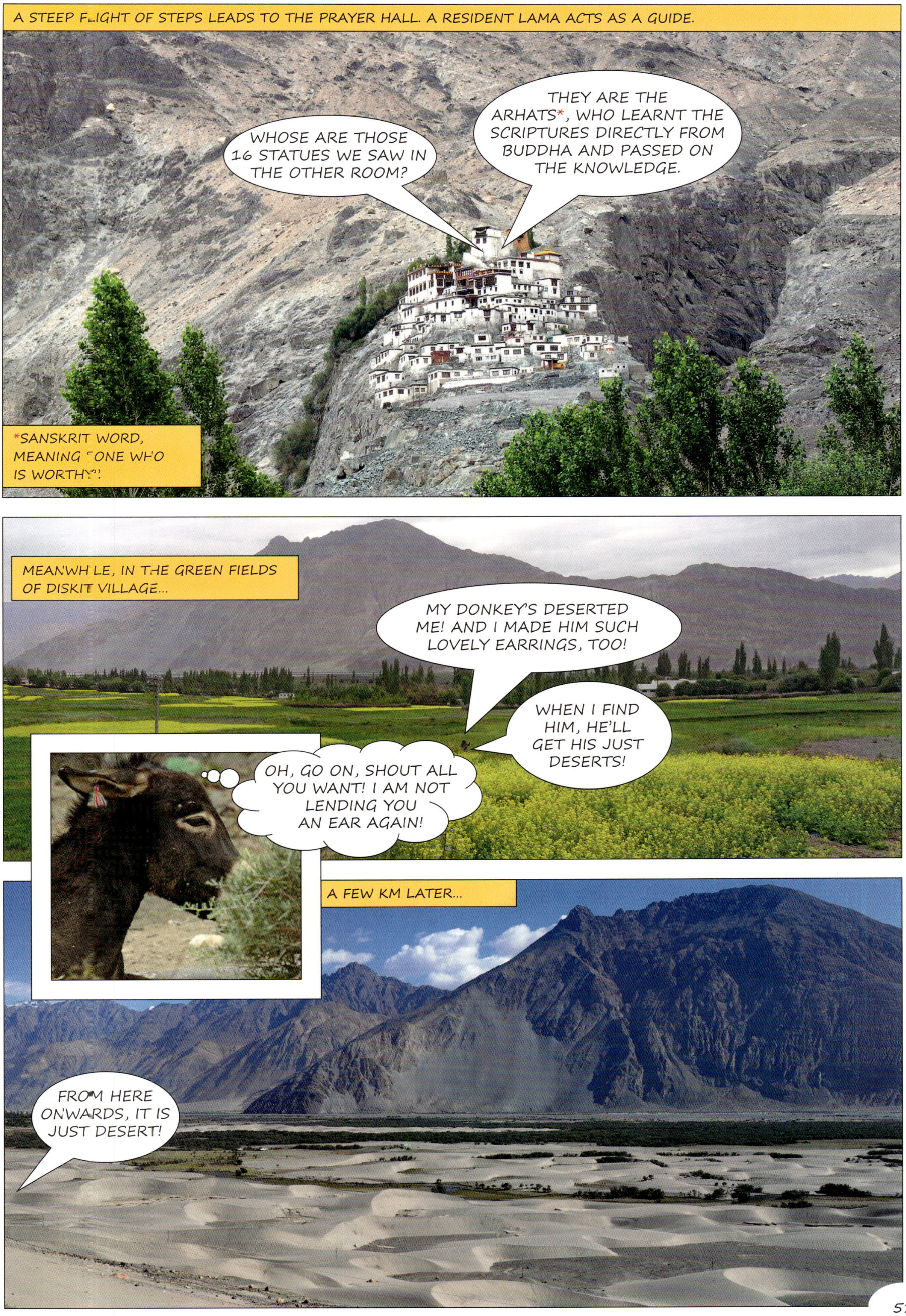
A STEEP FLIGHT OF STEPS LEADS TO THE PRAYER HALL. A RESIDENT LAMA ACTS AS A GUIDE.
WHOSE ARE THOSE 16 STATUES WE SAW IN THE OTHER ROOM?
THEY ARE THE ARHATS*, WHO LEARNT THE SCRIPTURES DIRECTLY FROM BUDDHA AND PASSED ON THE KNOWLEDGE.
*SANSKRIT WORD, MEANING 'ONE WHO IS WORTHY'.
MEANWHILE, IN THE GREEN FIELDS OF DISKIT VILLAGE...
MY DONKEY'S DESERTED ME! AND I MADE HIM SUCH LOVELY EARRINGS, TOO!
WHEN I FIND HIM, HE'LL GET HIS JUST DESERTS!
OH, GO ON, SHOUT ALL YOU WANT! I AM NOT LENDING YOU AN EAR AGAIN!
A FEW KM LATER...
FROM HERE ONWARDS, IT IS JUST DESERT!

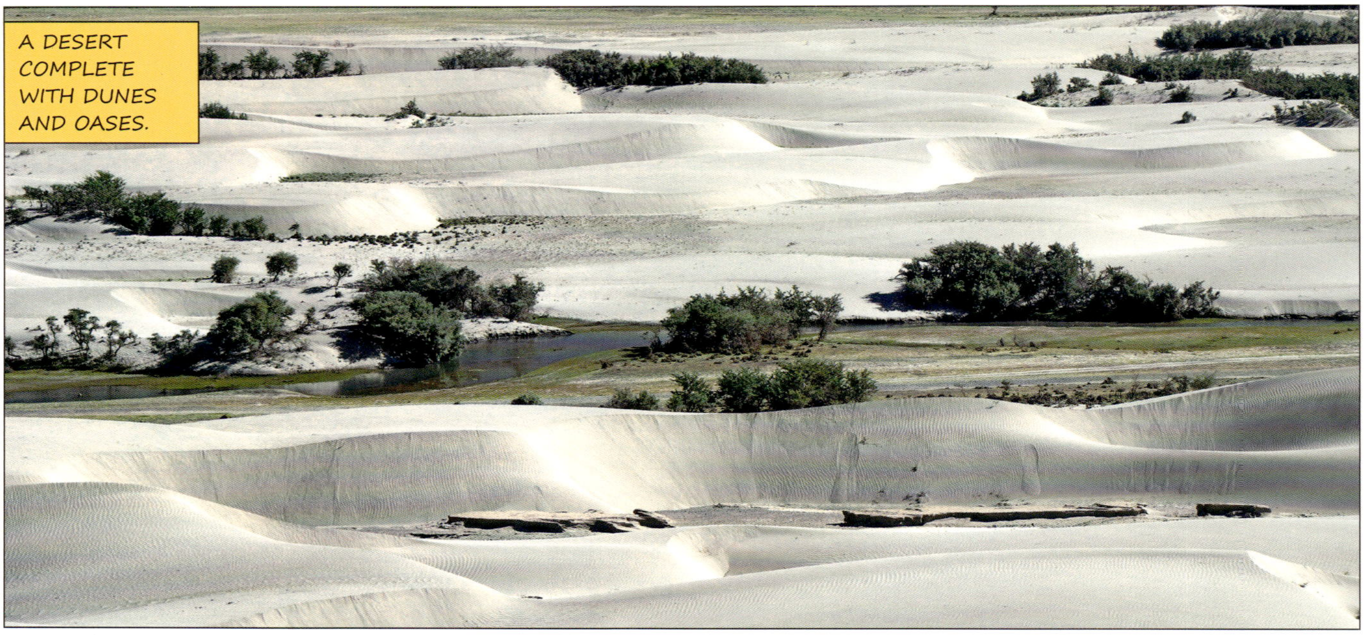
A DESERT COMPLETE WITH DUNES AND OASES.

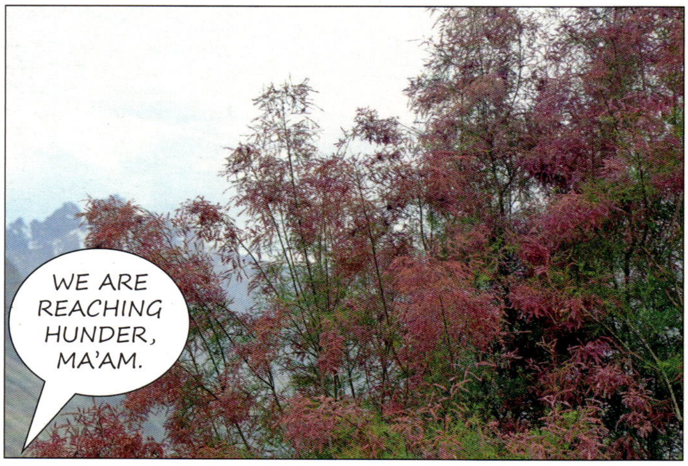
WE ARE REACHING HUNDER, MA'AM.

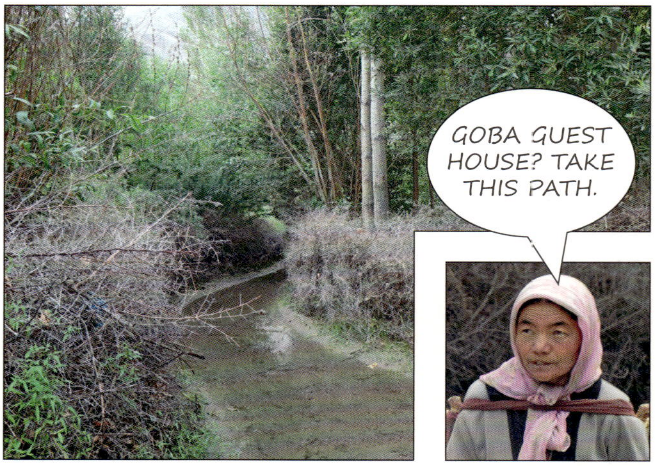
GOBA GUEST HOUSE? TAKE THIS PATH.

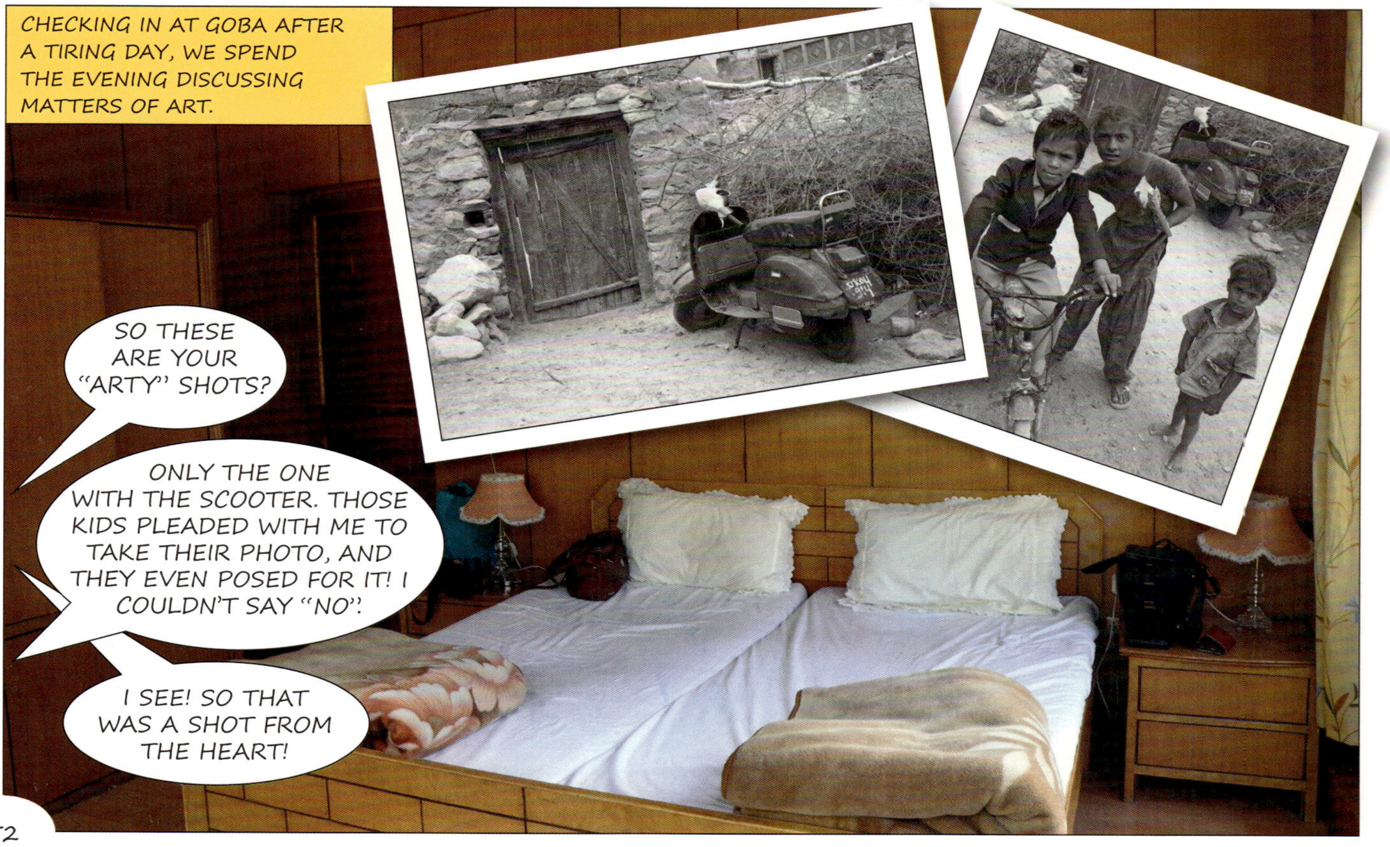
CHECKING IN AT GOBA AFTER A TIRING DAY, WE SPEND THE EVENING DISCUSSING MATTERS OF ART.
SO THESE ARE YOUR "ARTY" SHOTS?
ONLY THE ONE WITH THE SCOOTER. THOSE KIDS PLEADED WITH ME TO TAKE THEIR PHOTO, AND THEY EVEN POSED FOR IT! I COULDN'T SAY "NO".
I SEE! SO THAT WAS A SHOT FROM THE HEART!

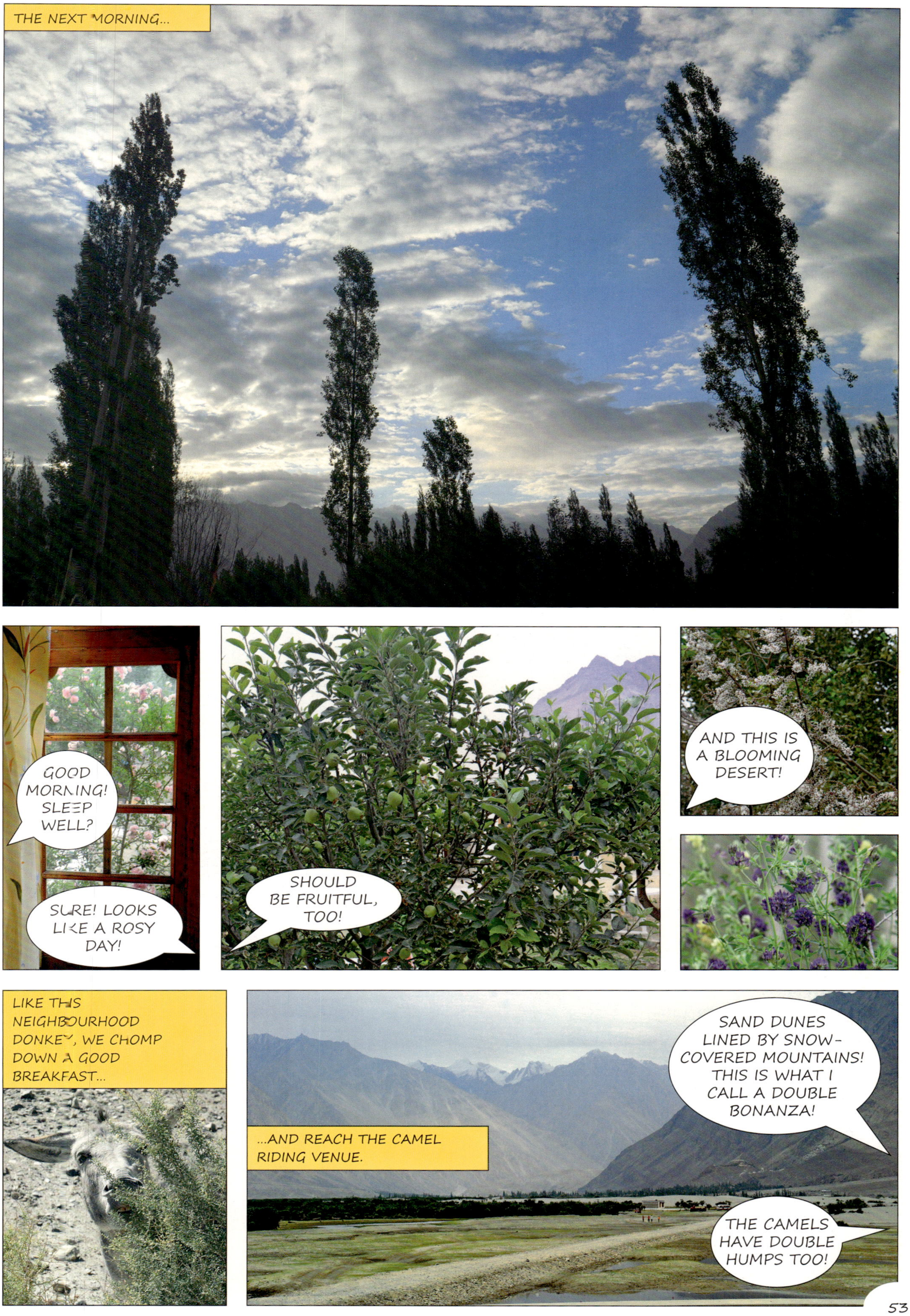
THE NEXT MORNING...
GOOD MORNING! SLEEP WELL?
SURE! LOOKS LIKE A ROSY DAY!
SHOULD BE FRUITFUL, TOO!
AND THIS IS A BLOOMING DESERT!
LIKE THIS NEIGHBOURHOOD DONKEY, WE CHOMP DOWN A GOOD BREAKFAST...
...AND REACH THE CAMEL RIDING VENUE.
SAND DUNES LINED BY SNOW-COVERED MOUNTAINS! THIS IS WHAT I CALL A DOUBLE BONANZA!
THE CAMELS HAVE DOUBLE HUMPS TOO!

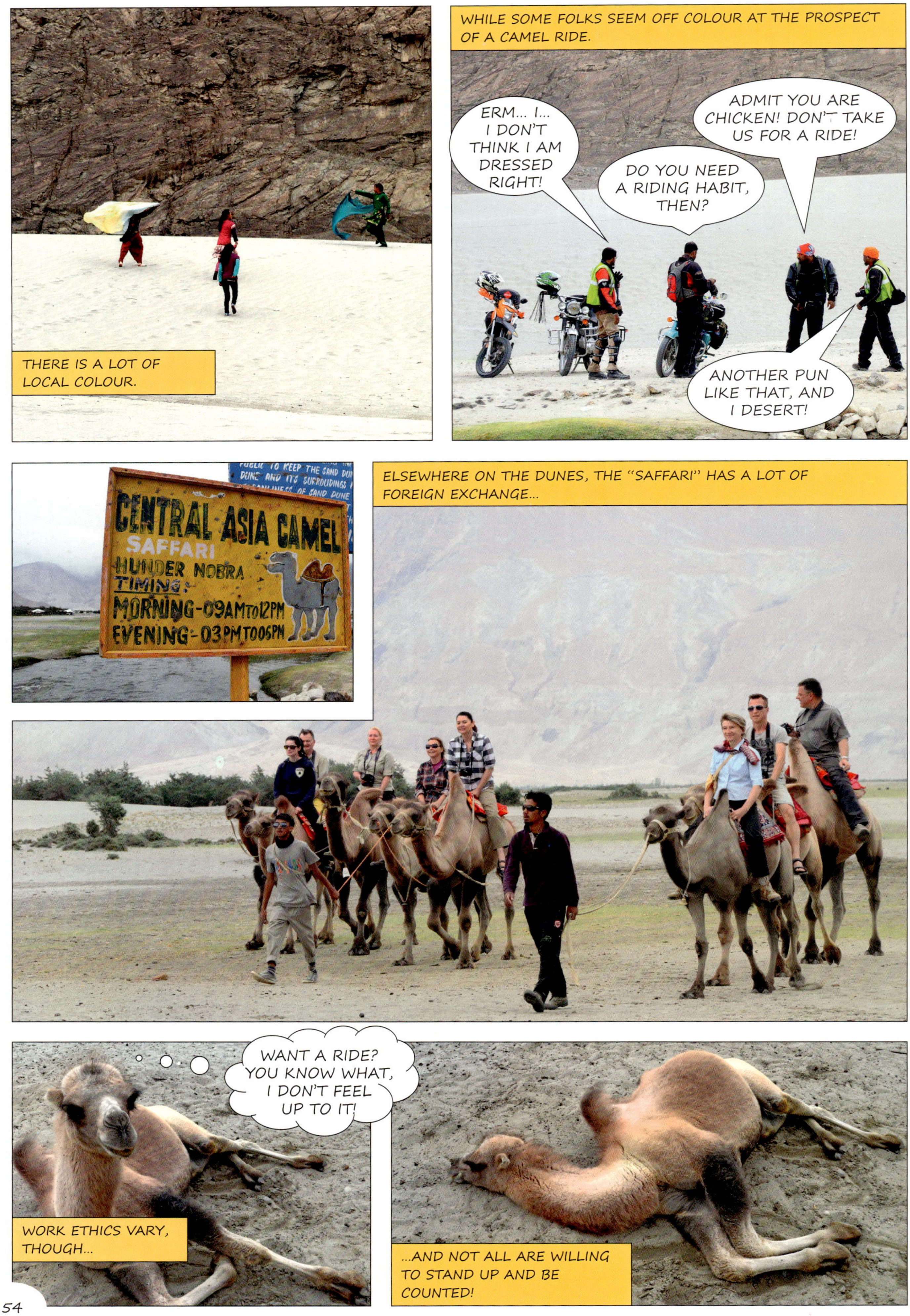
THERE IS A LOT OF LOCAL COLOUR.
WHILE SOME FOLKS SEEM OFF COLOUR AT THE PROSPECT OF A CAMEL RIDE.
ERM... I... I DON'T THINK I AM DRESSED RIGHT!
DO YOU NEED A RIDING HABIT, THEN?
ADMIT YOU ARE CHICKEN! DON'T TAKE US FOR A RIDE!
ANOTHER PUN LIKE THAT, AND I DESERT!
CENTRAL ASIA CAMEL
SAFFARI
HUNDER NOBRA
TIMING:
MORNING-09AM TO 12PM
EVENING-03PM TO 06PM
ELSEWHERE ON THE DUNES, THE "SAFFARI" HAS A LOT OF FOREIGN EXCHANGE...
WANT A RIDE? YOU KNOW WHAT, I DON'T FEEL UP TO IT!
WORK ETHICS VARY, THOUGH...
...AND NOT ALL ARE WILLING TO STAND UP AND BE COUNTED!

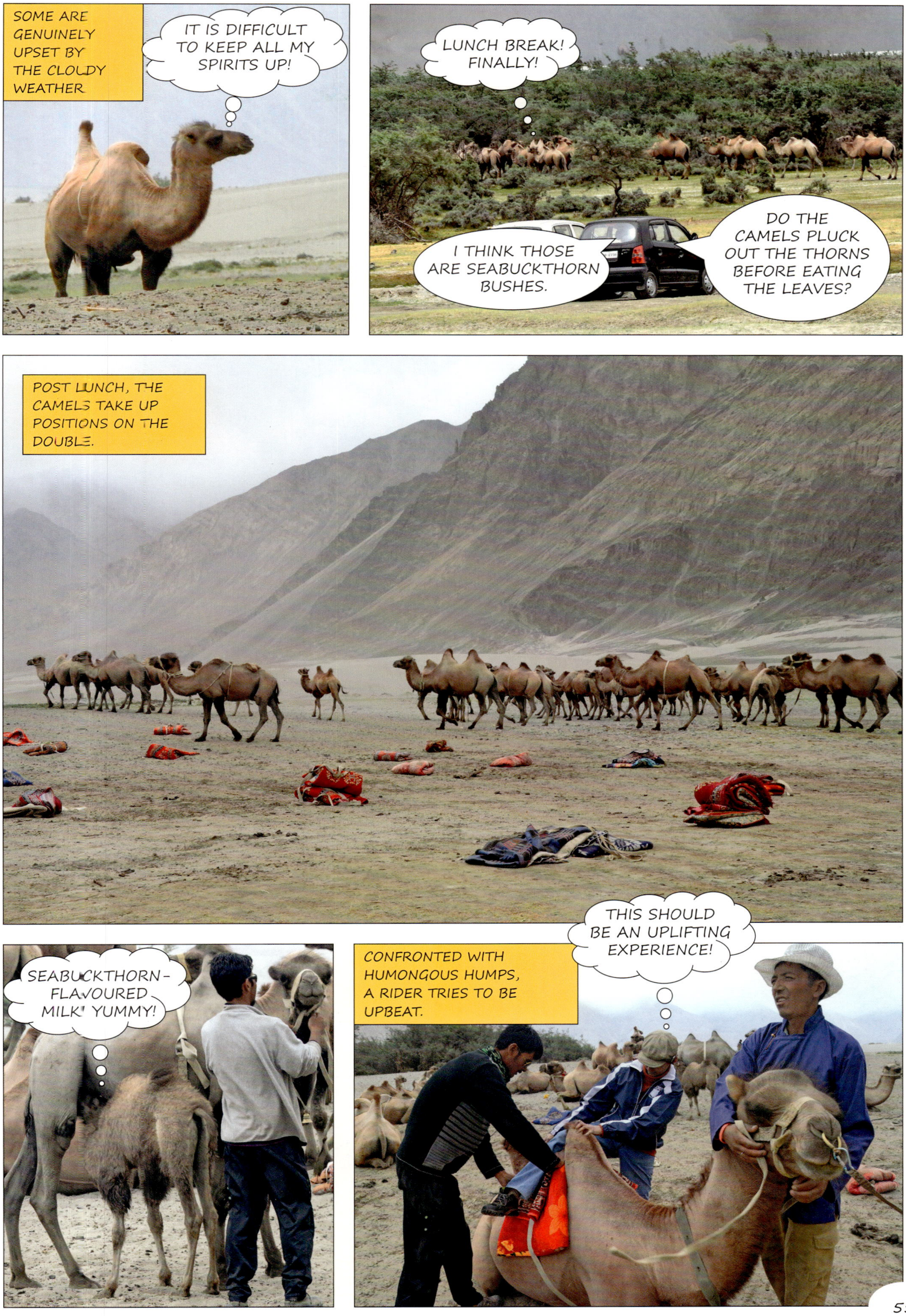
SOME ARE GENUINELY UPSET BY THE CLOUDY WEATHER
IT IS DIFFICULT TO KEEP ALL MY SPIRITS UP!
LUNCH BREAK! FINALLY!
I THINK THOSE ARE SEABUCKTHORN BUSHES.
DO THE CAMELS PLUCK OUT THE THORNS BEFORE EATING THE LEAVES?
POST LUNCH, THE CAMELS TAKE UP POSITIONS ON THE DOUBLE.
SEABUCKTHORN-FLAVOURED MILK! YUMMY!
CONFRONTED WITH HUMONGOUS HUMPS, A RIDER TRIES TO BE UPBEAT.
THIS SHOULD BE AN UPLIFTING EXPERIENCE!

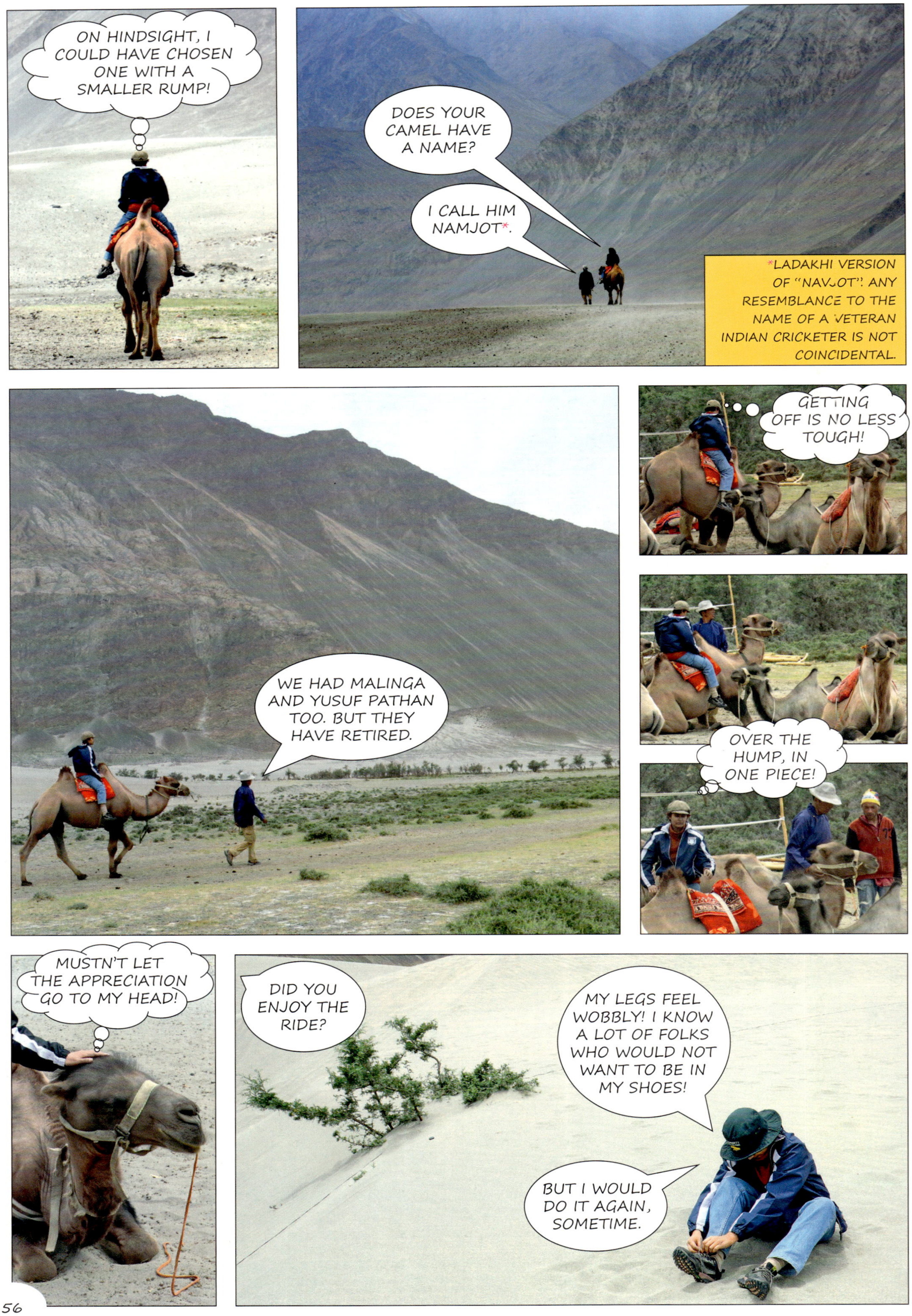
ON HINDSIGHT, I COULD HAVE CHOSEN ONE WITH A SMALLER RUMP!
DOES YOUR CAMEL HAVE A NAME?
I CALL HIM NAMJOT*.
*LADAKHI VERSION OF "NAVJOT". ANY RESEMBLANCE TO THE NAME OF A VETERAN INDIAN CRICKETER IS NOT COINCIDENTAL.
WE HAD MALINGA AND YUSUF PATHAN TOO. BUT THEY HAVE RETIRED.
GETTING OFF IS NO LESS TOUGH!
OVER THE HUMP, IN ONE PIECE!
MUSTN'T LET THE APPRECIATION GO TO MY HEAD!
DID YOU ENJOY THE RIDE?
MY LEGS FEEL WOBBLY! I KNOW A LOT OF FOLKS WHO WOULD NOT WANT TO BE IN MY SHOES!
BUT I WOULD DO IT AGAIN, SOMETIME.

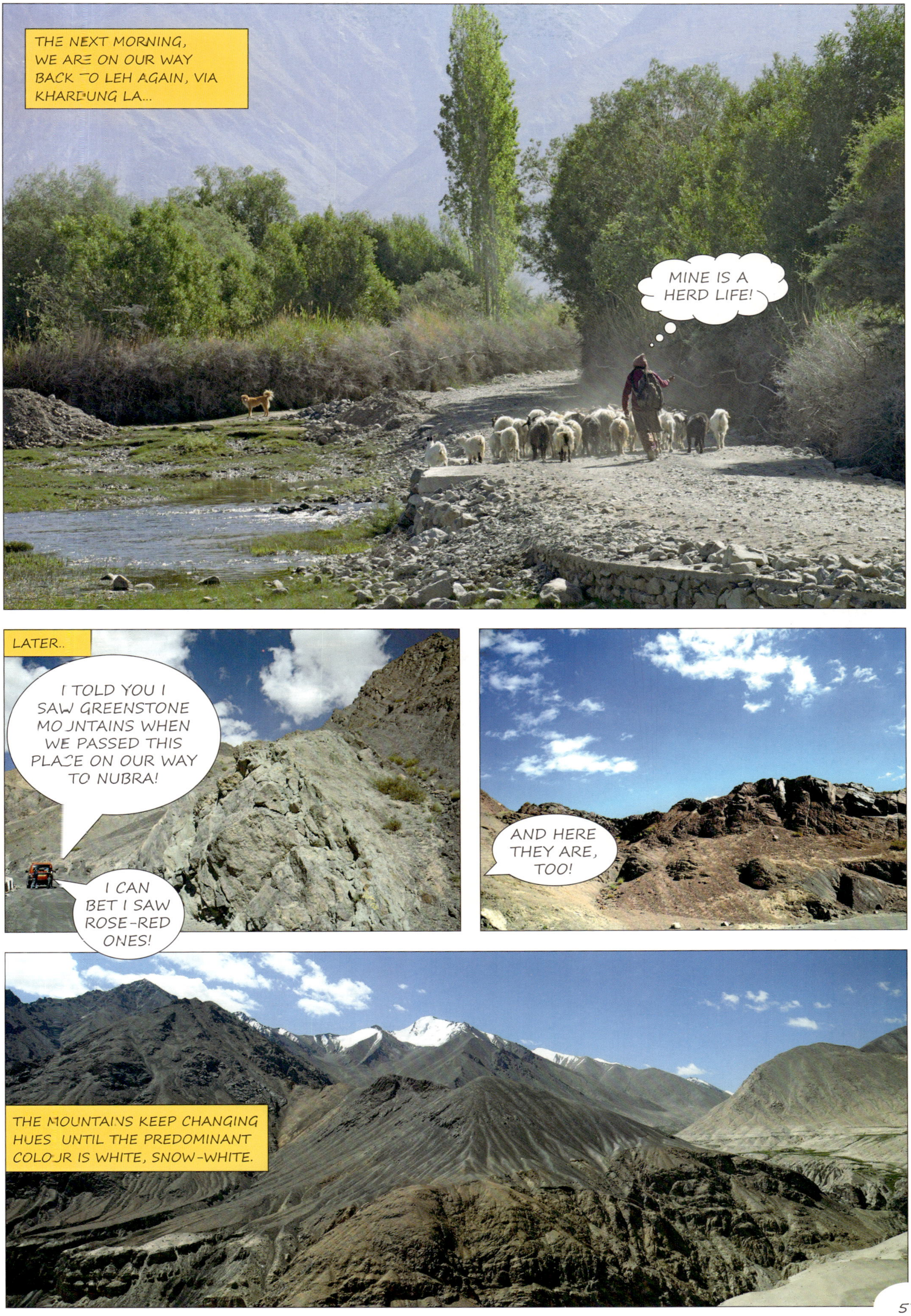
THE NEXT MORNING, WE ARE ON OUR WAY BACK TO LEH AGAIN, VIA KHARDUNG LA...
MINE IS A HERD LIFE!
LATER..
I TOLD YOU I SAW GREENSTONE MOUNTAINS WHEN WE PASSED THIS PLACE ON OUR WAY TO NUBRA!
I CAN BET I SAW ROSE-RED ONES!
AND HERE THEY ARE, TOO!
THE MOUNTAINS KEEP CHANGING HUES UNTIL THE PREDOMINANT COLOUR IS WHITE, SNOW-WHITE.

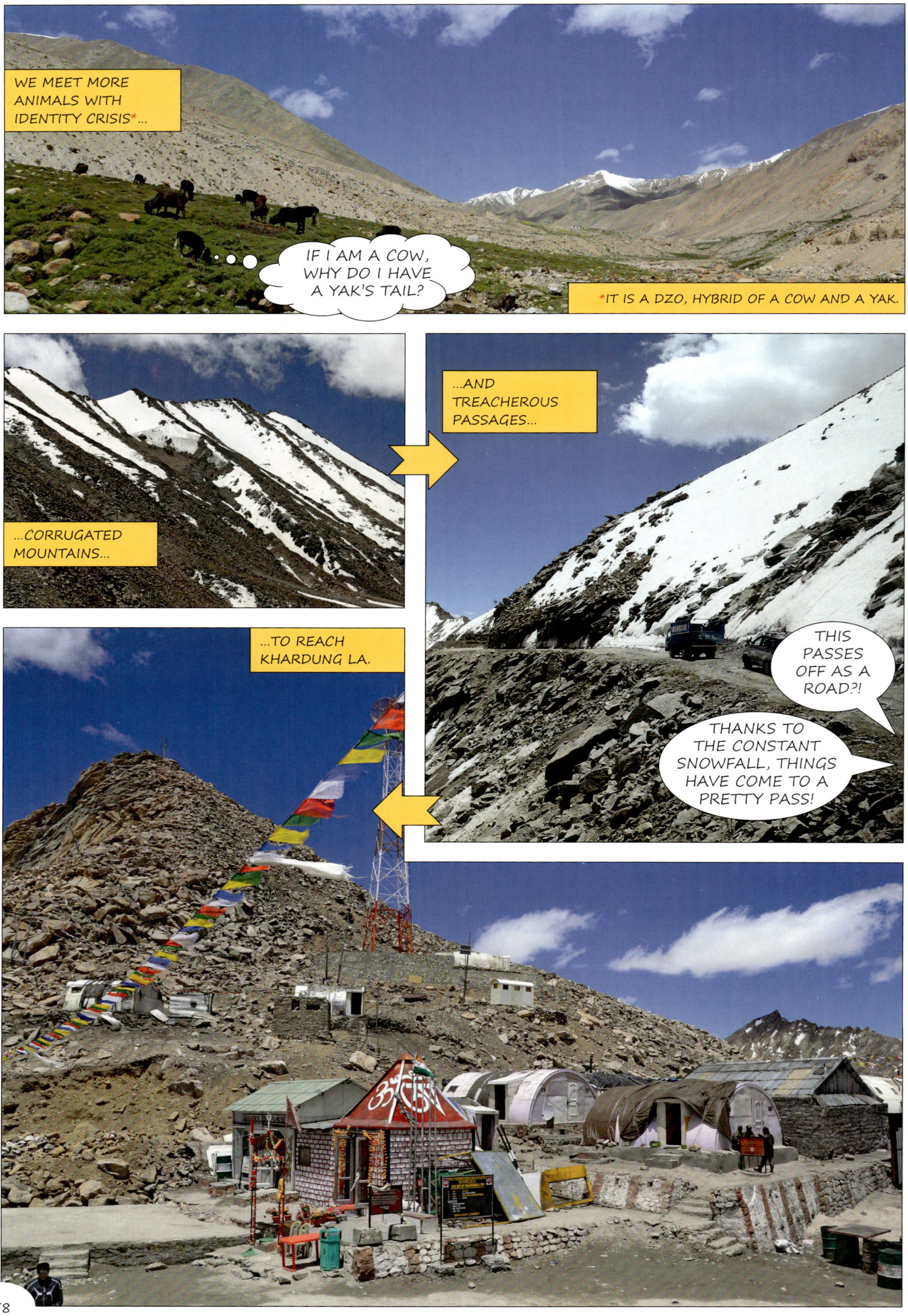
WE MEET MORE ANIMALS WITH IDENTITY CRISIS*...
IF I AM A COW, WHY DO I HAVE A YAK'S TAIL?
*IT IS A DZO, HYBRID OF A COW AND A YAK.
...CORRUGATED MOUNTAINS...
...AND TREACHEROUS PASSAGES...
THIS PASSES OFF AS A ROAD?!
THANKS TO THE CONSTANT SNOWFALL, THINGS HAVE COME TO A PRETTY PASS!
...TO REACH KHARDUNG LA.

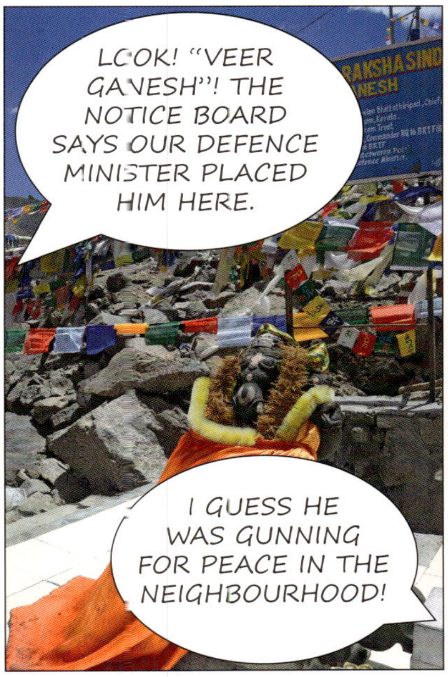
LOOK! "VEER GANESH"! THE NOTICE BOARD SAYS OUR DEFENCE MINISTER PLACED HIM HERE.
I GUESS HE WAS GUNNING FOR PEACE IN THE NEIGHBOURHOOD!

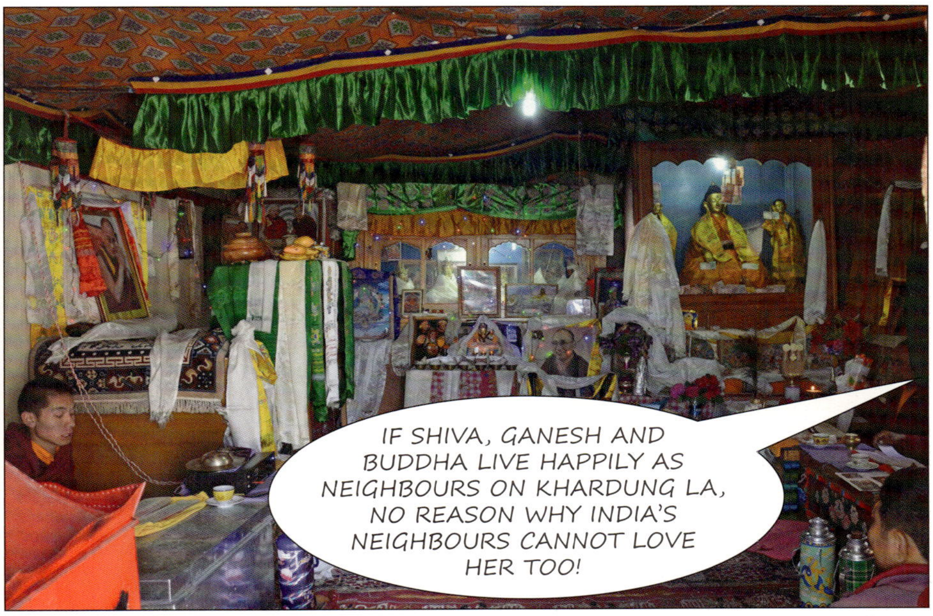
IF SHIVA, GANESH AND BUDDHA LIVE HAPPILY AS NEIGHBOURS ON KHARDUNG LA, NO REASON WHY INDIA'S NEIGHBOURS CANNOT LOVE HER TOO!

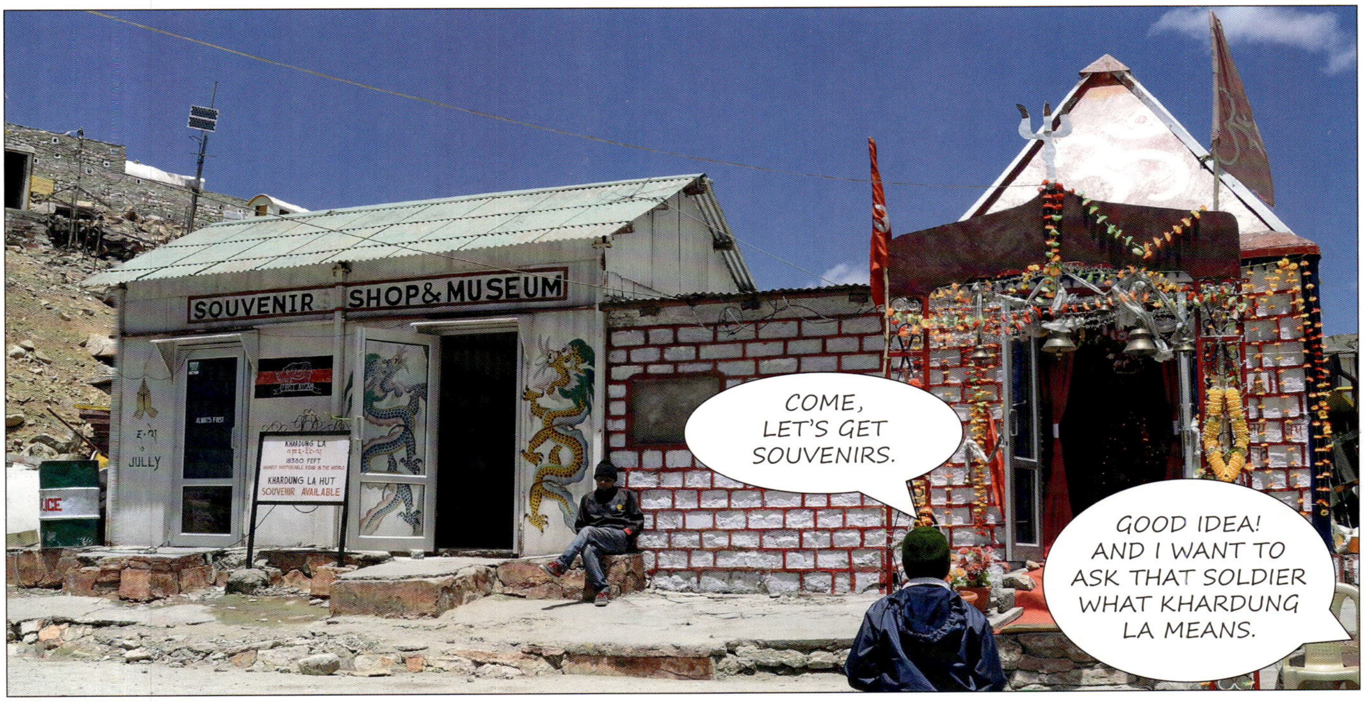
SOUVENIR SHOP&MUSEUM
JULLY
KHARDUNG LA HUT
SOUVENIR AVAILABLE
COME, LET'S GET SOUVENIRS.
GOOD IDEA! AND I WANT TO ASK THAT SOLDIER WHAT KHARDUNG LA MEANS.

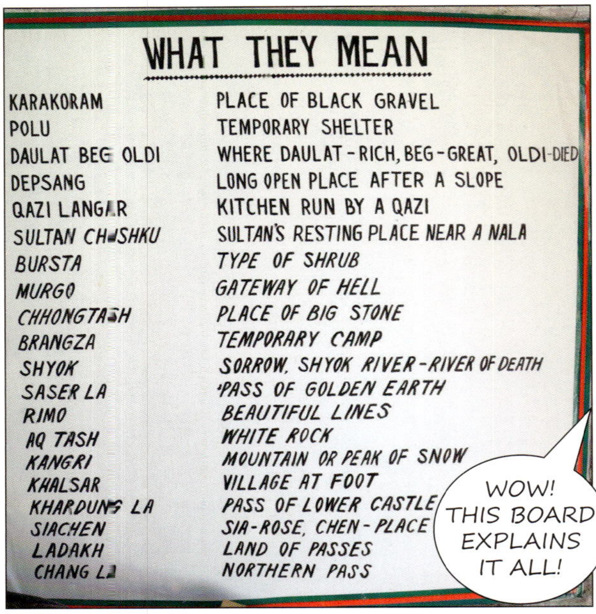
WHAT THEY MEAN
KARAKORAM PLACE OF BLACK GRAVEL
POLU TEMPORARY SHELTER
DAULAT BEG OLDI WHERE DAULAT-RICH, BEG-GREAT, OLDI-DIED
DEPSANG LONG OPEN PLACE AFTER A SLOPE
QAZI LANGAR KITCHEN RUN BY A QAZI
SULTAN CHUSHKU SULTAN'S RESTING PLACE NEAR A NALA
BURSTA TYPE OF SHRUB
MURGO GATEWAY OF HELL
CHHONGTASH PLACE OF BIG STONE
BRANGZA TEMPORARY CAMP
SHYOK SORROW, SHYOK RIVER-RIVER OF DEATH
SASER LA PASS OF GOLDEN EARTH
RIMO BEAUTIFUL LINES
AQ TASH WHITE ROCK
KANGRI MOUNTAIN OR PEAK OF SNOW
KHALSAR VILLAGE AT FOOT
KHARDUNG LA PASS OF LOWER CASTLE
SIACHEN SIA-ROSE, CHEN-PLACE
LADAKH LAND OF PASSES
CHANG LA NORTHERN PASS
WOW! THIS BOARD EXPLAINS IT ALL!

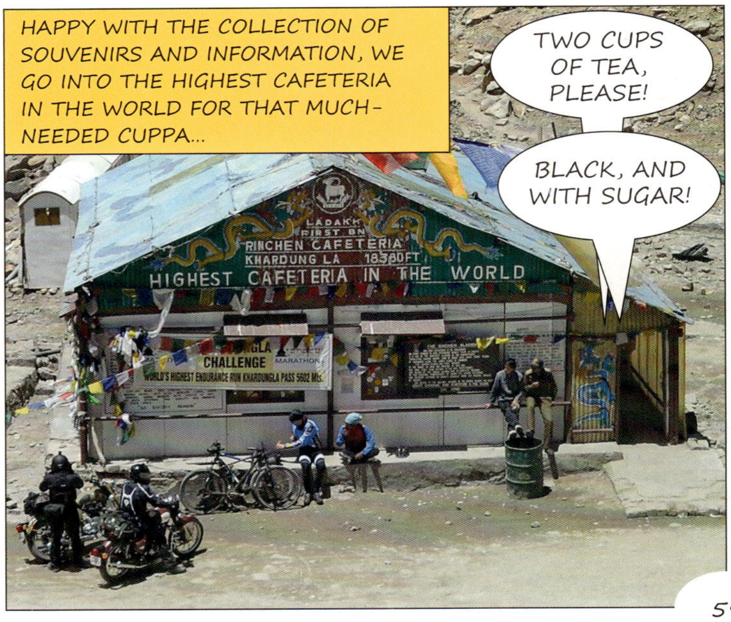
HAPPY WITH THE COLLECTION OF SOUVENIRS AND INFORMATION, WE GO INTO THE HIGHEST CAFETERIA IN THE WORLD FOR THAT MUCH-NEEDED CUPPA...
TWO CUPS OF TEA, PLEASE!
BLACK, AND WITH SUGAR!
RINCHEN CAFETERIA
KHARDUNG LA 18380FT
HIGHEST CAFETERIA IN THE WORLD
CHALLENGE

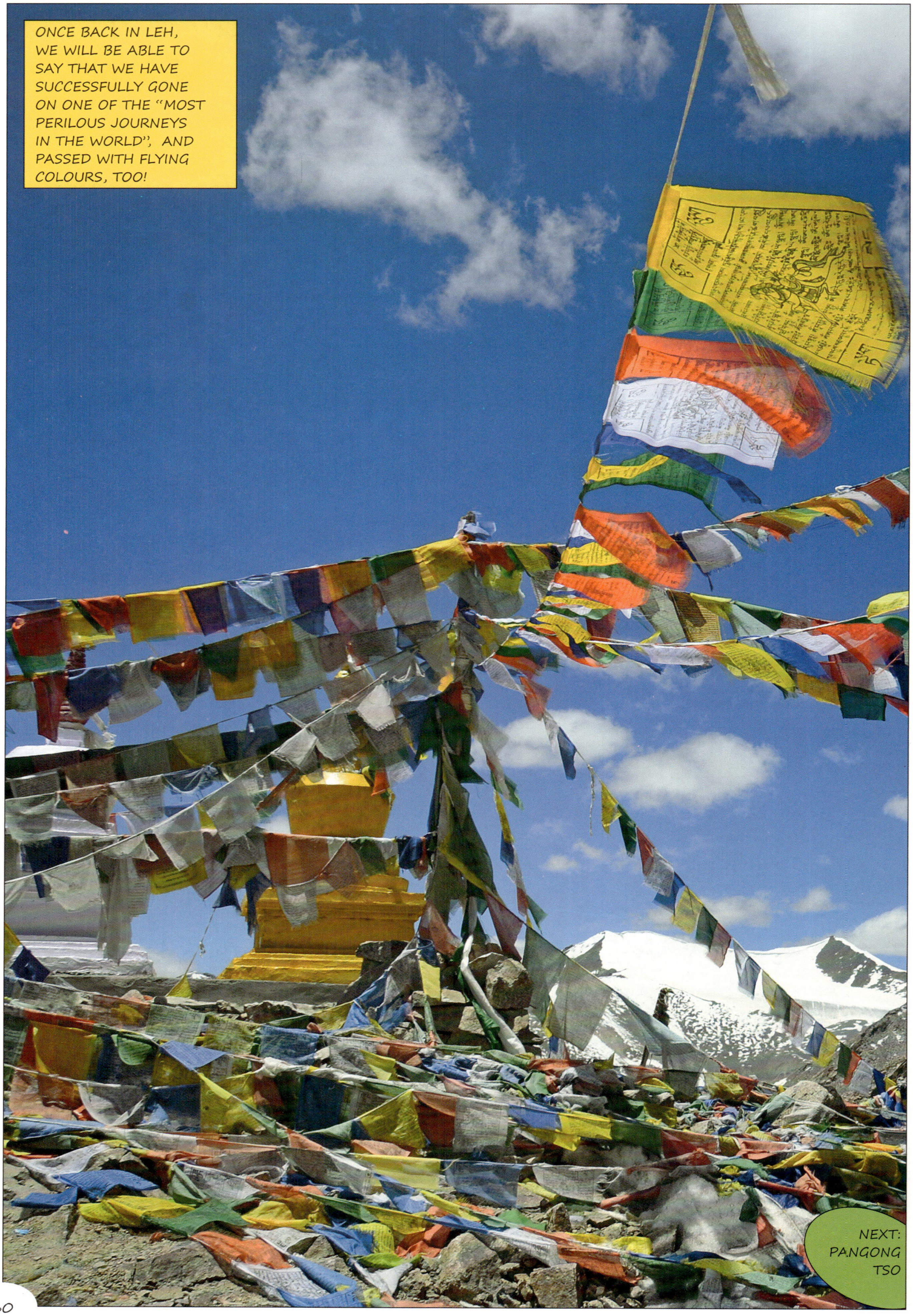
ONCE BACK IN LEH, WE WILL BE ABLE TO SAY THAT WE HAVE SUCCESSFULLY GONE ON ONE OF THE "MOST PERILOUS JOURNEYS IN THE WORLD", AND PASSED WITH FLYING COLOURS, TOO!
NEXT: PANGONG TSO

Chapter IV: Pangong Tso

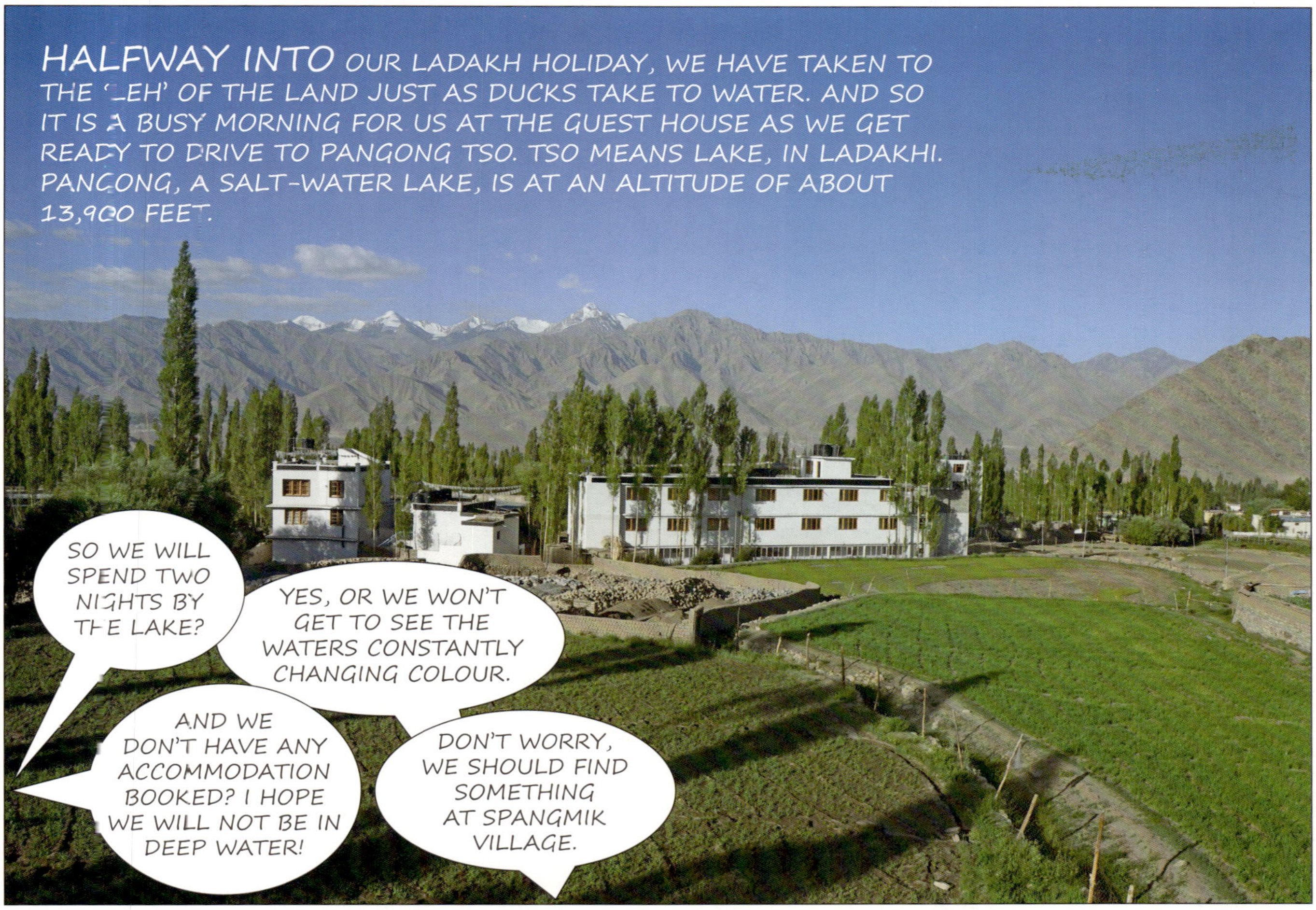

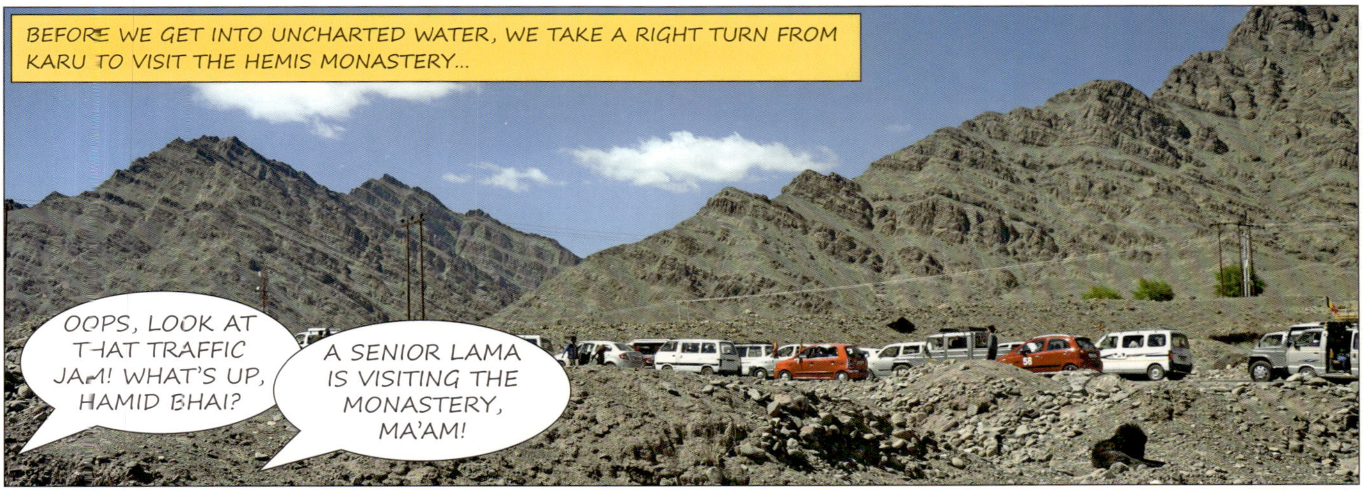

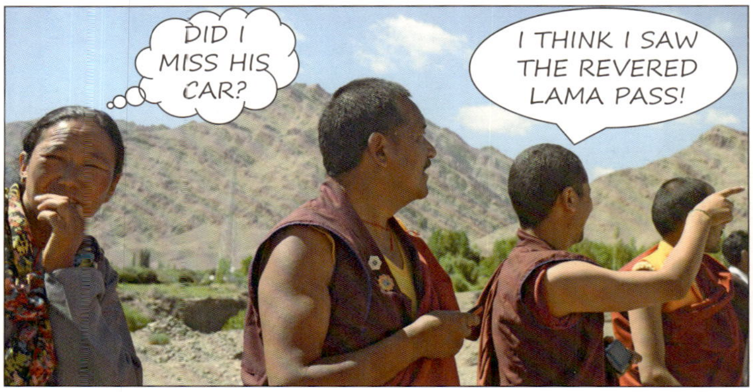

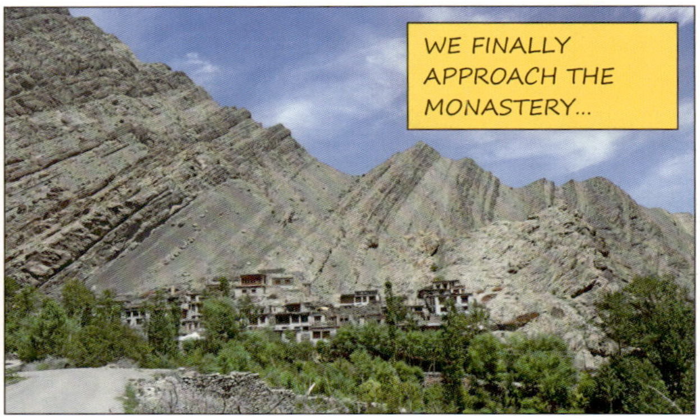

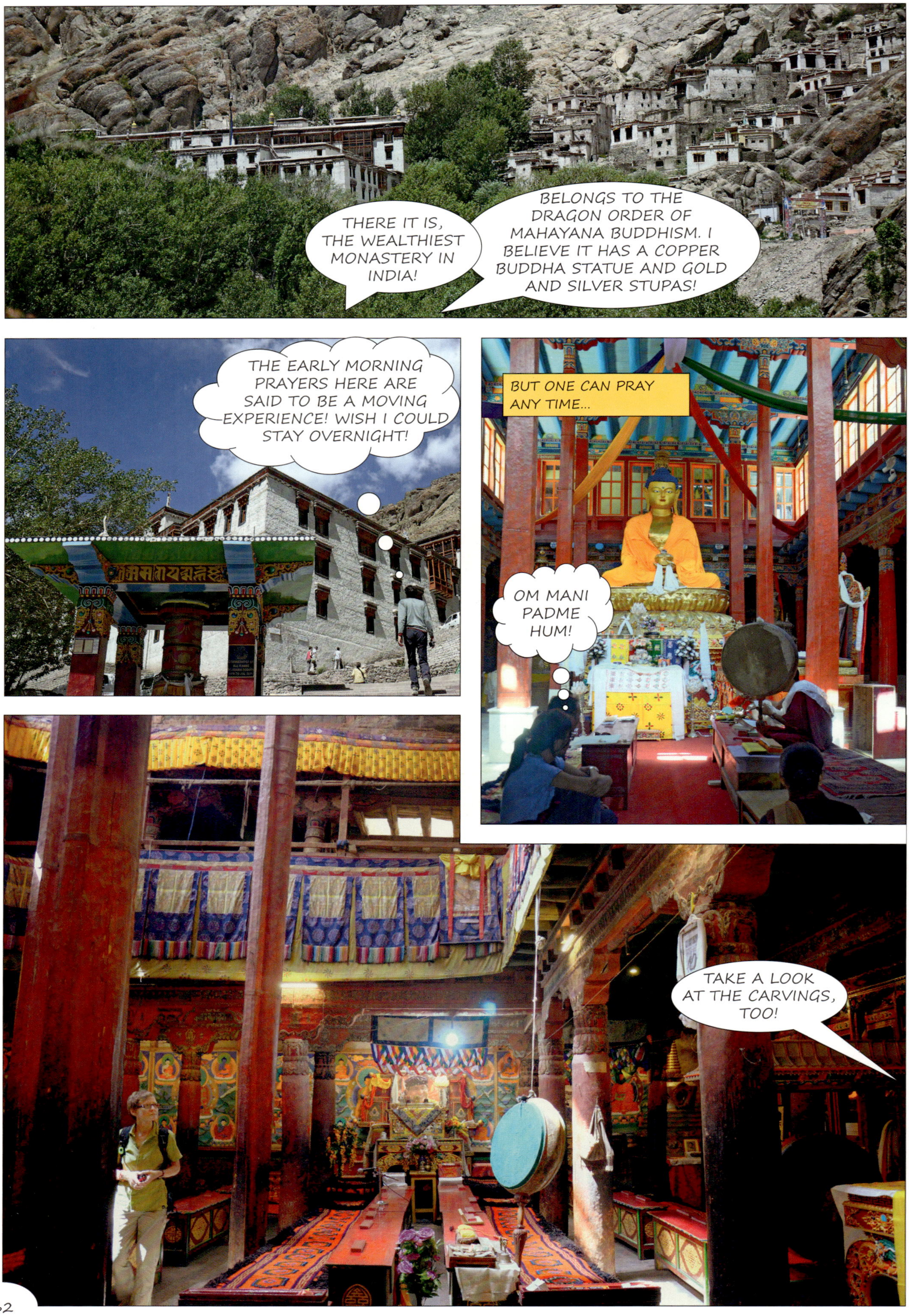
THERE IT IS, THE WEALTHIEST MONASTERY IN INDIA!
BELONGS TO THE DRAGON ORDER OF MAHAYANA BUDDHISM. I BELIEVE IT HAS A COPPER BUDDHA STATUE AND GOLD AND SILVER STUPAS!
THE EARLY MORNING PRAYERS HERE ARE SAID TO BE A MOVING EXPERIENCE! WISH I COULD STAY OVERNIGHT!
BUT ONE CAN PRAY ANY TIME...
OM MANI PADME HUM!
TAKE A LOOK AT THE CARVINGS, TOO!

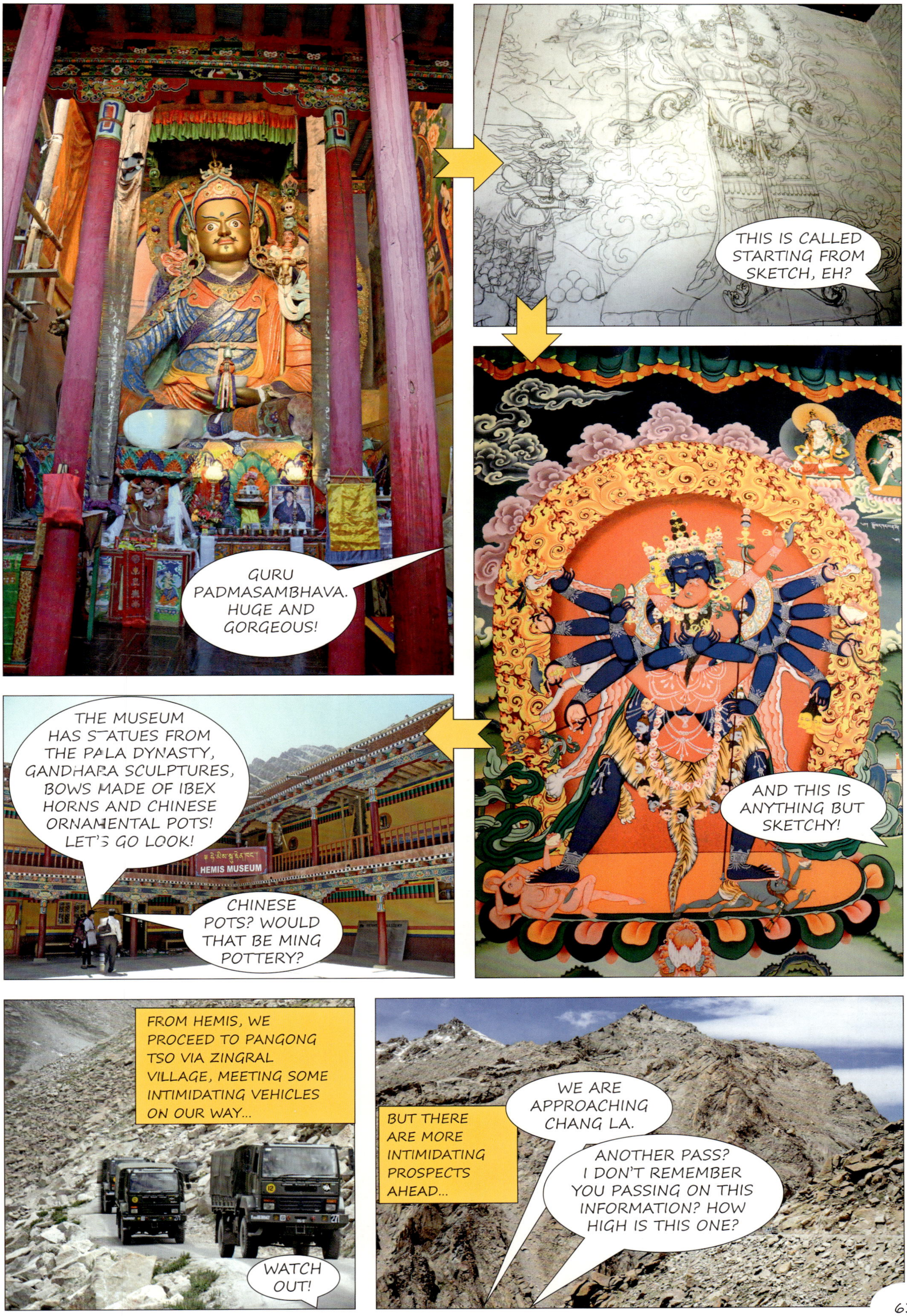
GURU PADMASAMBHAVA. HUGE AND GORGEOUS!
THIS IS CALLED STARTING FROM SKETCH, EH?
AND THIS IS ANYTHING BUT SKETCHY!
THE MUSEUM HAS STATUES FROM THE PALA DYNASTY, GANDHARA SCULPTURES, BOWS MADE OF IBEX HORNS AND CHINESE ORNAMENTAL POTS! LET'S GO LOOK!
HEMIS MUSEUM
CHINESE POTS? WOULD THAT BE MING POTTERY?
FROM HEMIS, WE PROCEED TO PANGONG TSO VIA ZINGRAL VILLAGE, MEETING SOME INTIMIDATING VEHICLES ON OUR WAY...
WATCH OUT!
BUT THERE ARE MORE INTIMIDATING PROSPECTS AHEAD...
WE ARE APPROACHING CHANG LA.
ANOTHER PASS? I DON'T REMEMBER YOU PASSING ON THIS INFORMATION? HOW HIGH IS THIS ONE?

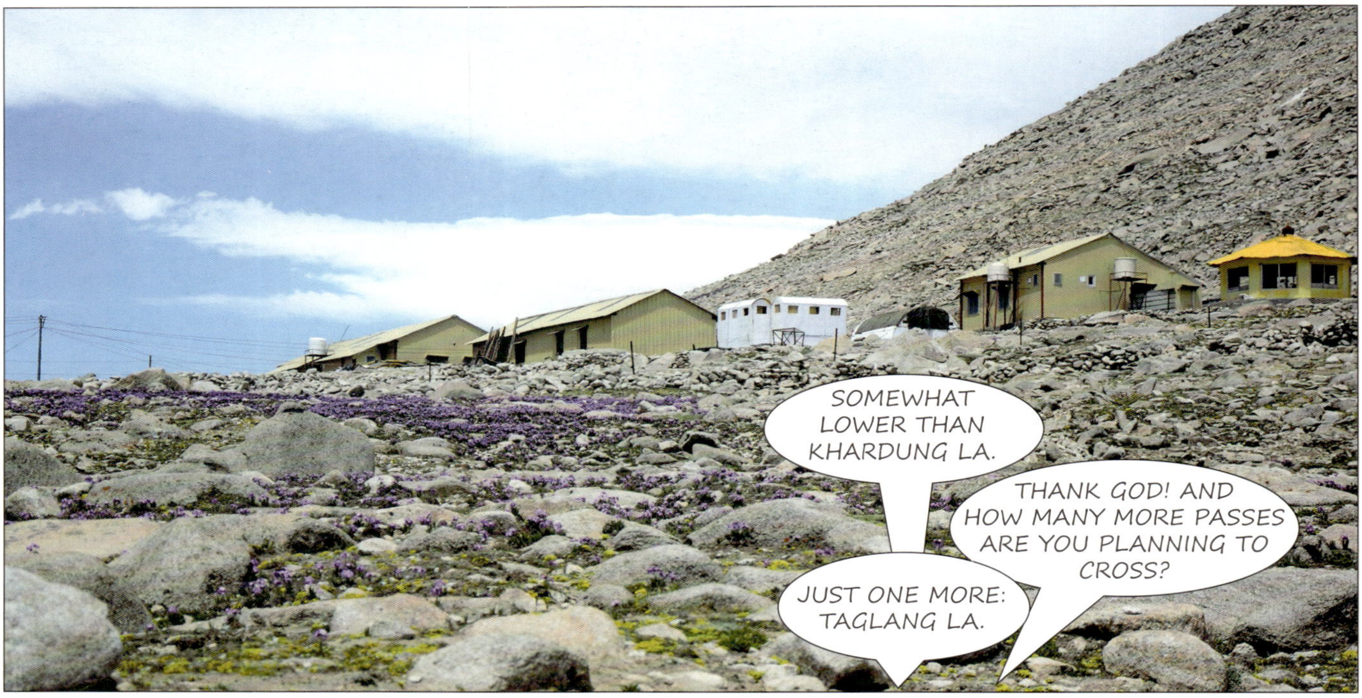
SOMEWHAT LOWER THAN KHARDUNG LA.
THANK GOD! AND HOW MANY MORE PASSES ARE YOU PLANNING TO CROSS?
JUST ONE MORE: TAGLANG LA.

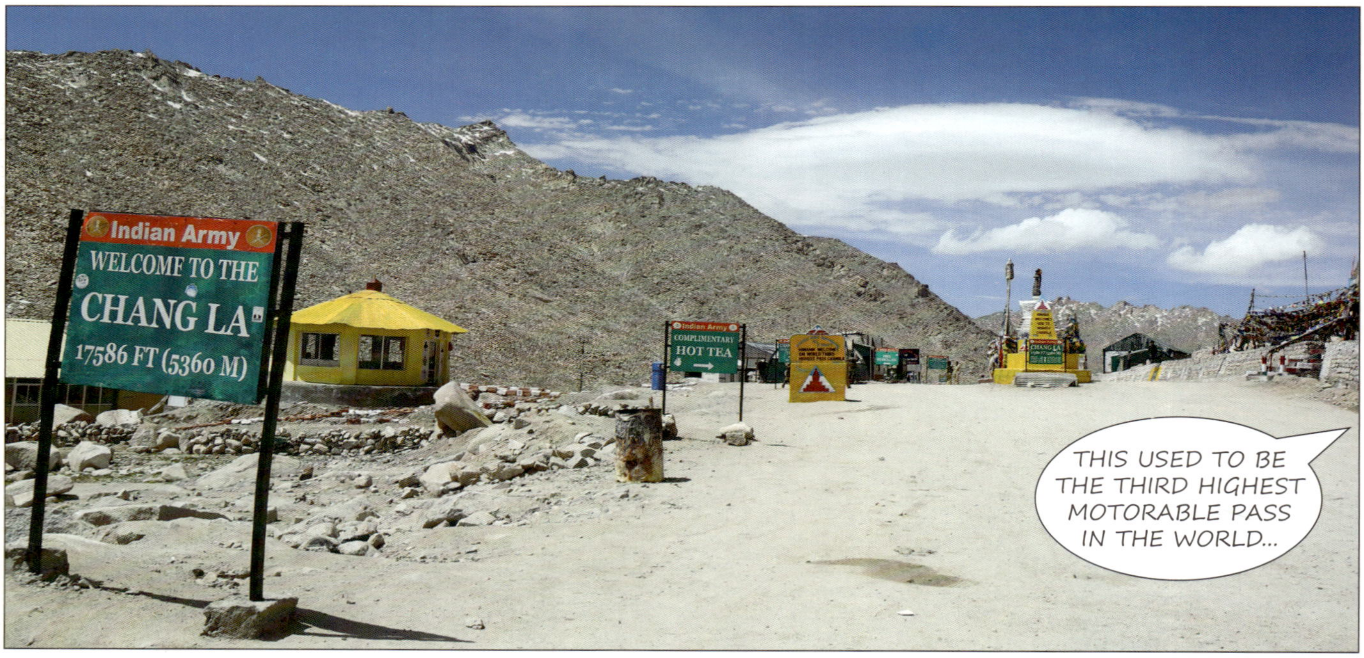
Indian Army
WELCOMF TO THE
CHANG LA
17586 FT (5360 M)
HOT TEA
THIS USED TO BE THE THIRD HIGHEST MOTORABLE PASS IN THE WORLD...

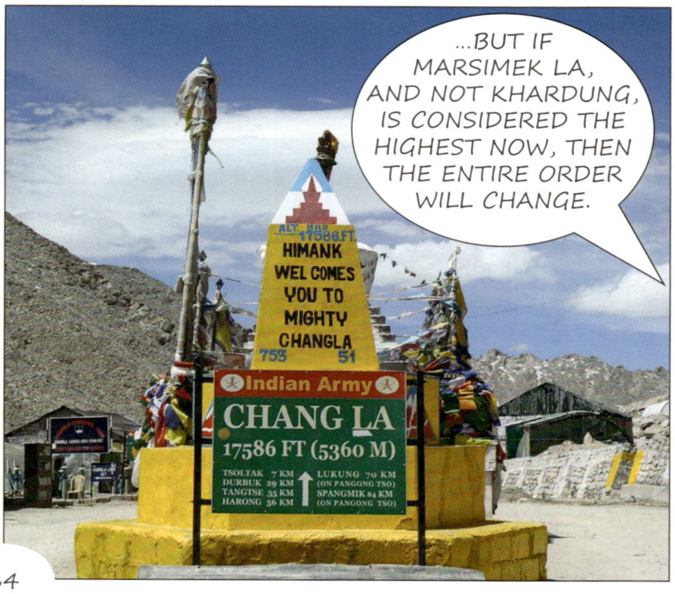
...BUT IF MARSIMEK LA, AND NOT KHARDUNG, IS CONSIDERED THE HIGHEST NOW, THEN THE ENTIRE ORDER WILL CHANGE.
HIMANK WEL COMES YOU TO MIGHTY CHANGLA
Indian Army
CHANG LA
17586 FT (5360 M)

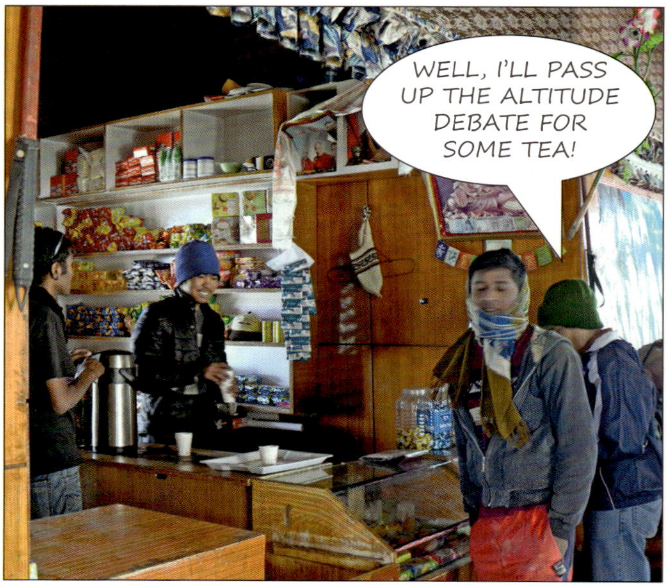
WELL, I'LL PASS UP THE ALTITUDE DEBATE FOR SOME TEA!

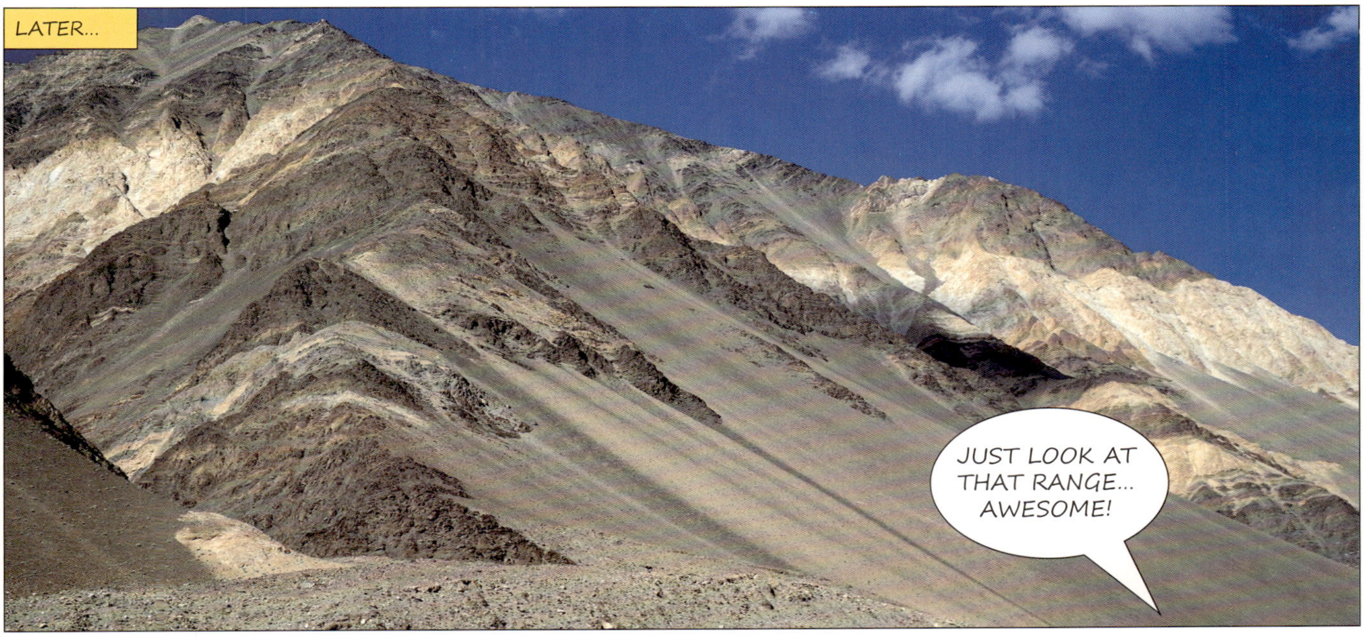
LATER...
JUST LOOK AT THAT RANGE... AWESOME!

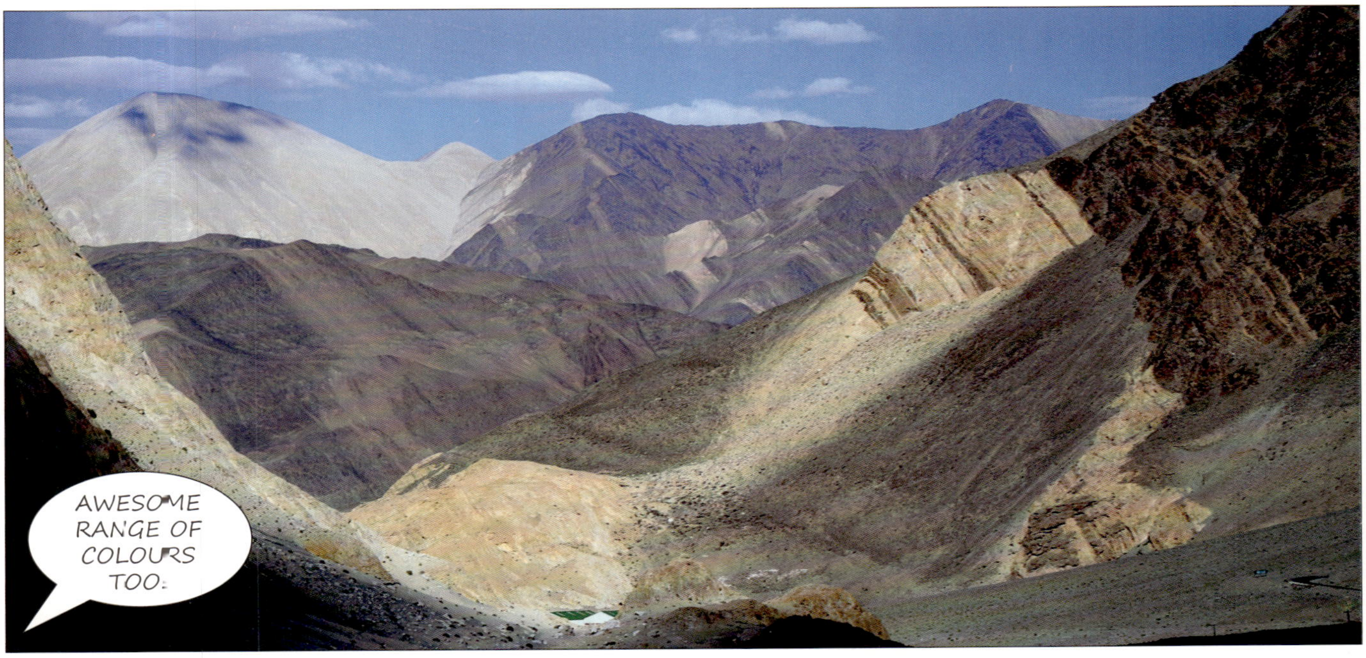
AWESOME RANGE OF COLOURS TOO!

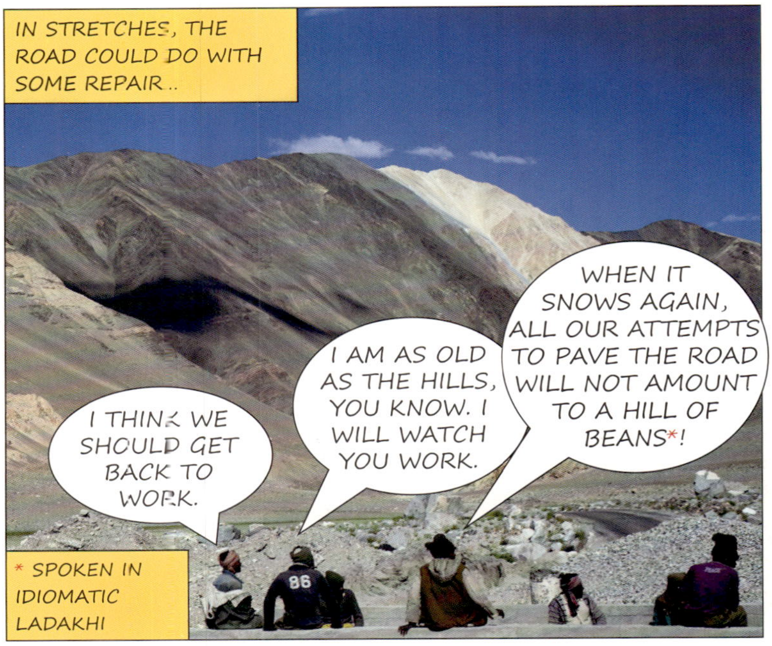
IN STRETCHES, THE ROAD COULD DO WITH SOME REPAIR...
I THINK WE SHOULD GET BACK TO WORK.
I AM AS OLD AS THE HILLS, YOU KNOW. I WILL WATCH YOU WORK.
WHEN IT SNOWS AGAIN, ALL OUR ATTEMPTS TO PAVE THE ROAD WILL NOT AMOUNT TO A HILL OF BEANS*!
* SPOKEN IN IDIOMATIC LADAKHI

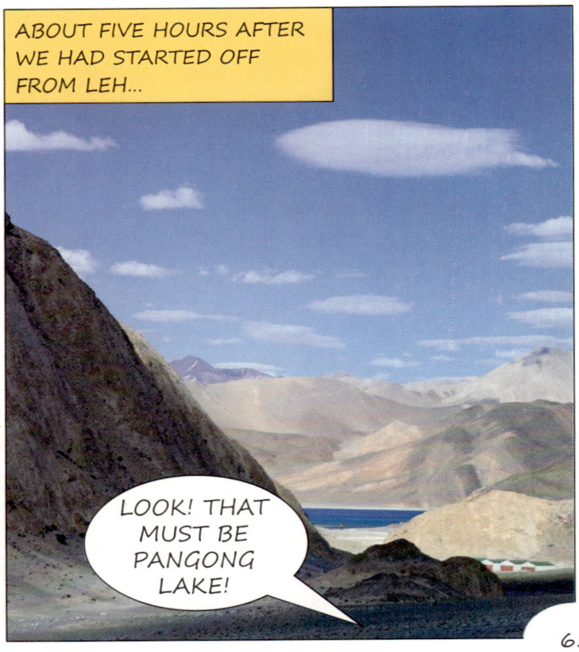
ABOUT FIVE HOURS AFTER WE HAD STARTED OFF FROM LEH...
LOOK! THAT MUST BE PANGONG LAKE!

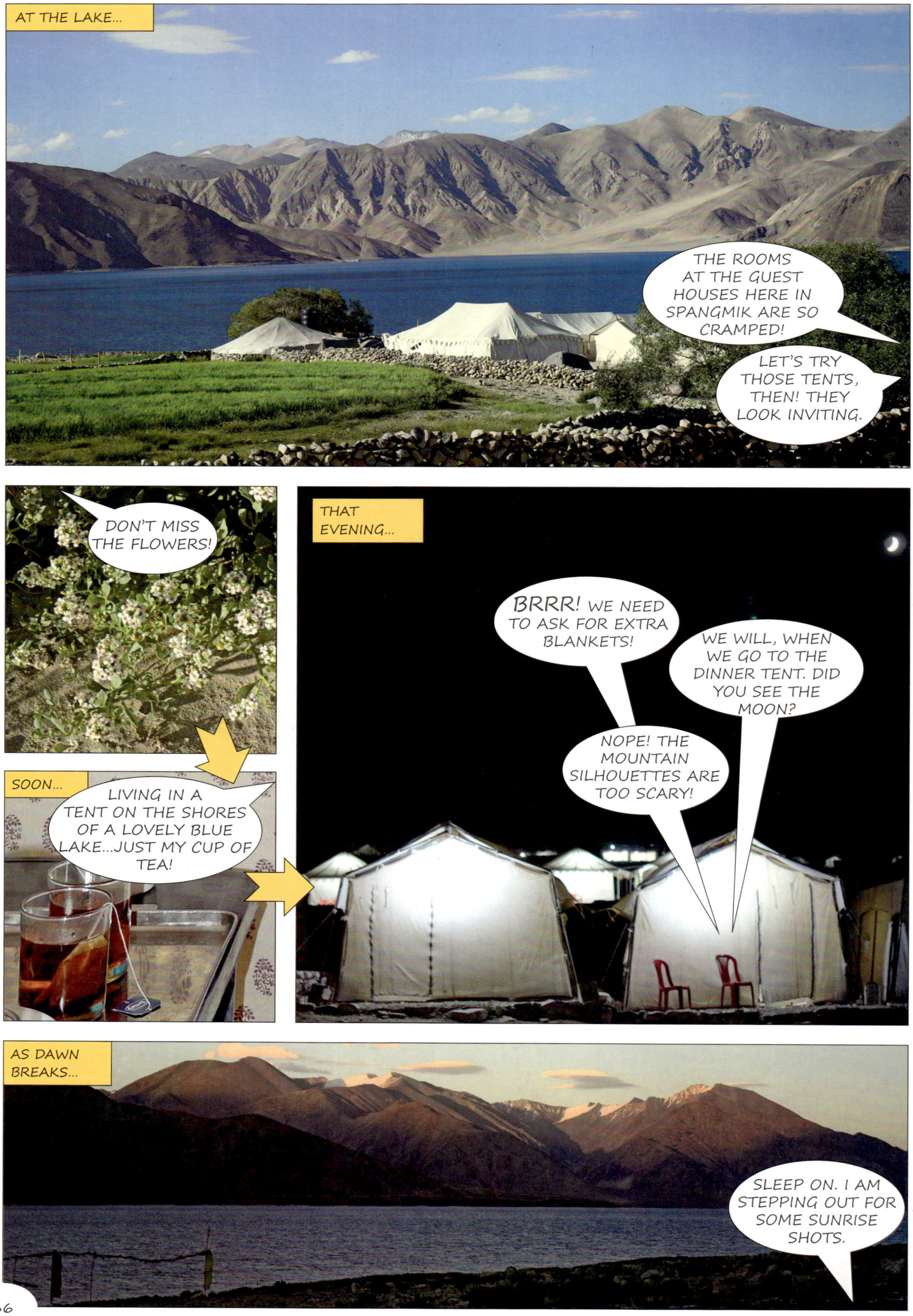

AT THE LAKE...
THE ROOMS AT THE GUEST HOUSES HERE IN SPANGMIK ARE SO CRAMPED!
LET'S TRY THOSE TENTS, THEN! THEY LOOK INVITING.
DON'T MISS THE FLOWERS!
SOON...
LIVING IN A TENT ON THE SHORES OF A LOVELY BLUE LAKE...JUST MY CUP OF TEA!
THAT EVENING...
BRRR! WE NEED TO ASK FOR EXTRA BLANKETS!
WE WILL, WHEN WE GO TO THE DINNER TENT. DID YOU SEE THE MOON?
NOPE! THE MOUNTAIN SILHOUETTES ARE TOO SCARY!
AS DAWN BREAKS...
SLEEP ON. I AM STEPPING OUT FOR SOME SUNRISE SHOTS.

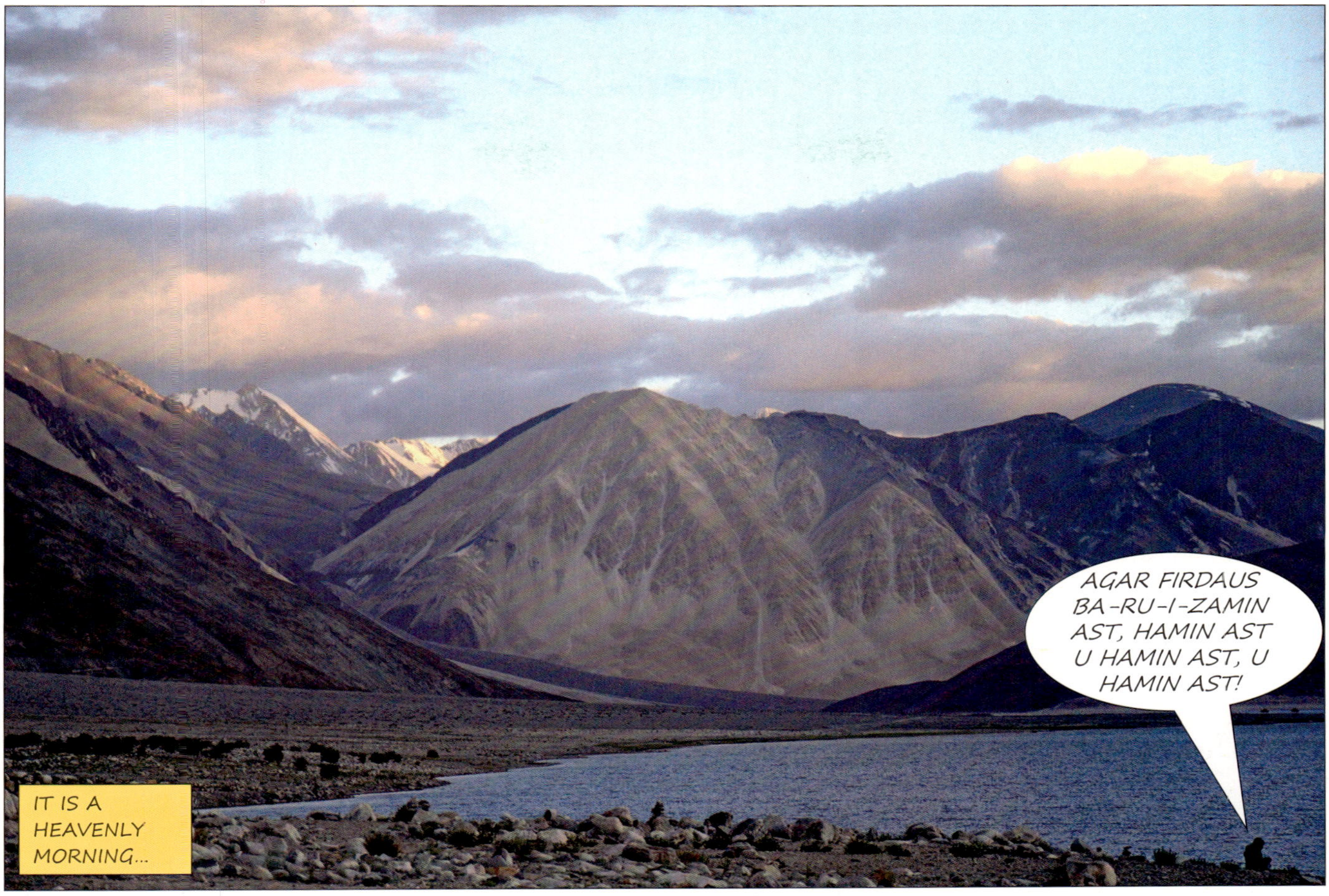
IT IS A HEAVENLY MORNING...
AGAR FIRDAUS BA-RU-I-ZAMIN AST, HAMIN AST U HAMIN AST, U HAMIN AST!

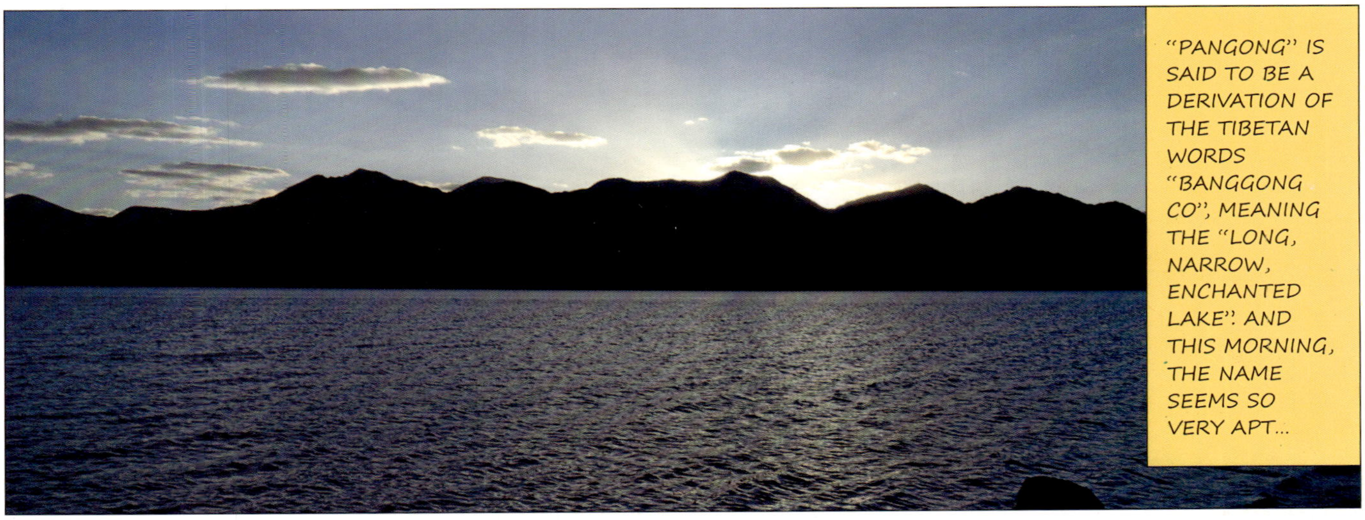
"PANGONG" IS SAID TO BE A DERIVATION OF THE TIBETAN WORDS "BANGGONG CO", MEANING THE "LONG, NARROW, ENCHANTED LAKE". AND THIS MORNING, THE NAME SEEMS SO VERY APT...

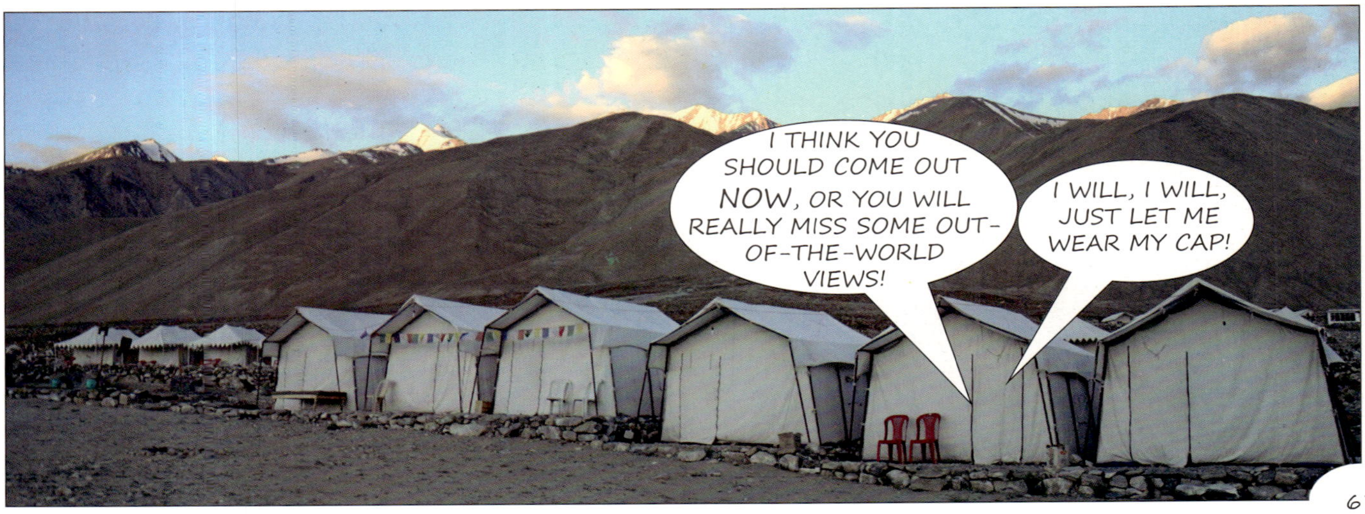
I THINK YOU SHOULD COME OUT NOW, OR YOU WILL REALLY MISS SOME OUT-OF-THE-WORLD VIEWS!
I WILL, I WILL, JUST LET ME WEAR MY CAP!

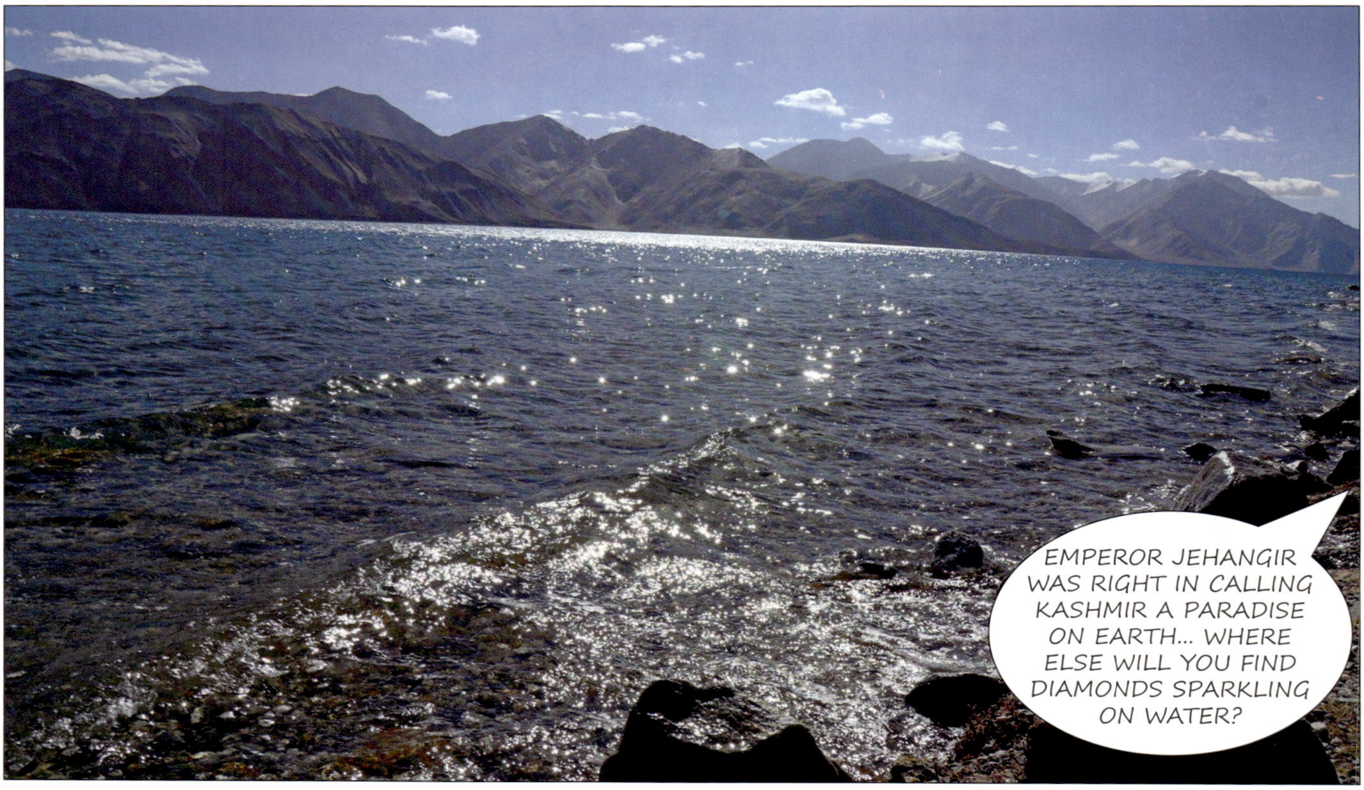
EMPEROR JEHANGIR WAS RIGHT IN CALLING KASHMIR A PARADISE ON EARTH... WHERE ELSE WILL YOU FIND DIAMONDS SPARKLING ON WATER?

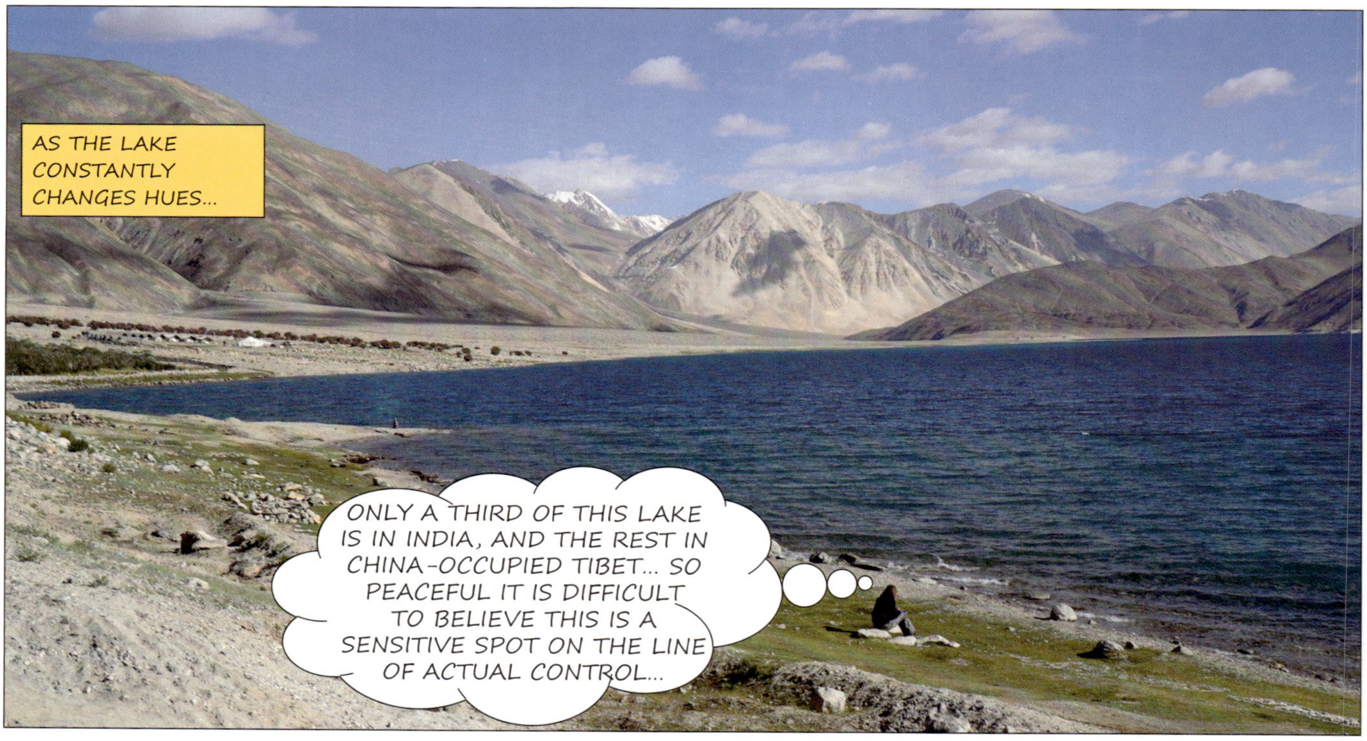
AS THE LAKE CONSTANTLY CHANGES HUES...
ONLY A THIRD OF THIS LAKE IS IN INDIA, AND THE REST IN CHINA-OCCUPIED TIBET... SO PEACEFUL IT IS DIFFICULT TO BELIEVE THIS IS A SENSITIVE SPOT ON THE LINE OF ACTUAL CONTROL...

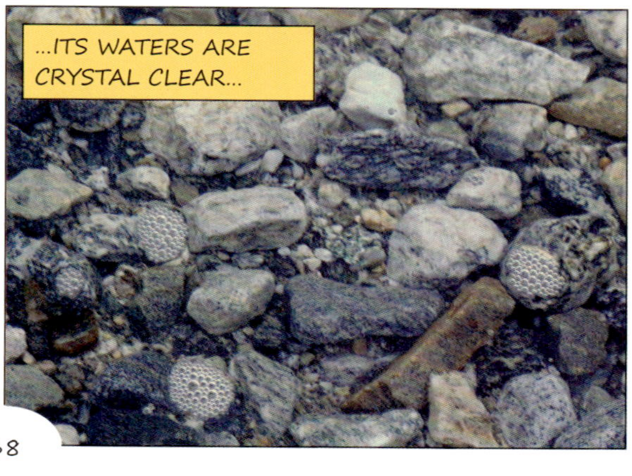
...ITS WATERS ARE CRYSTAL CLEAR...

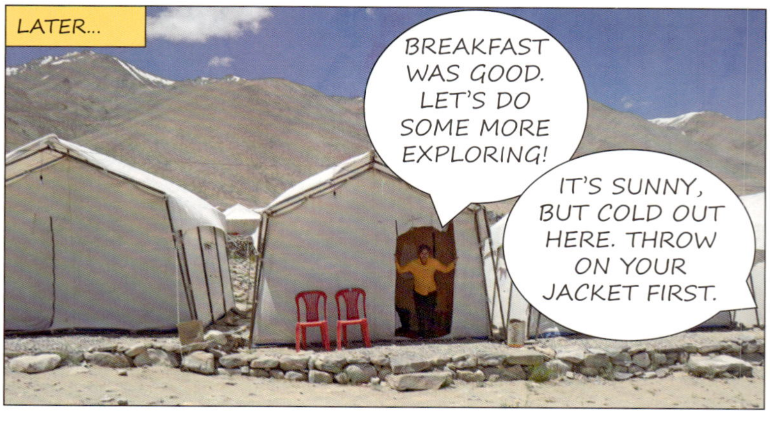
LATER...
BREAKFAST WAS GOOD. LET'S DO SOME MORE EXPLORING!
IT'S SUNNY, BUT COLD OUT HERE. THROW ON YOUR JACKET FIRST.

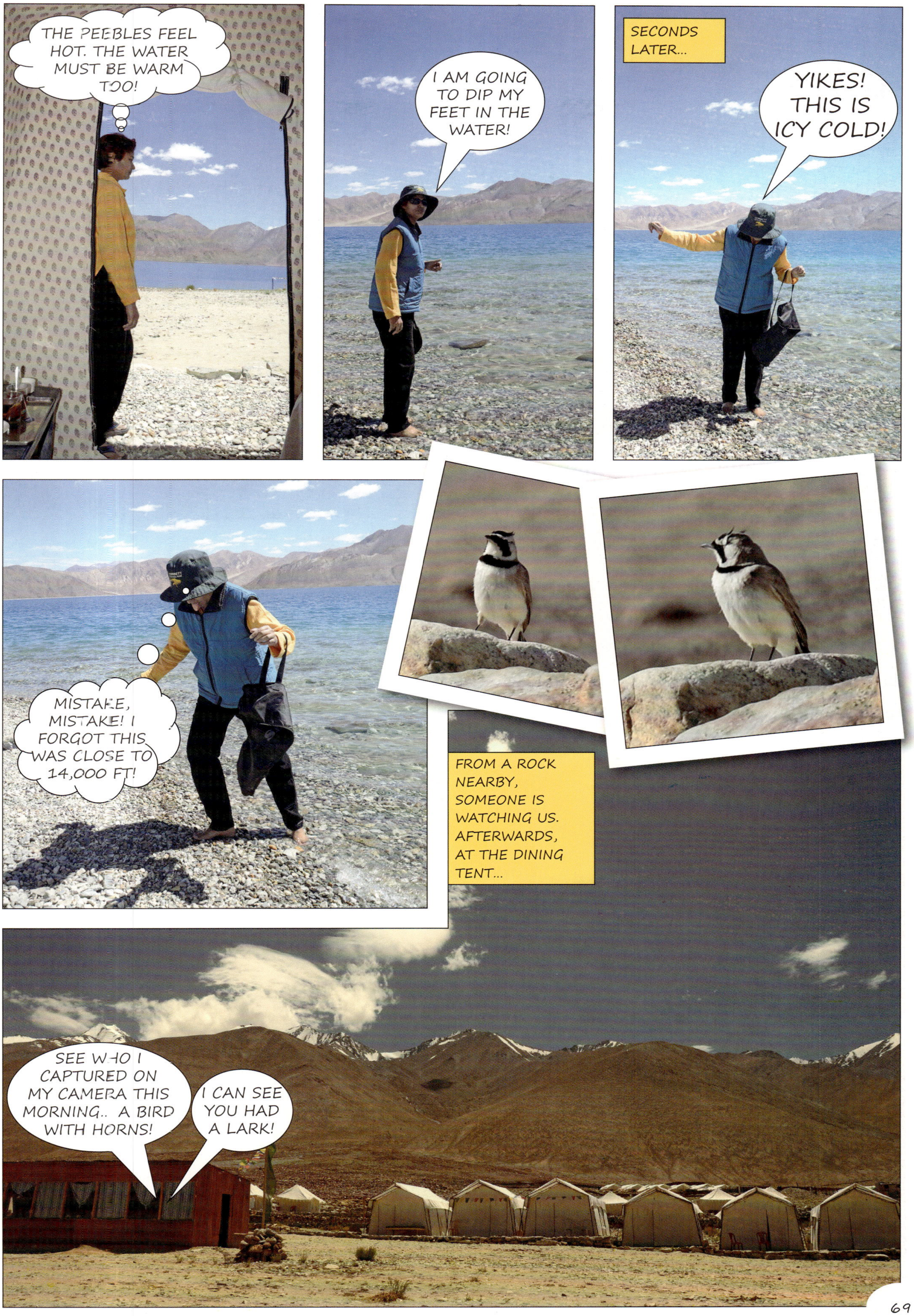

THE PEEBLES FEEL HOT. THE WATER MUST BE WARM TOO!
I AM GOING TO DIP MY FEET IN THE WATER!
SECONDS LATER...
YIKES! THIS IS ICY COLD!
MISTAKE, MISTAKE! I FORGOT THIS WAS CLOSE TO 14,000 FT!
FROM A ROCK NEARBY, SOMEONE IS WATCHING US. AFTERWARDS, AT THE DINING TENT...
SEE WHO I CAPTURED ON MY CAMERA THIS MORNING.. A BIRD WITH HORNS!
I CAN SEE YOU HAD A LARK!

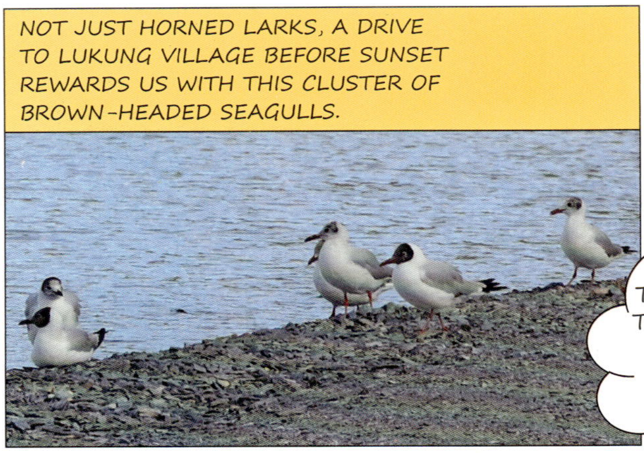
NOT JUST HORNED LARKS, A DRIVE TO LUKUNG VILLAGE BEFORE SUNSET REWARDS US WITH THIS CLUSTER OF BROWN-HEADED SEAGULLS.

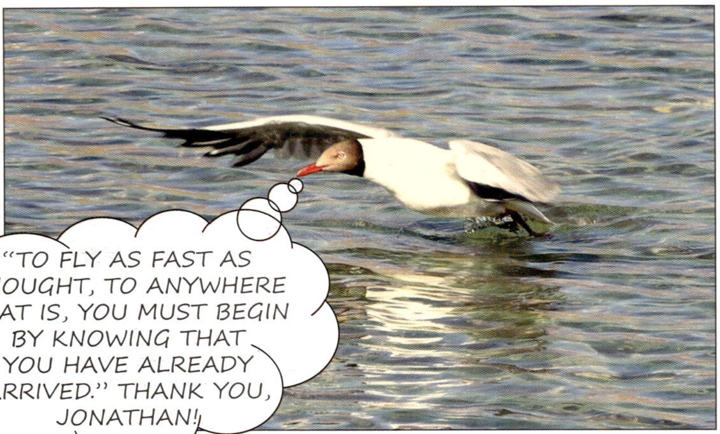
"TO FLY AS FAST AS THOUGHT, TO ANYWHERE THAT IS, YOU MUST BEGIN BY KNOWING THAT YOU HAVE ALREADY ARRIVED." THANK YOU, JONATHAN!

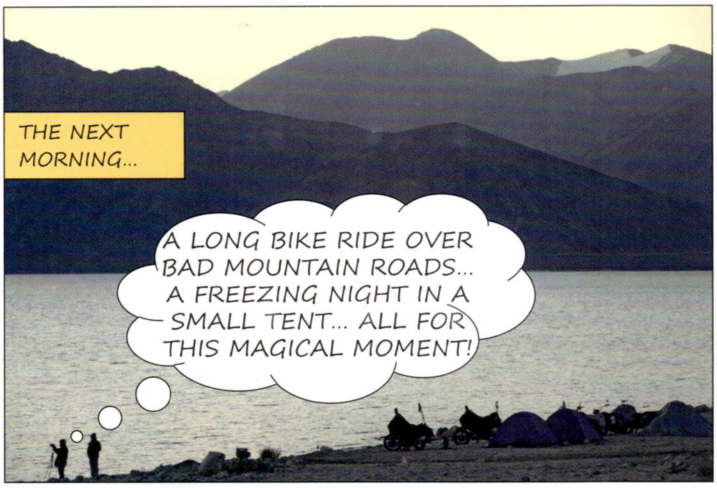
THE NEXT MORNING...
A LONG BIKE RIDE OVER BAD MOUNTAIN ROADS... A FREEZING NIGHT IN A SMALL TENT... ALL FOR THIS MAGICAL MOMENT!

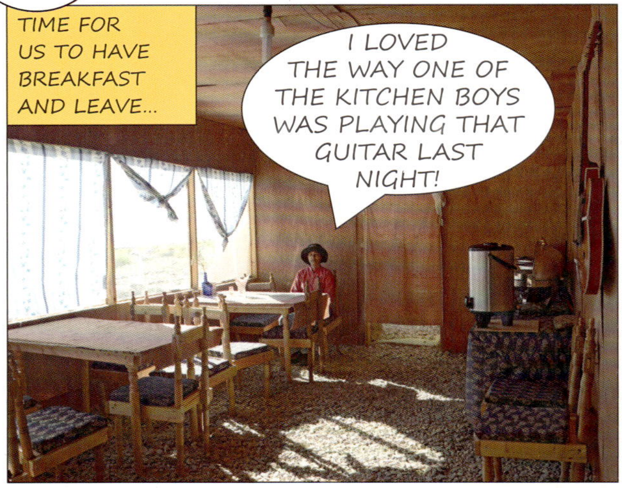
TIME FOR US TO HAVE BREAKFAST AND LEAVE...
I LOVED THE WAY ONE OF THE KITCHEN BOYS WAS PLAYING THAT GUITAR LAST NIGHT!

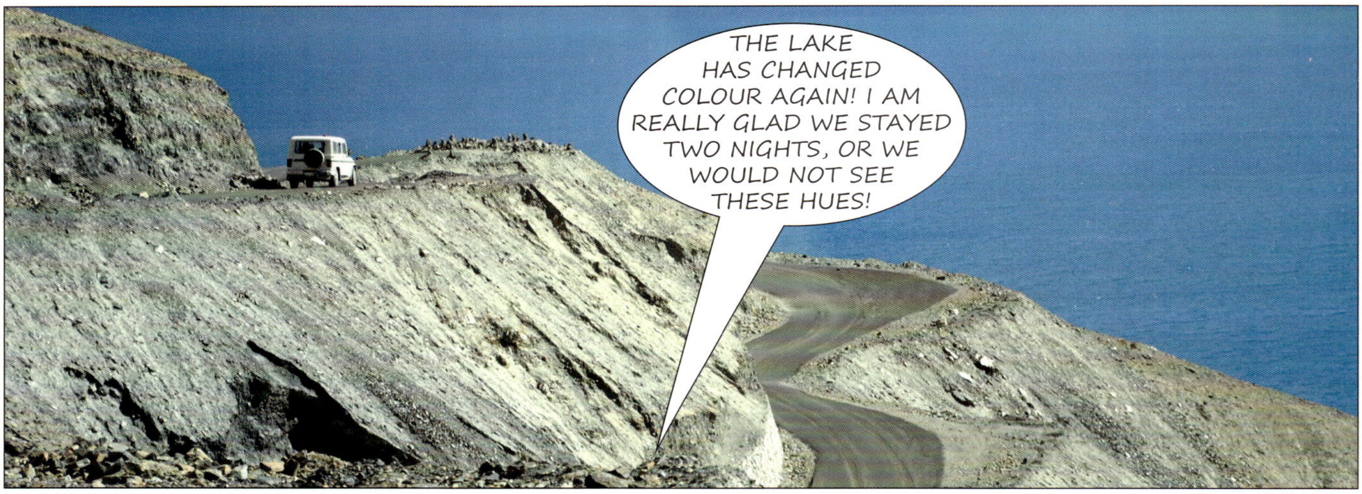
THE LAKE HAS CHANGED COLOUR AGAIN! I AM REALLY GLAD WE STAYED TWO NIGHTS, OR WE WOULD NOT SEE THESE HUES!

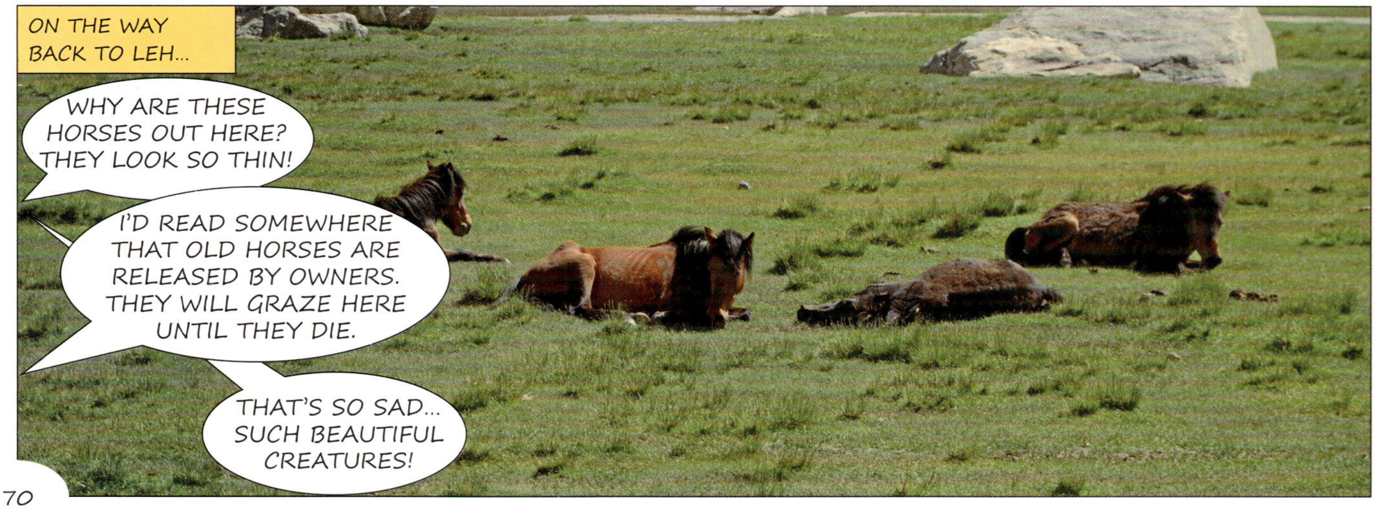
ON THE WAY BACK TO LEH...
WHY ARE THESE HORSES OUT HERE? THEY LOOK SO THIN!
I'D READ SOMEWHERE THAT OLD HORSES ARE RELEASED BY OWNERS. THEY WILL GRAZE HERE UNTIL THEY DIE.
THAT'S SO SAD... SUCH BEAUTIFUL CREATURES!

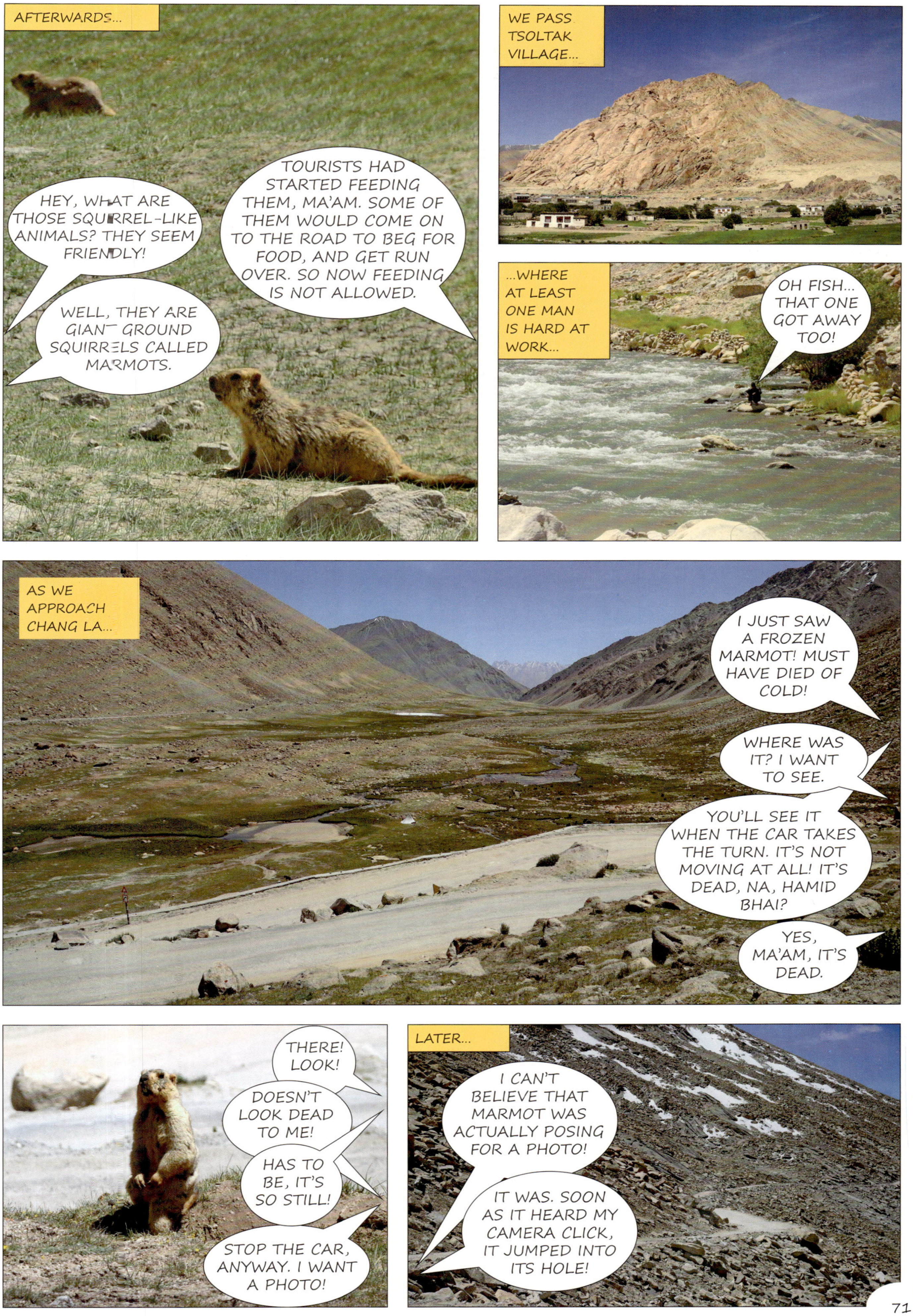
AFTERWARDS...
HEY, WHAT ARE THOSE SQUIRREL-LIKE ANIMALS? THEY SEEM FRIENDLY!
WELL, THEY ARE GIANT GROUND SQUIRRELS CALLED MARMOTS.
TOURISTS HAD STARTED FEEDING THEM, MA'AM. SOME OF THEM WOULD COME ON TO THE ROAD TO BEG FOR FOOD, AND GET RUN OVER. SO NOW FEEDING IS NOT ALLOWED.
WE PASS TSOLTAK VILLAGE...
...WHERE AT LEAST ONE MAN IS HARD AT WORK...
OH FISH... THAT ONE GOT AWAY TOO!
AS WE APPROACH CHANG LA...
I JUST SAW A FROZEN MARMOT! MUST HAVE DIED OF COLD!
WHERE WAS IT? I WANT TO SEE.
YOU'LL SEE IT WHEN THE CAR TAKES THE TURN. IT'S NOT MOVING AT ALL! IT'S DEAD, NA, HAMID BHAI?
YES, MA'AM, IT'S DEAD.
THERE! LOOK!
DOESN'T LOOK DEAD TO ME!
HAS TO BE, IT'S SO STILL!
STOP THE CAR, ANYWAY. I WANT A PHOTO!
LATER...
I CAN'T BELIEVE THAT MARMOT WAS ACTUALLY POSING FOR A PHOTO!
IT WAS. SOON AS IT HEARD MY CAMERA CLICK, IT JUMPED INTO ITS HOLE!

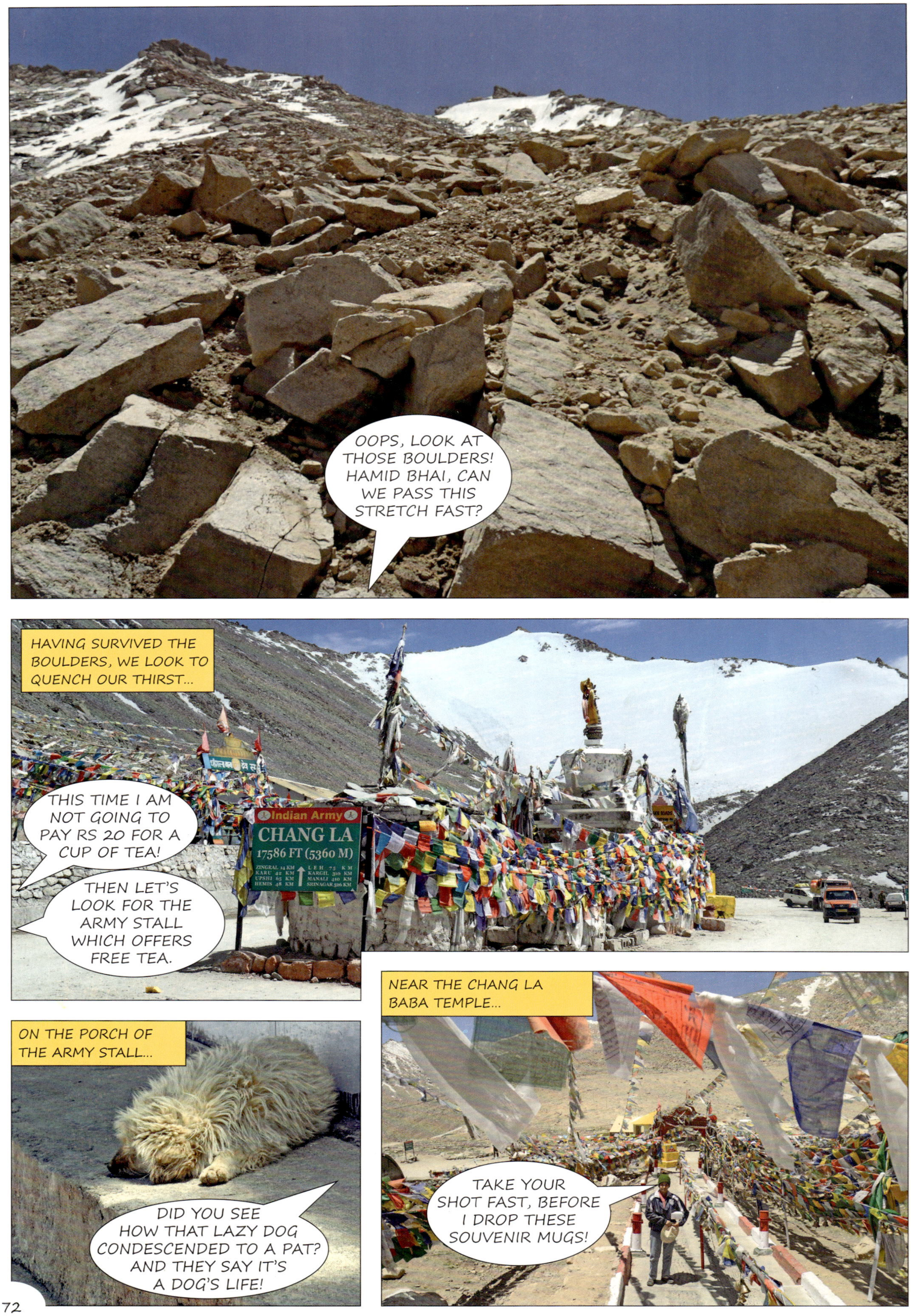
OOPS, LOOK AT THOSE BOULDERS! HAMID BHAI, CAN WE PASS THIS STRETCH FAST?
HAVING SURVIVED THE BOULDERS, WE LOOK TO QUENCH OUR THIRST...
Indian Army
CHANG LA
17586 FT (5360 M)
THIS TIME I AM NOT GOING TO PAY RS 20 FOR A CUP OF TEA!
THEN LET'S LOOK FOR THE ARMY STALL WHICH OFFERS FREE TEA.
ON THE PORCH OF THE ARMY STALL...
DID YOU SEE HOW THAT LAZY DOG CONDESCENDED TO A PAT? AND THEY SAY IT'S A DOG'S LIFE!
NEAR THE CHANG LA BABA TEMPLE...
TAKE YOUR SHOT FAST, BEFORE I DROP THESE SOUVENIR MUGS!

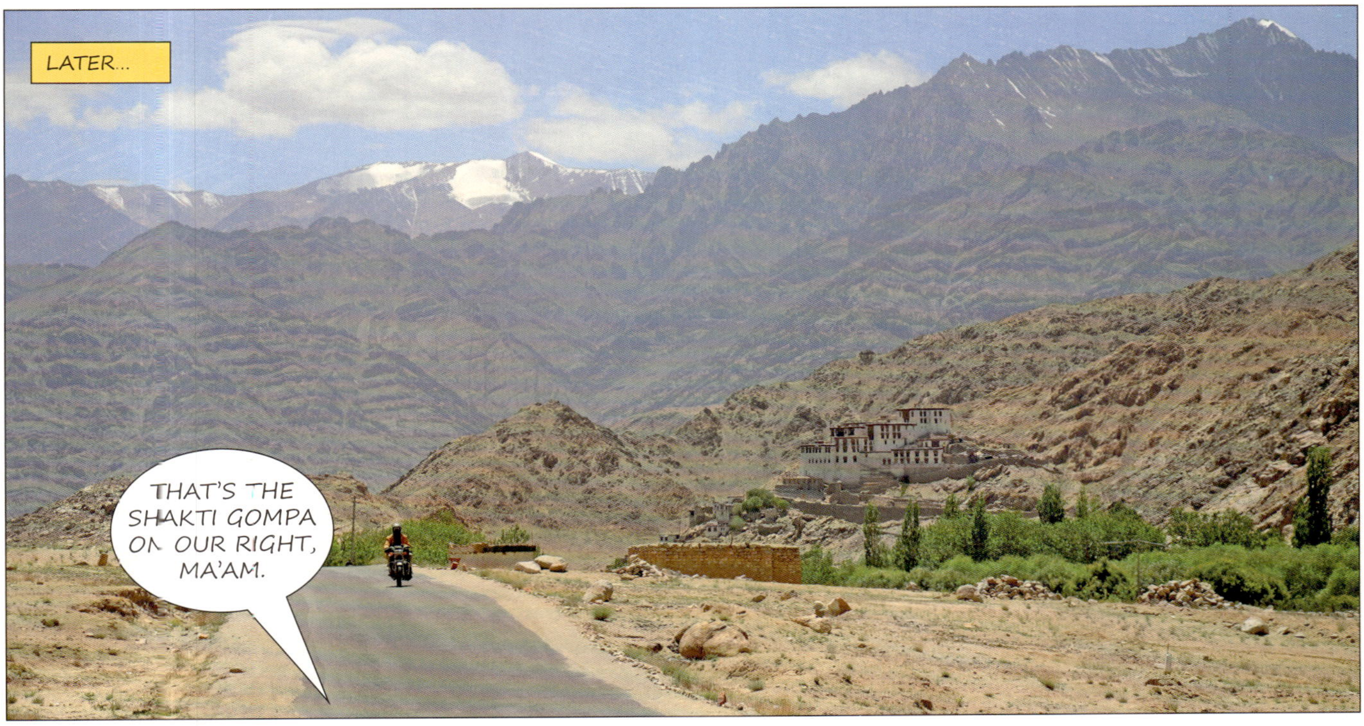
LATER...
THAT'S THE SHAKTI GOMPA ON OUR RIGHT, MA'AM.

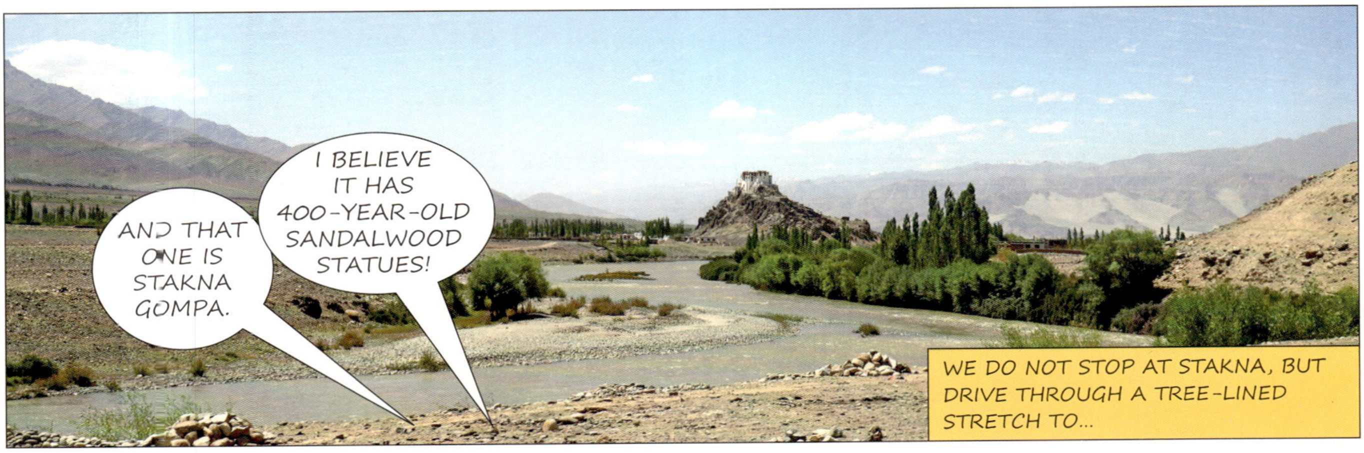
AND THAT ONE IS STAKNA GOMPA.
I BELIEVE IT HAS 400-YEAR-OLD SANDALWOOD STATUES!
WE DO NOT STOP AT STAKNA, BUT DRIVE THROUGH A TREE-LINED STRETCH TO...

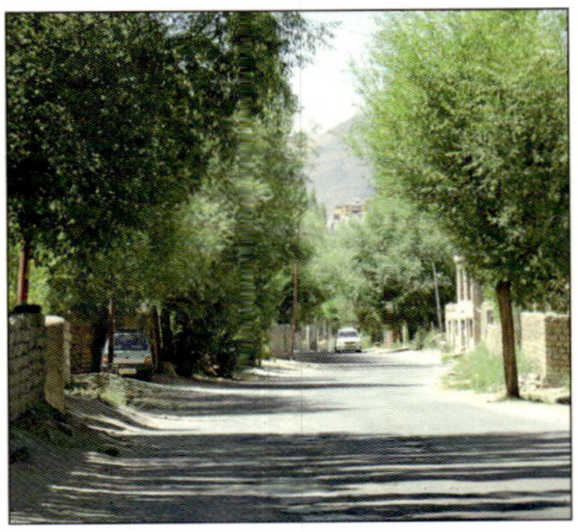

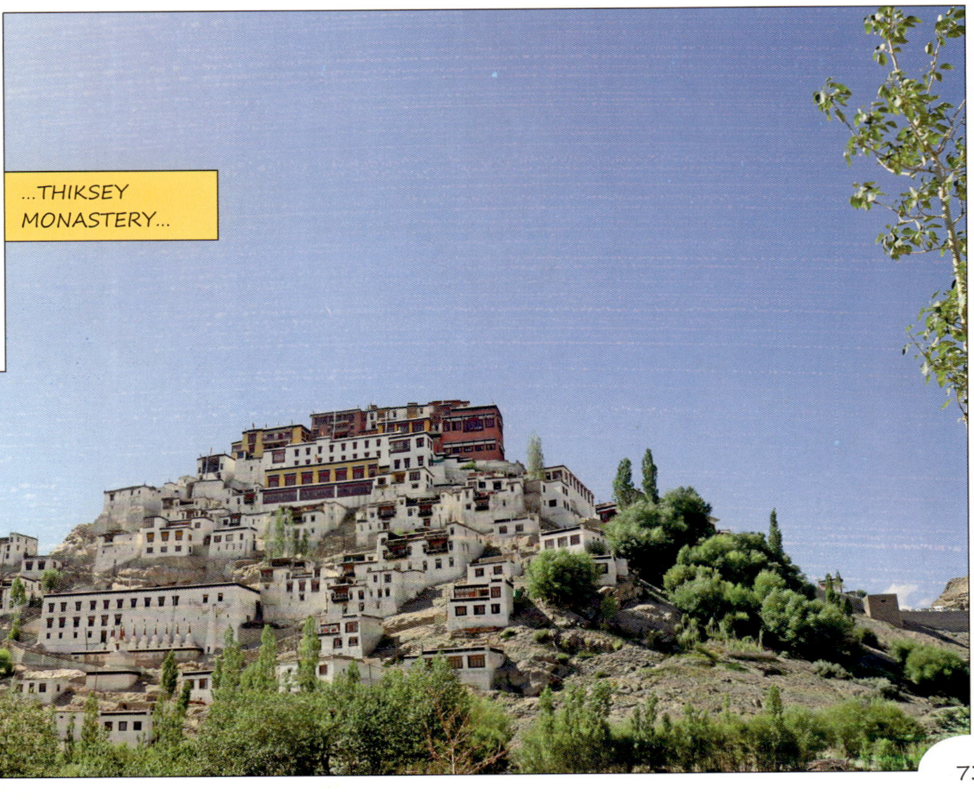
...THIKSEY MONASTERY...

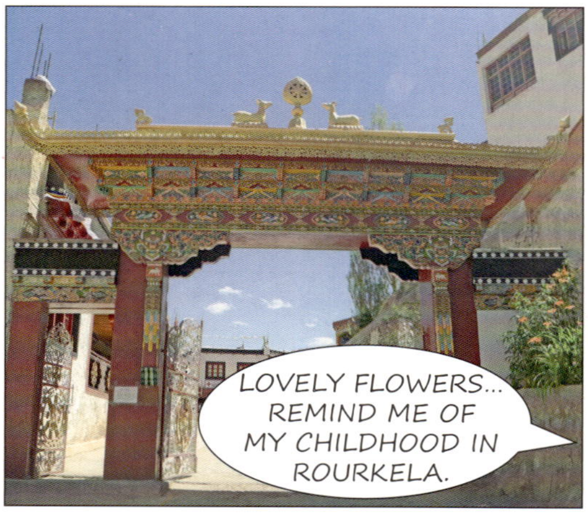
LOVELY FLOWERS... REMIND ME OF MY CHILDHOOD IN ROURKELA.

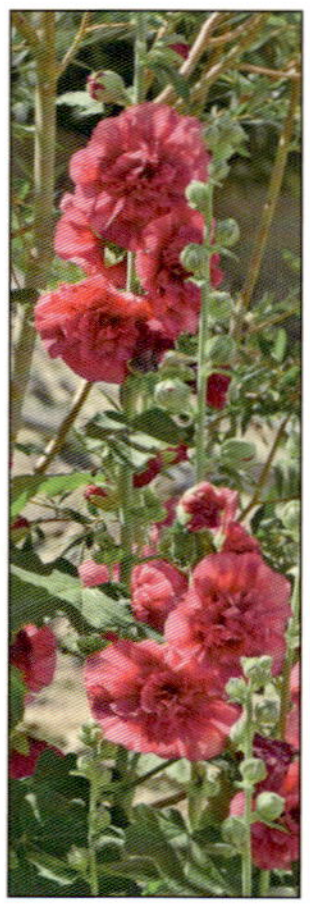

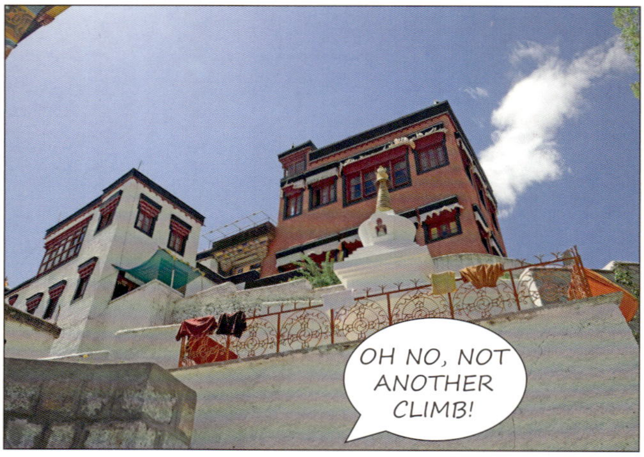
OH NO, NOT ANOTHER CLIMB!

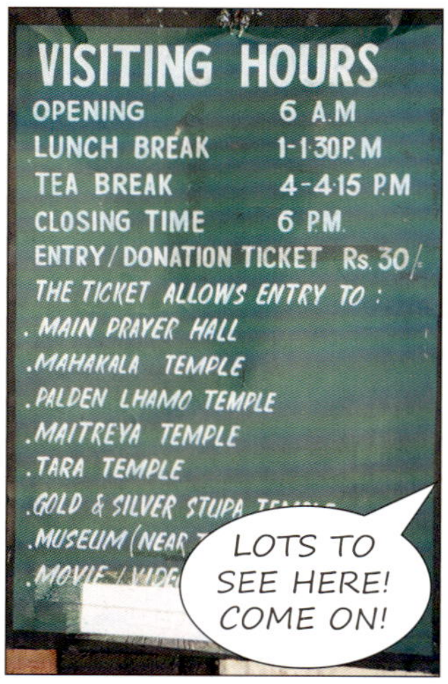
VISITING HOURS
OPENING 6 A.M
LUNCH BREAK 1-1:30P.M
TEA BREAK 4-4:15 P.M
CLOSING TIME 6 P.M.
ENTRY/DONATION TICKET Rs. 30/-
THE TICKET ALLOWS ENTRY TO :
. MAIN PRAYER HALL
.MAHAKALA TEMPLE
.PALDEN LHAMO TEMPLE
.MAITREYA TEMPLE
.TARA TEMPLE
.GOLD & SILVER STUPA
.MUSEUM (NEAR
LOTS TO SEE HERE! COME ON!

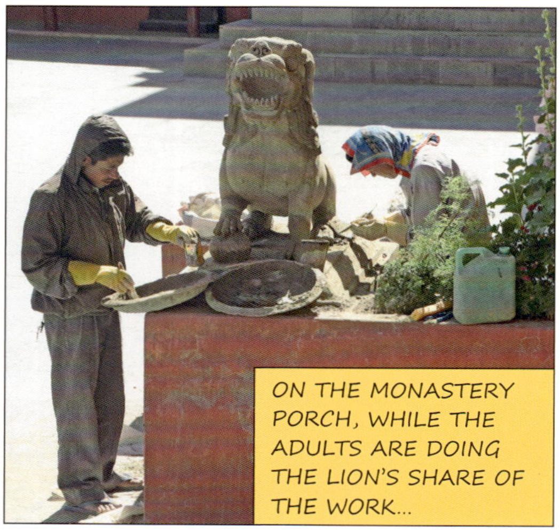
ON THE MONASTERY PORCH, WHILE THE ADULTS ARE DOING THE LION'S SHARE OF THE WORK...

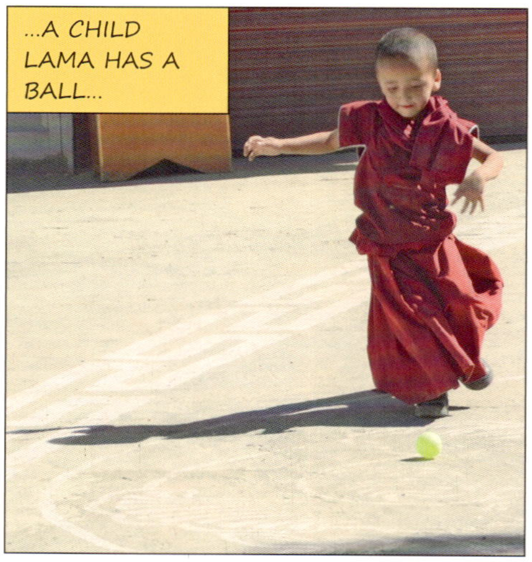
...A CHILD LAMA HAS A BALL...

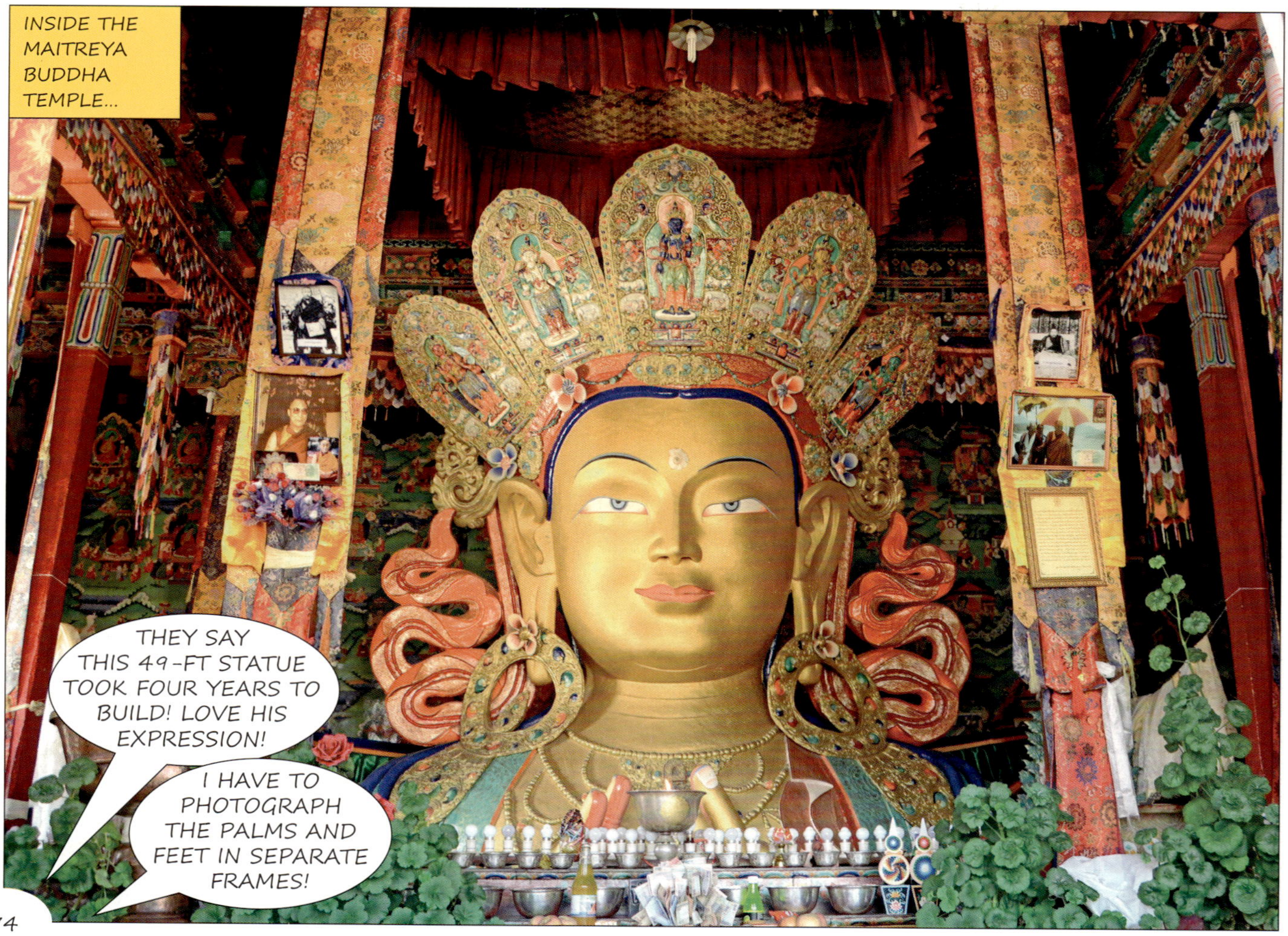
INSIDE THE MAITREYA BUDDHA TEMPLE...
THEY SAY THIS 49-FT STATUE TOOK FOUR YEARS TO BUILD! LOVE HIS EXPRESSION!
I HAVE TO PHOTOGRAPH THE PALMS AND FEET IN SEPARATE FRAMES!

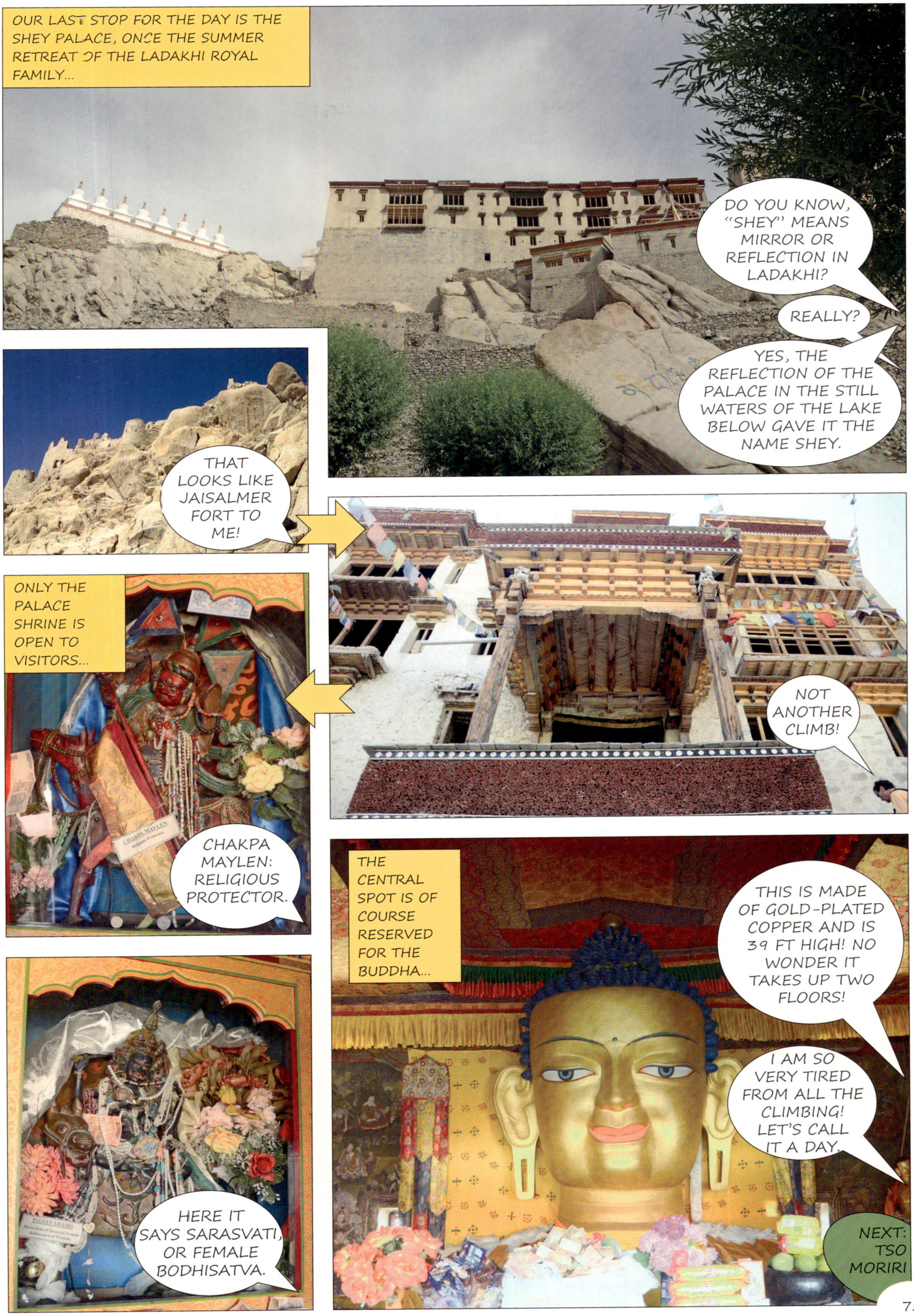

OUR LAST STOP FOR THE DAY IS THE SHEY PALACE, ONCE THE SUMMER RETREAT OF THE LADAKHI ROYAL FAMILY...
DO YOU KNOW, "SHEY" MEANS MIRROR OR REFLECTION IN LADAKHI?
REALLY?
YES, THE REFLECTION OF THE PALACE IN THE STILL WATERS OF THE LAKE BELOW GAVE IT THE NAME SHEY.
THAT LOOKS LIKE JAISALMER FORT TO ME!
NOT ANOTHER CLIMB!
ONLY THE PALACE SHRINE IS OPEN TO VISITORS...
CHAKPA MAYLEN: RELIGIOUS PROTECTOR.
HERE IT SAYS SARASVATI, OR FEMALE BODHISATVA.
THE CENTRAL SPOT IS OF COURSE RESERVED FOR THE BUDDHA...
THIS IS MADE OF GOLD-PLATED COPPER AND IS 39 FT HIGH! NO WONDER IT TAKES UP TWO FLOORS!
I AM SO VERY TIRED FROM ALL THE CLIMBING! LET'S CALL IT A DAY.
NEXT: TSO MORIRI

Chapter V: Tso Moriri

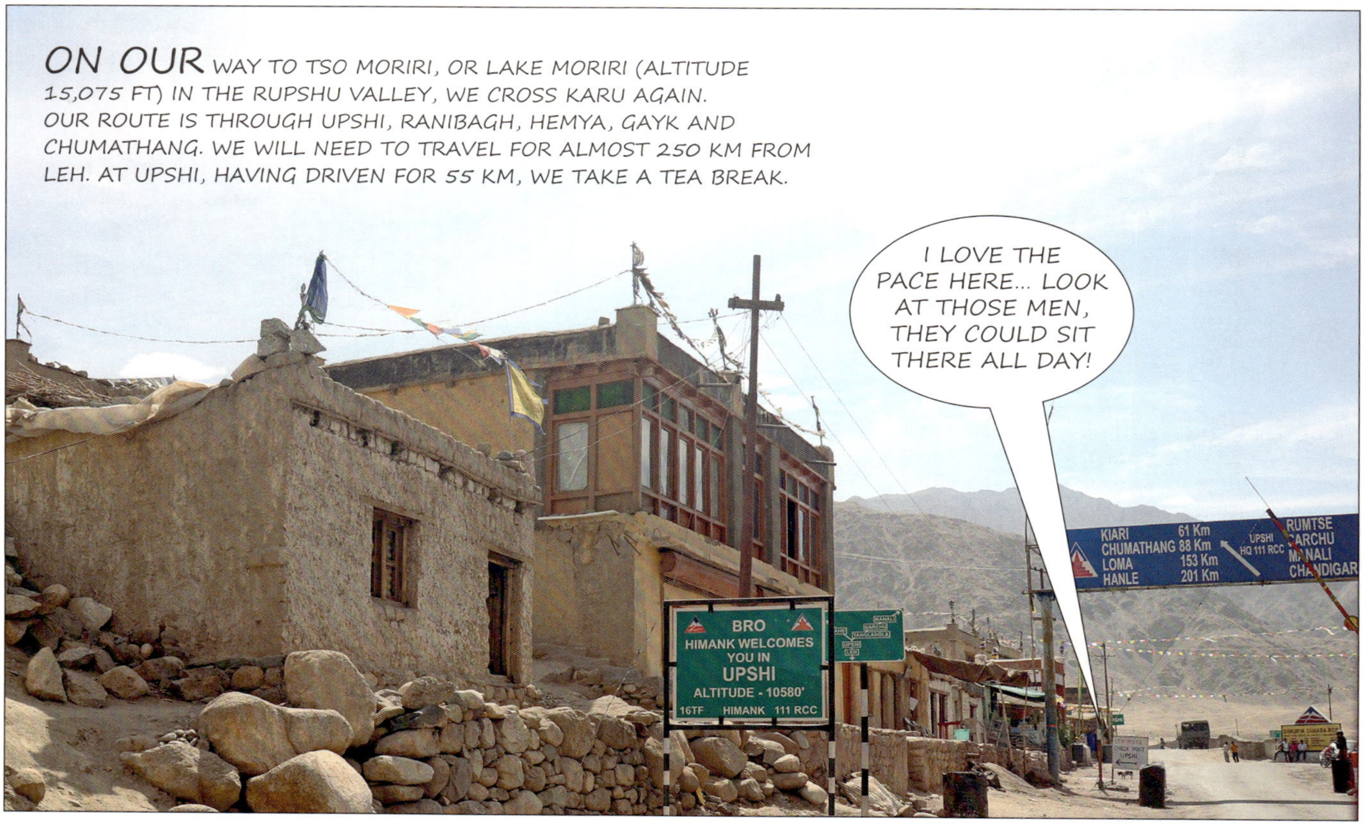

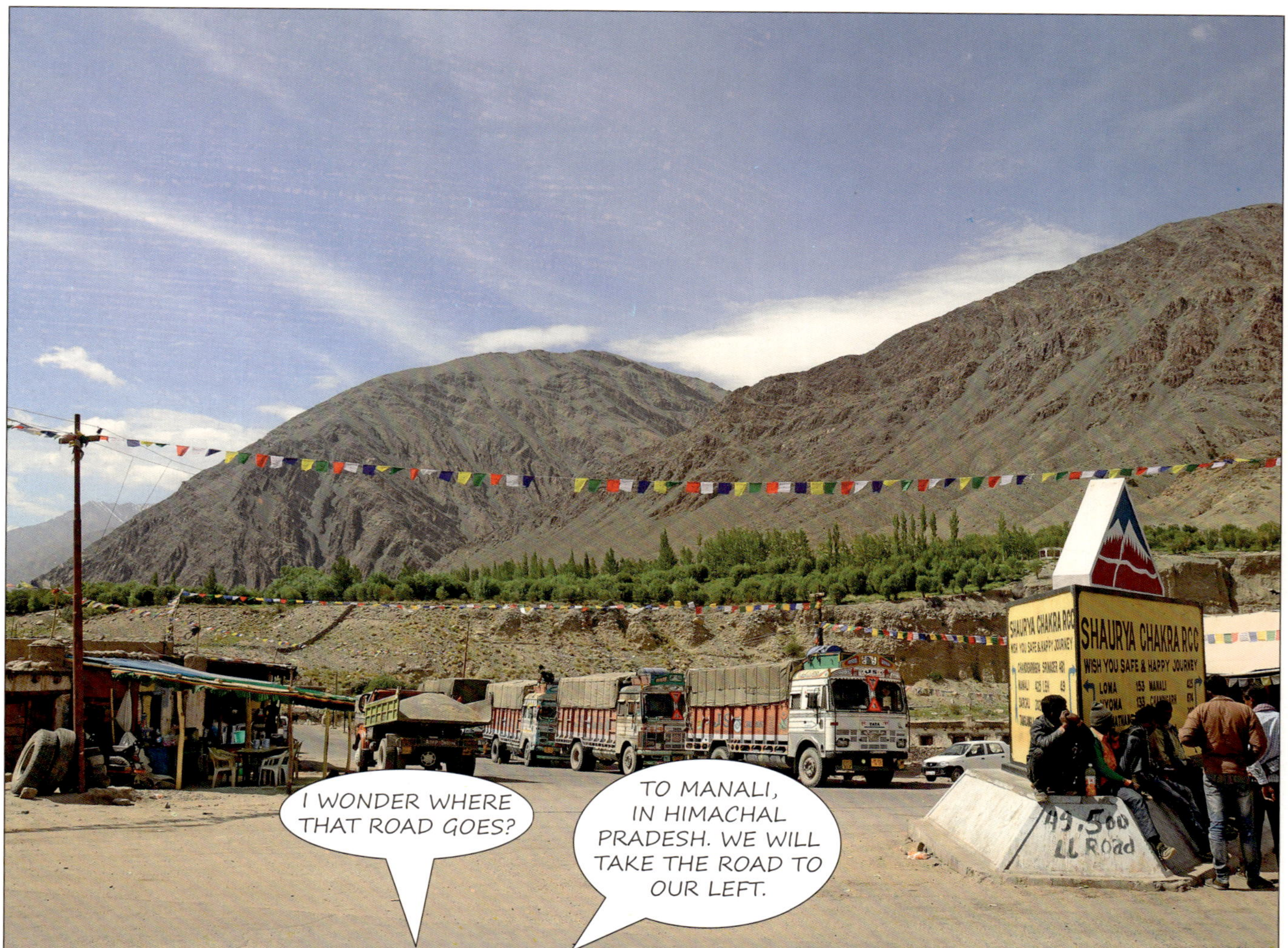

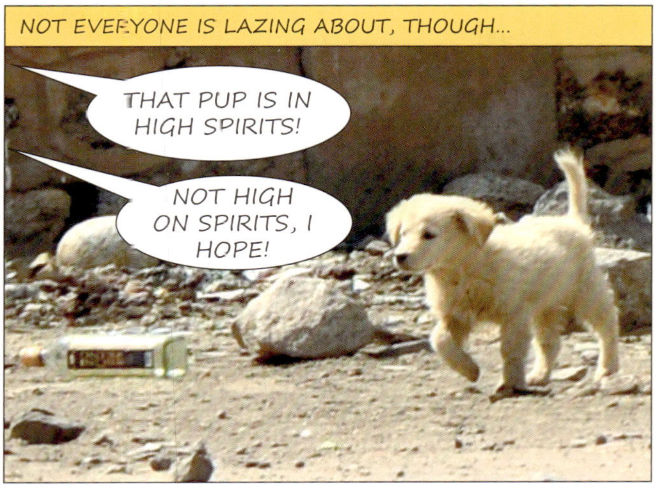
NOT EVERYONE IS LAZING ABOUT, THOUGH...
THAT PUP IS IN HIGH SPIRITS!
NOT HIGH ON SPIRITS, I HOPE!

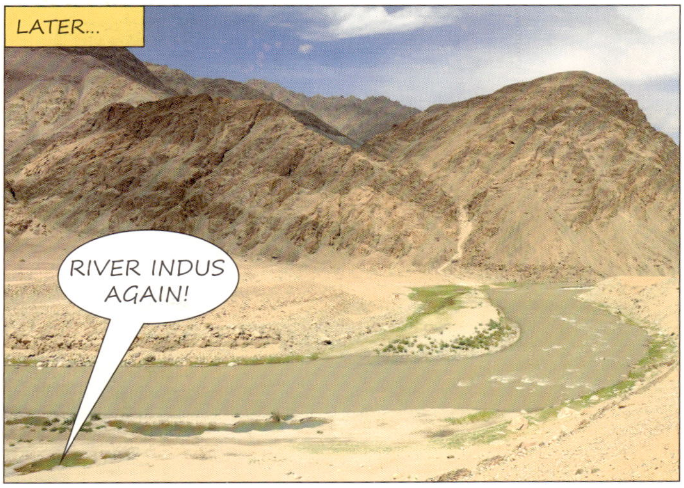
LATER...
RIVER INDUS AGAIN!

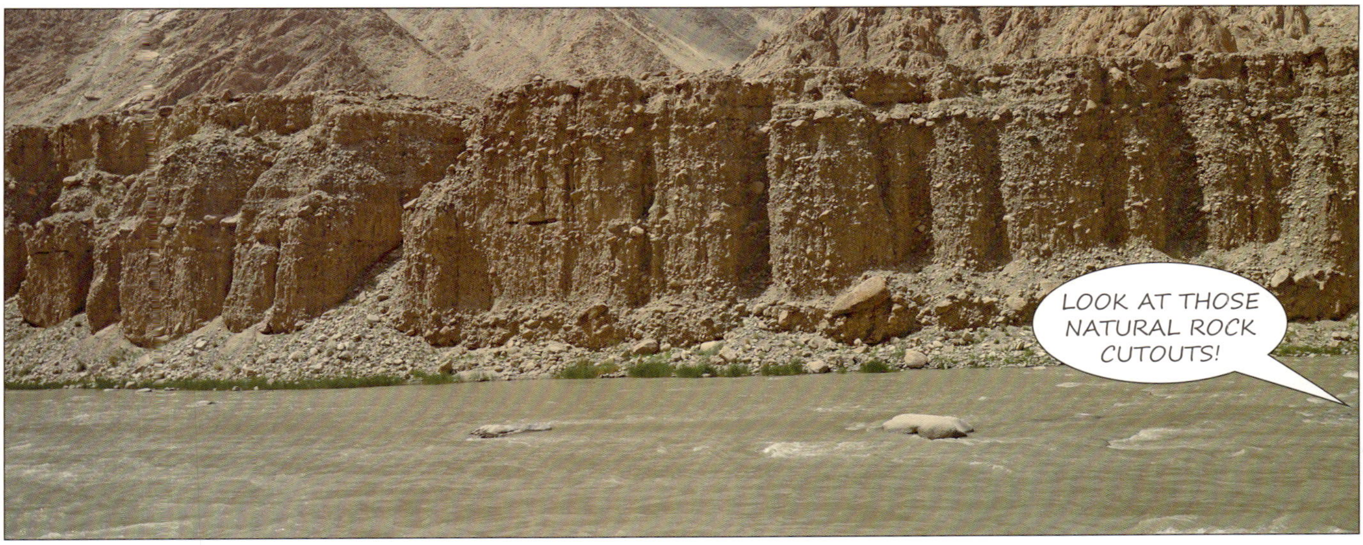
LOOK AT THOSE NATURAL ROCK CUTOUTS!

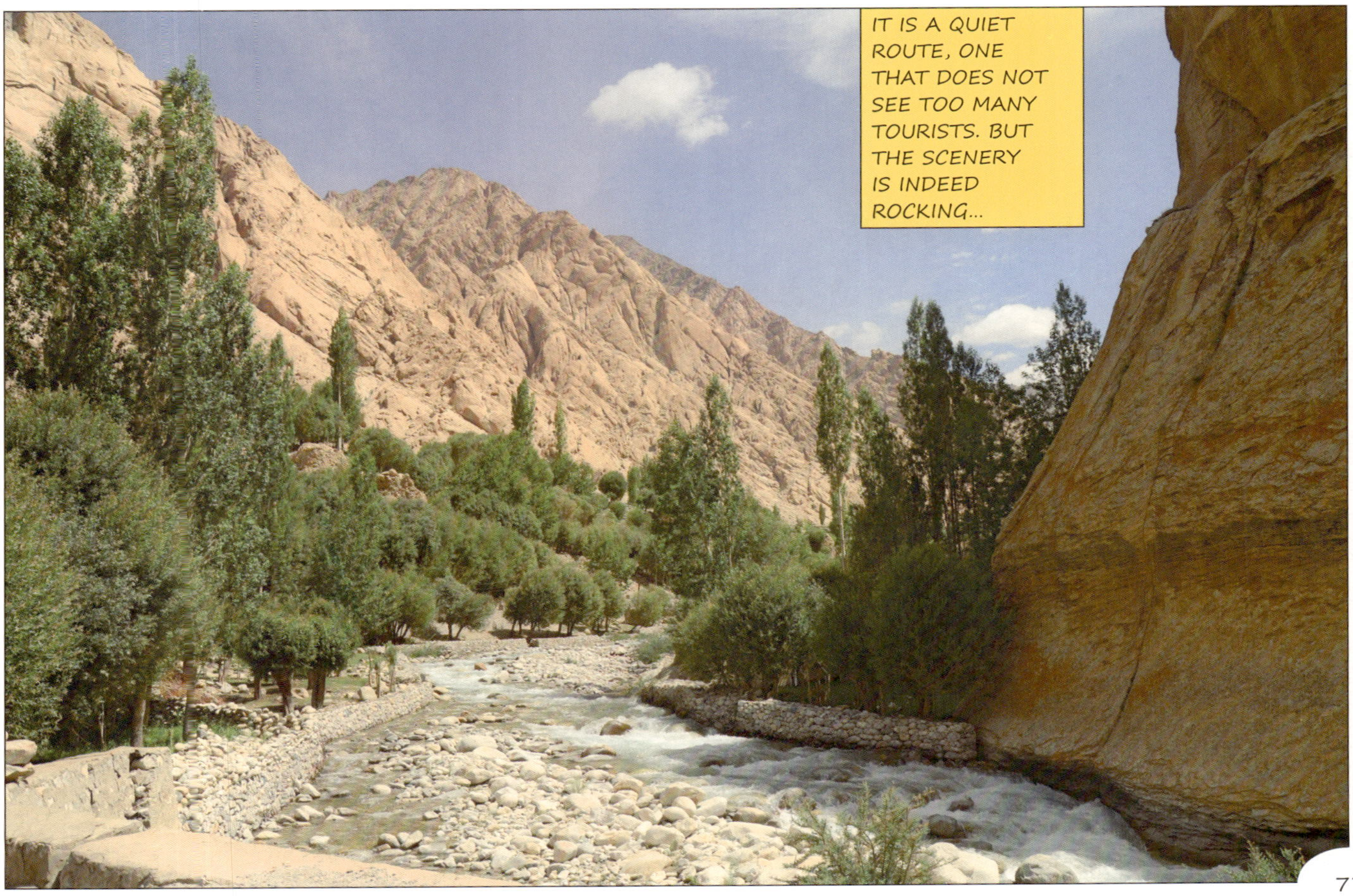
IT IS A QUIET ROUTE, ONE THAT DOES NOT SEE TOO MANY TOURISTS. BUT THE SCENERY IS INDEED ROCKING...

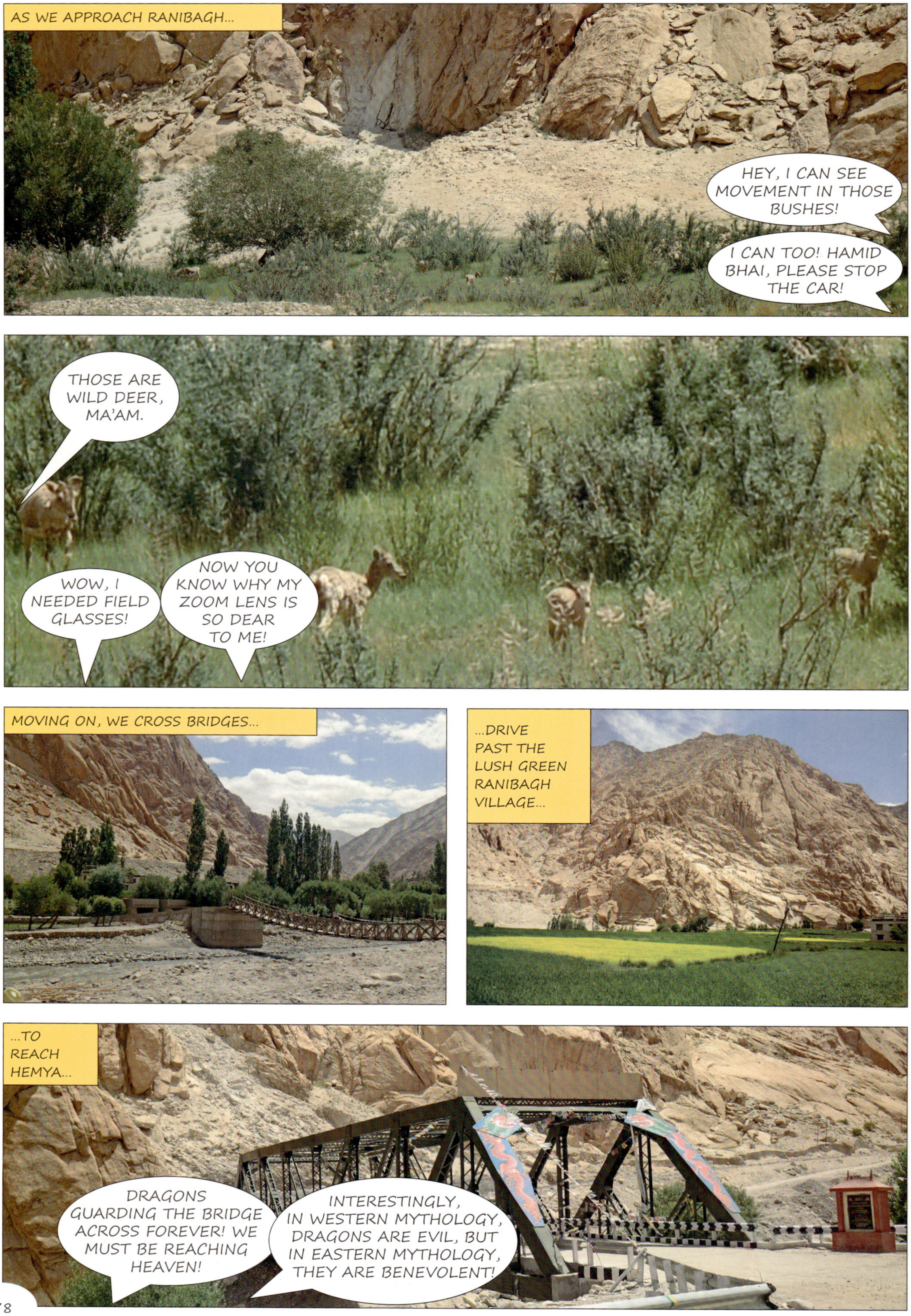
AS WE APPROACH RANIBAGH...
HEY, I CAN SEE MOVEMENT IN THOSE BUSHES!
I CAN TOO! HAMID BHAI, PLEASE STOP THE CAR!
THOSE ARE WILD DEER, MA'AM.
WOW, I NEEDED FIELD GLASSES!
NOW YOU KNOW WHY MY ZOOM LENS IS SO DEAR TO ME!
MOVING ON, WE CROSS BRIDGES...
...DRIVE PAST THE LUSH GREEN RANIBAGH VILLAGE...
...TO REACH HEMYA...
DRAGONS GUARDING THE BRIDGE ACROSS FOREVER! WE MUST BE REACHING HEAVEN!
INTERESTINGLY, IN WESTERN MYTHOLOGY, DRAGONS ARE EVIL, BUT IN EASTERN MYTHOLOGY, THEY ARE BENEVOLENT!

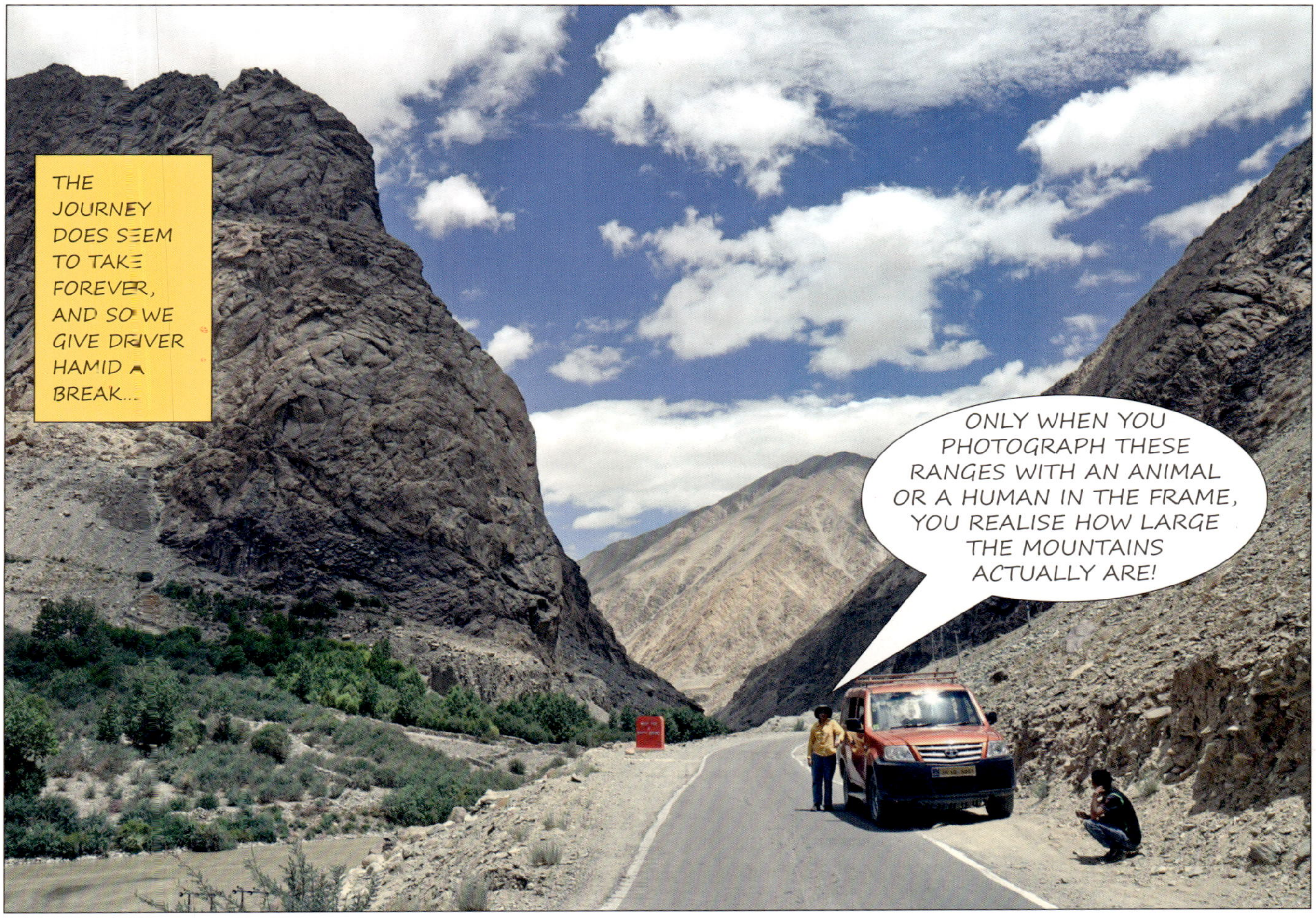
THE JOURNEY DOES SEEM TO TAKE FOREVER, AND SO WE GIVE DRIVER HAMID A BREAK...
ONLY WHEN YOU PHOTOGRAPH THESE RANGES WITH AN ANIMAL OR A HUMAN IN THE FRAME, YOU REALISE HOW LARGE THE MOUNTAINS ACTUALLY ARE!

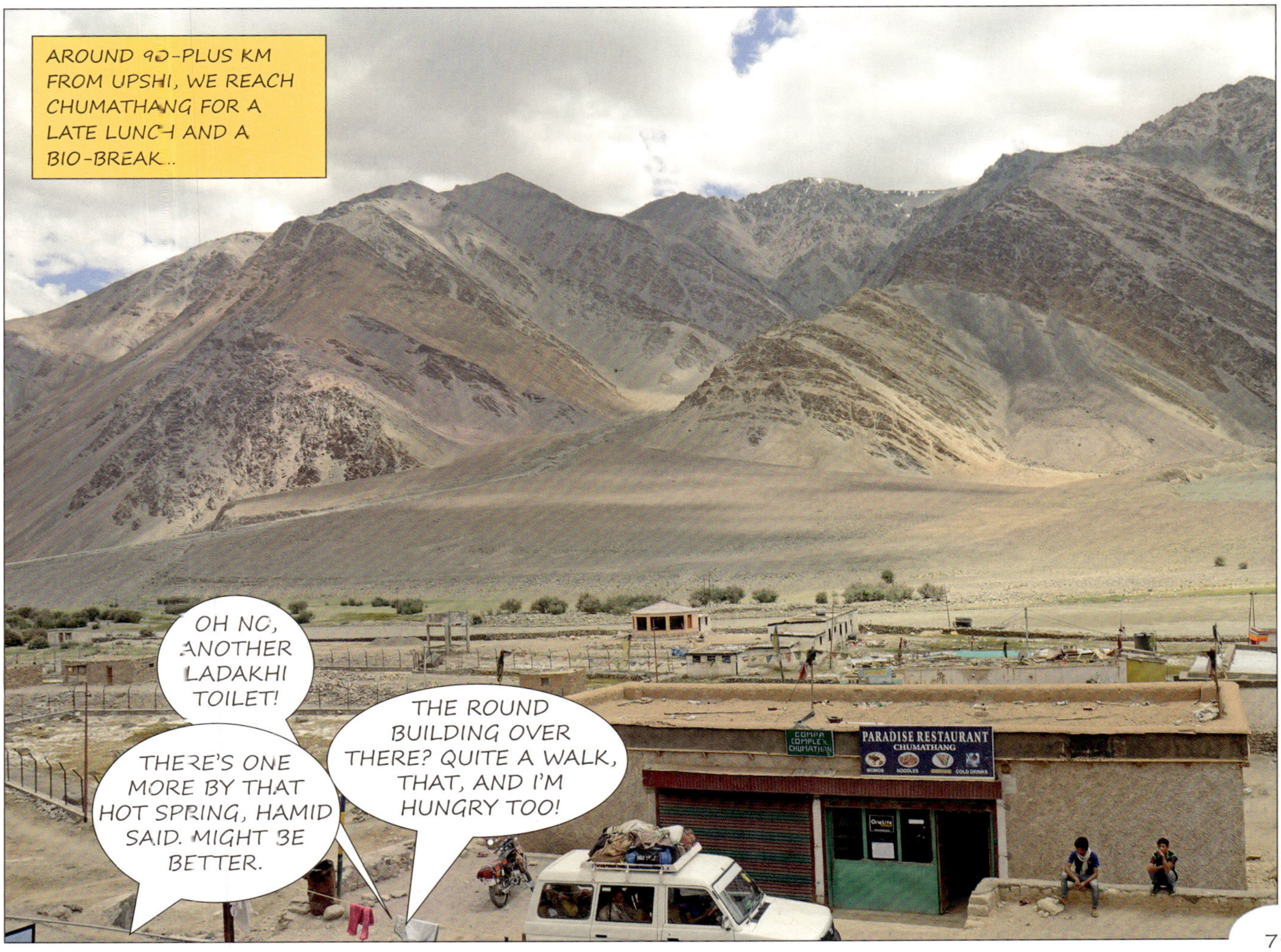
AROUND 90-PLUS KM FROM UPSHI, WE REACH CHUMATHANG FOR A LATE LUNCH AND A BIO-BREAK...
OH NO, ANOTHER LADAKHI TOILET!
THERE'S ONE MORE BY THAT HOT SPRING, HAMID SAID. MIGHT BE BETTER.
THE ROUND BUILDING OVER THERE? QUITE A WALK, THAT, AND I'M HUNGRY TOO!
PARADISE RESTAURANT
CHUMATHANG

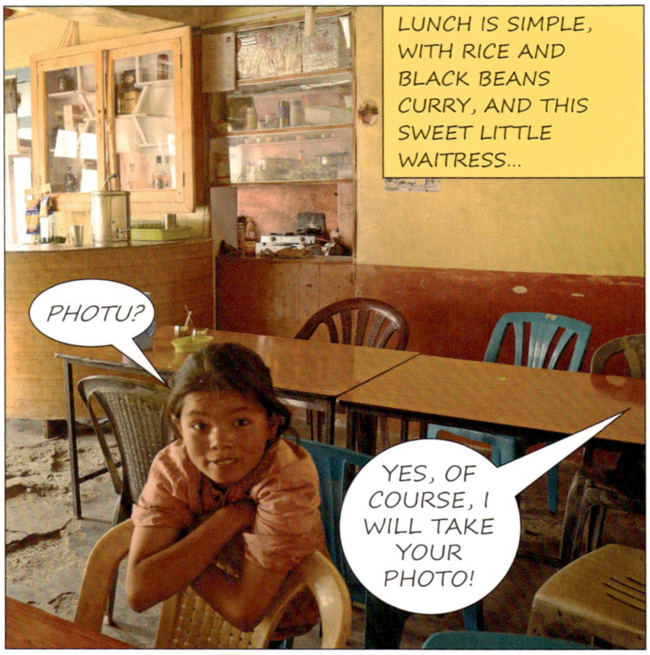
LUNCH IS SIMPLE, WITH RICE AND BLACK BEANS CURRY, AND THIS SWEET LITTLE WAITRESS...
PHOTU?
YES, OF COURSE, I WILL TAKE YOUR PHOTO!

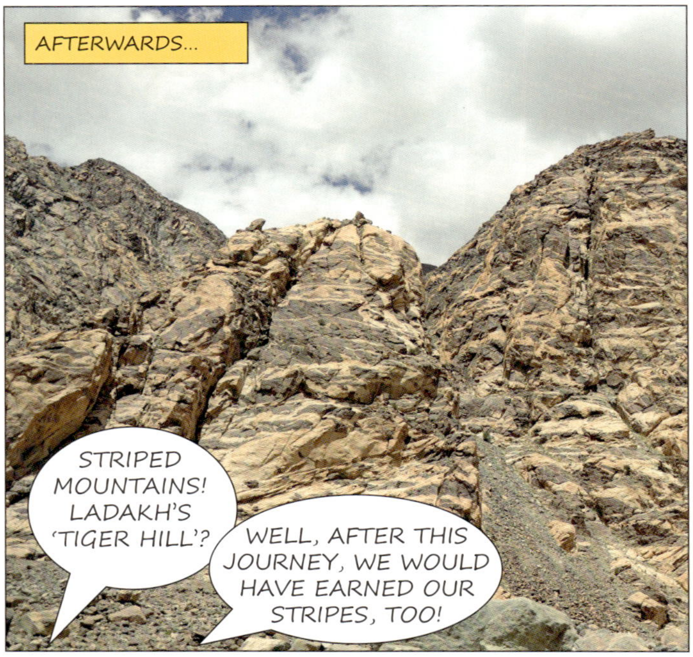
AFTERWARDS...
STRIPED MOUNTAINS! LADAKH'S 'TIGER HILL'?
WELL, AFTER THIS JOURNEY, WE WOULD HAVE EARNED OUR STRIPES, TOO!

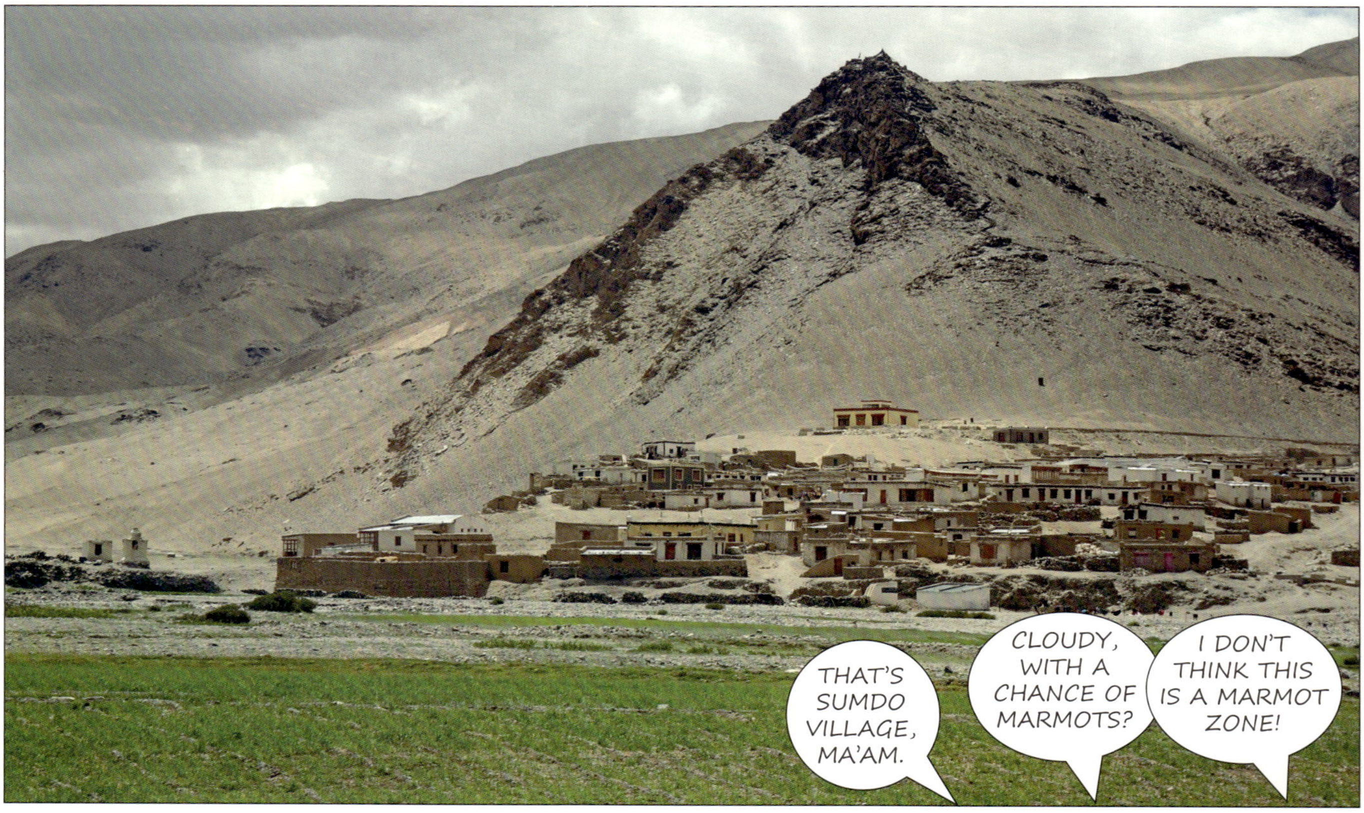
THAT'S SUMDO VILLAGE, MA'AM.
CLOUDY, WITH A CHANCE OF MARMOTS?
I DON'T THINK THIS IS A MARMOT ZONE!

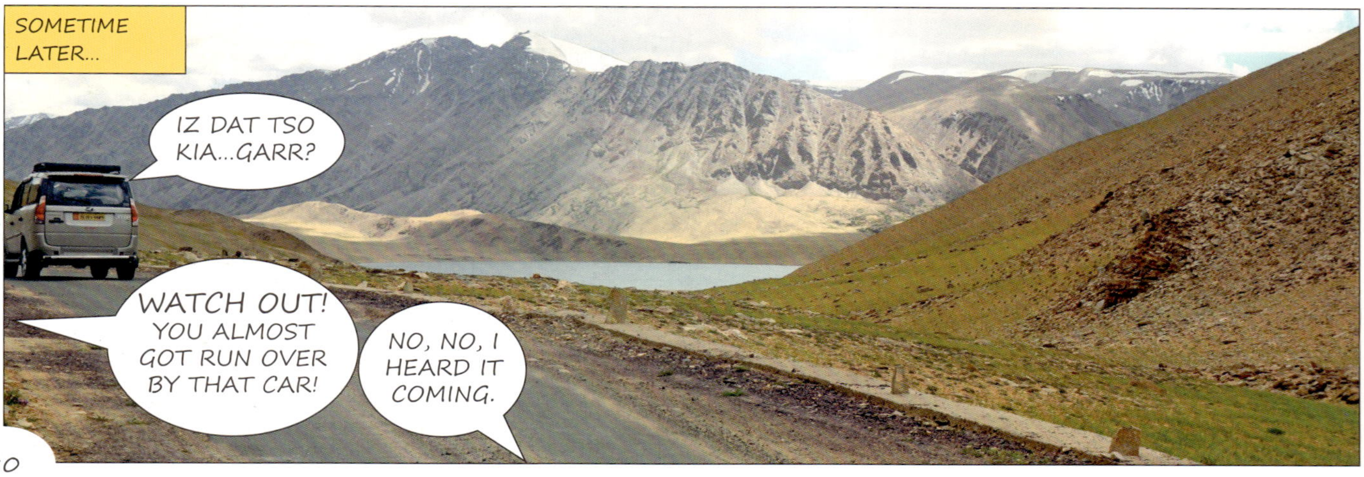
SOMETIME LATER...
IZ DAT TSO KIA...GARR?
WATCH OUT! YOU ALMOST GOT RUN OVER BY THAT CAR!
NO, NO, I HEARD IT COMING.

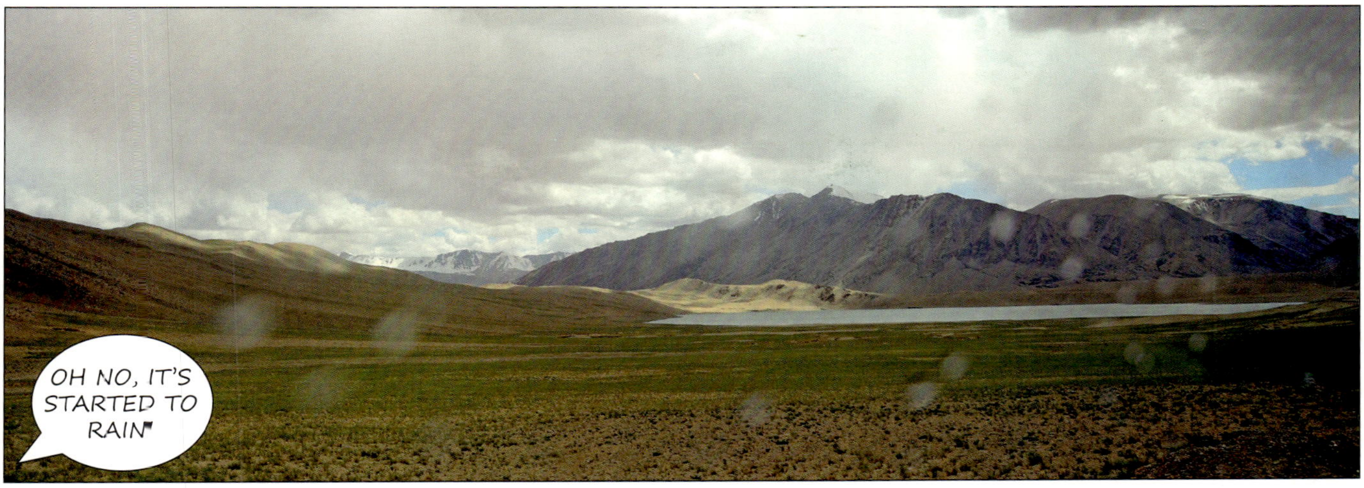
OH NO, IT'S STARTED TO RAIN!

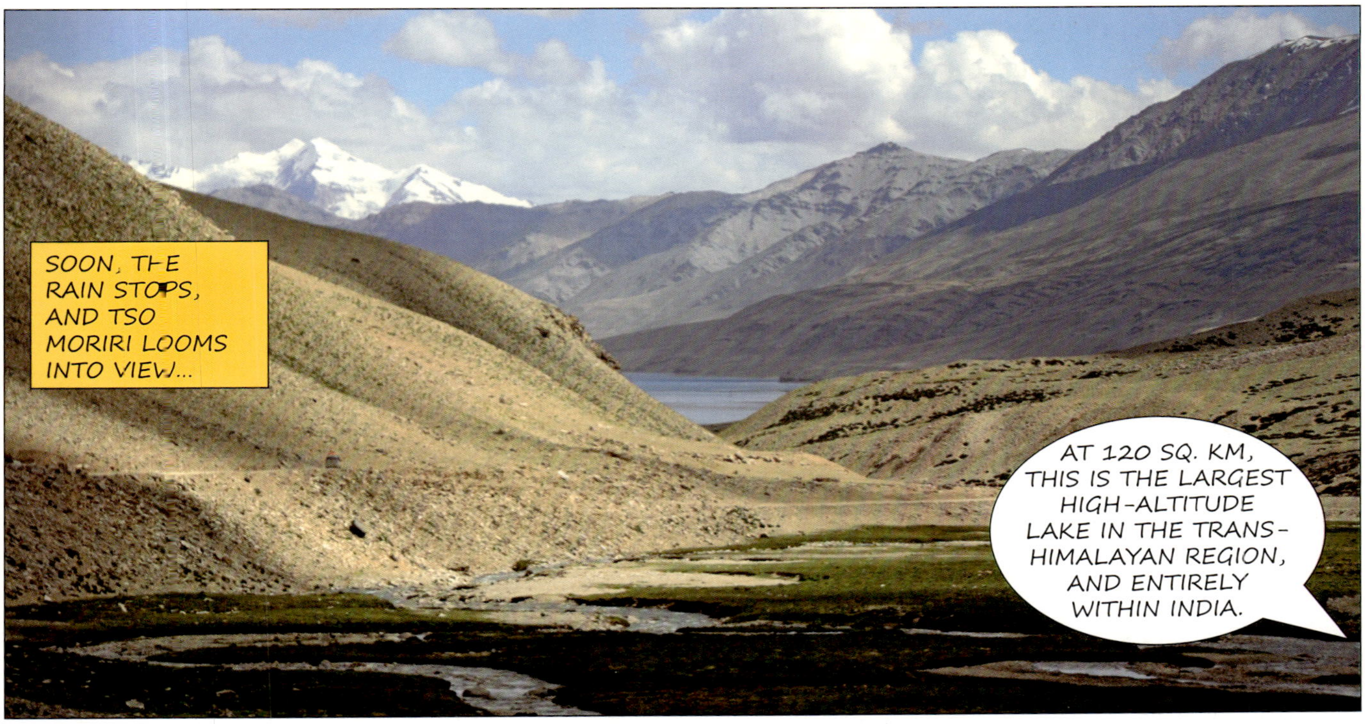
SOON, THE RAIN STOPS, AND TSO MORIRI LOOMS INTO VIEW...
AT 120 SQ. KM, THIS IS THE LARGEST HIGH-ALTITUDE LAKE IN THE TRANS-HIMALAYAN REGION, AND ENTIRELY WITHIN INDIA.

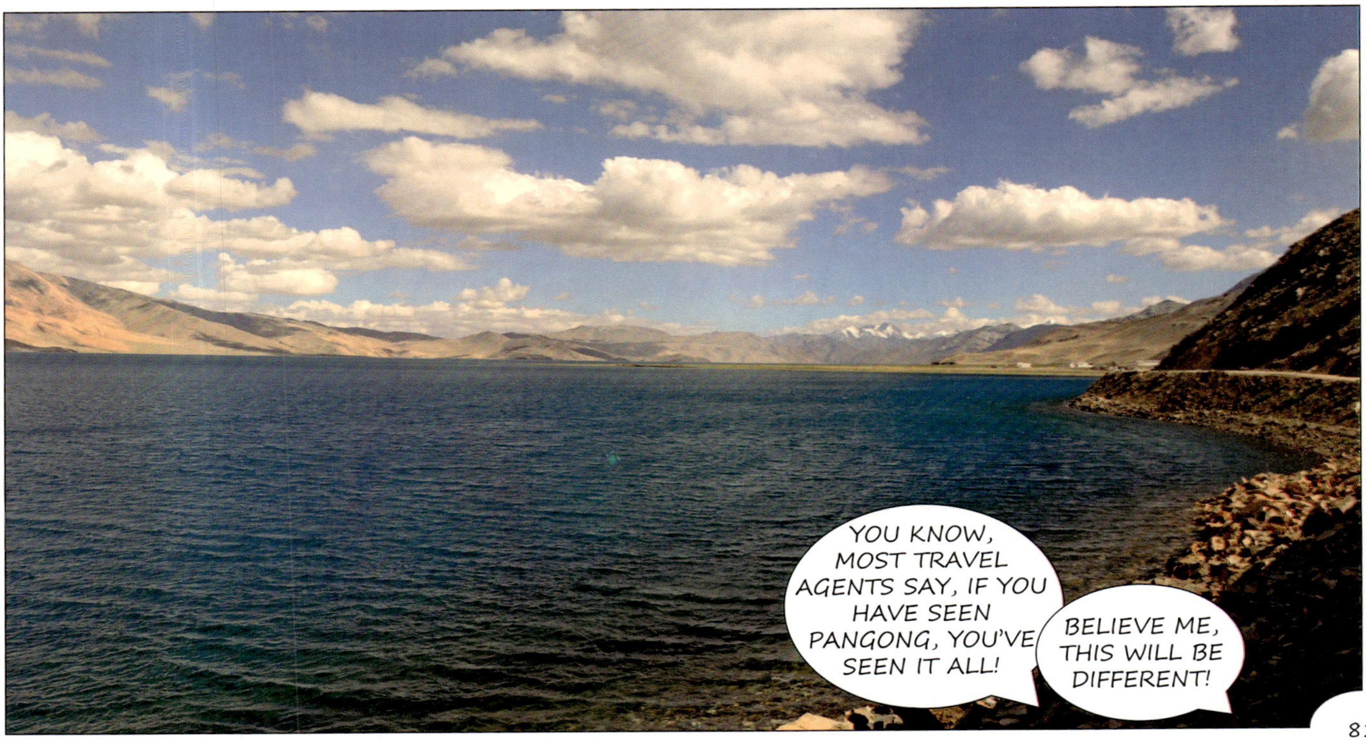
YOU KNOW, MOST TRAVEL AGENTS SAY, IF YOU HAVE SEEN PANGONG, YOU'VE SEEN IT ALL!
BELIEVE ME, THIS WILL BE DIFFERENT!

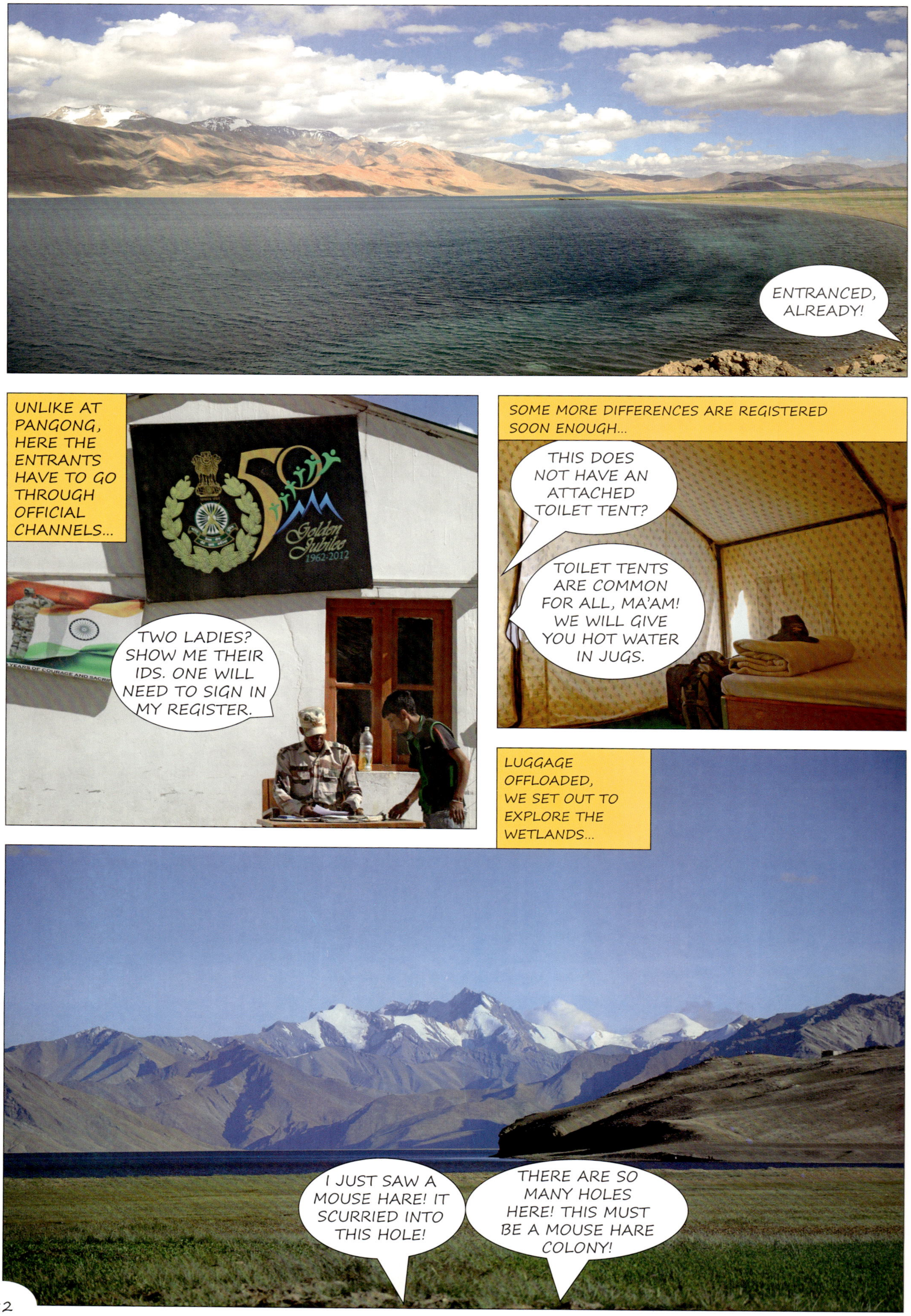
ENTRANCED, ALREADY!
UNLIKE AT PANGONG, HERE THE ENTRANTS HAVE TO GO THROUGH OFFICIAL CHANNELS...
TWO LADIES? SHOW ME THEIR IDS. ONE WILL NEED TO SIGN IN MY REGISTER.
SOME MORE DIFFERENCES ARE REGISTERED SOON ENOUGH...
THIS DOES NOT HAVE AN ATTACHED TOILET TENT?
TOILET TENTS ARE COMMON FOR ALL, MA'AM! WE WILL GIVE YOU HOT WATER IN JUGS.
LUGGAGE OFFLOADED, WE SET OUT TO EXPLORE THE WETLANDS...
I JUST SAW A MOUSE HARE! IT SCURRIED INTO THIS HOLE!
THERE ARE SO MANY HOLES HERE! THIS MUST BE A MOUSE HARE COLONY!

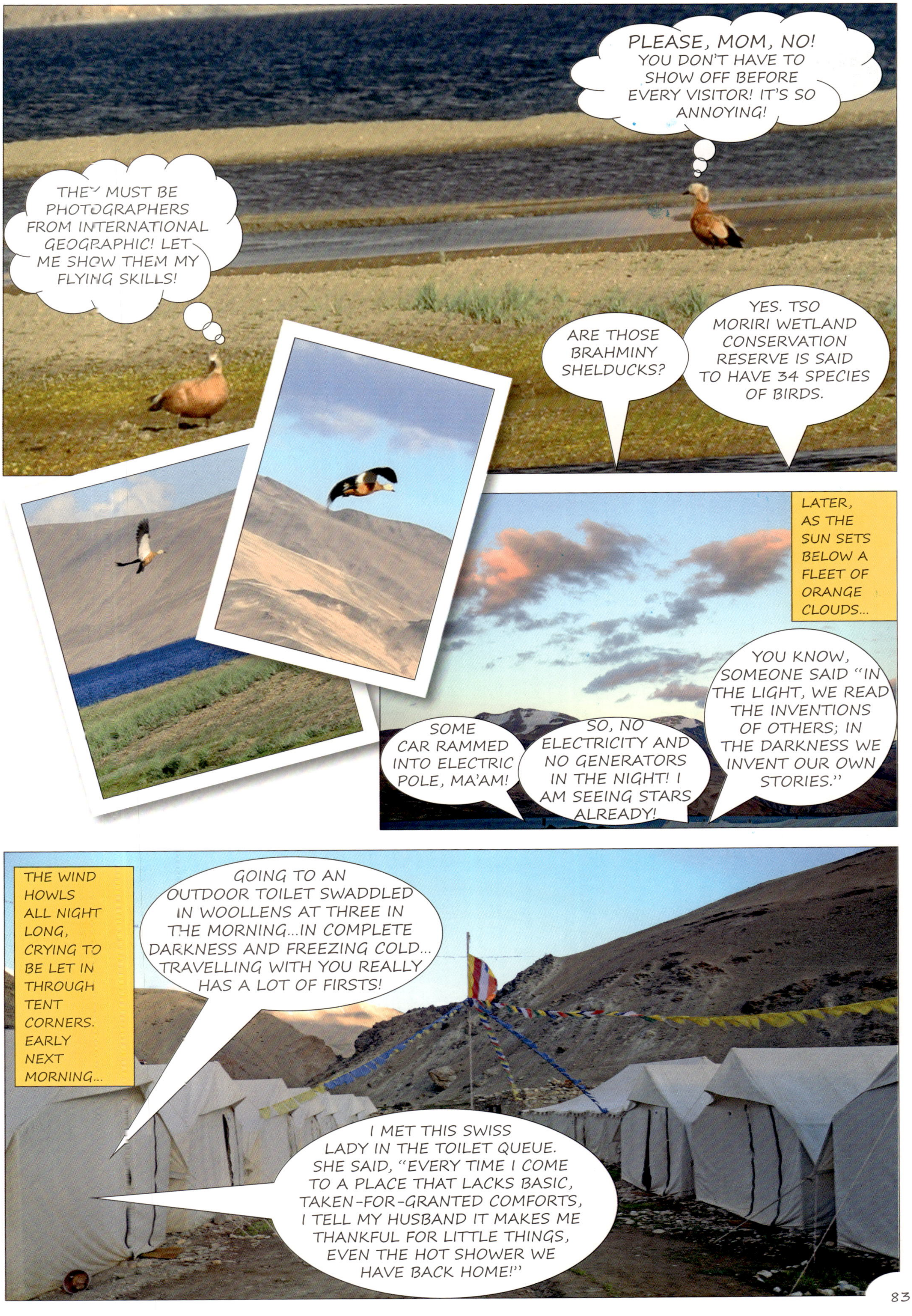
PLEASE, MOM, NO! YOU DON'T HAVE TO SHOW OFF BEFORE EVERY VISITOR! IT'S SO ANNOYING!
THEY MUST BE PHOTOGRAPHERS FROM INTERNATIONAL GEOGRAPHIC! LET ME SHOW THEM MY FLYING SKILLS!
ARE THOSE BRAHMINY SHELDUCKS?
YES. TSO MORIRI WETLAND CONSERVATION RESERVE IS SAID TO HAVE 34 SPECIES OF BIRDS.
LATER, AS THE SUN SETS BELOW A FLEET OF ORANGE CLOUDS...
SOME CAR RAMMED INTO ELECTRIC POLE, MA'AM!
SO, NO ELECTRICITY AND NO GENERATORS IN THE NIGHT! I AM SEEING STARS ALREADY!
YOU KNOW, SOMEONE SAID "IN THE LIGHT, WE READ THE INVENTIONS OF OTHERS; IN THE DARKNESS WE INVENT OUR OWN STORIES."
THE WIND HOWLS ALL NIGHT LONG, CRYING TO BE LET IN THROUGH TENT CORNERS. EARLY NEXT MORNING...
GOING TO AN OUTDOOR TOILET SWADDLED IN WOOLLENS AT THREE IN THE MORNING...IN COMPLETE DARKNESS AND FREEZING COLD... TRAVELLING WITH YOU REALLY HAS A LOT OF FIRSTS!
I MET THIS SWISS LADY IN THE TOILET QUEUE. SHE SAID, "EVERY TIME I COME TO A PLACE THAT LACKS BASIC, TAKEN-FOR-GRANTED COMFORTS, I TELL MY HUSBAND IT MAKES ME THANKFUL FOR LITTLE THINGS, EVEN THE HOT SHOWER WE HAVE BACK HOME!"

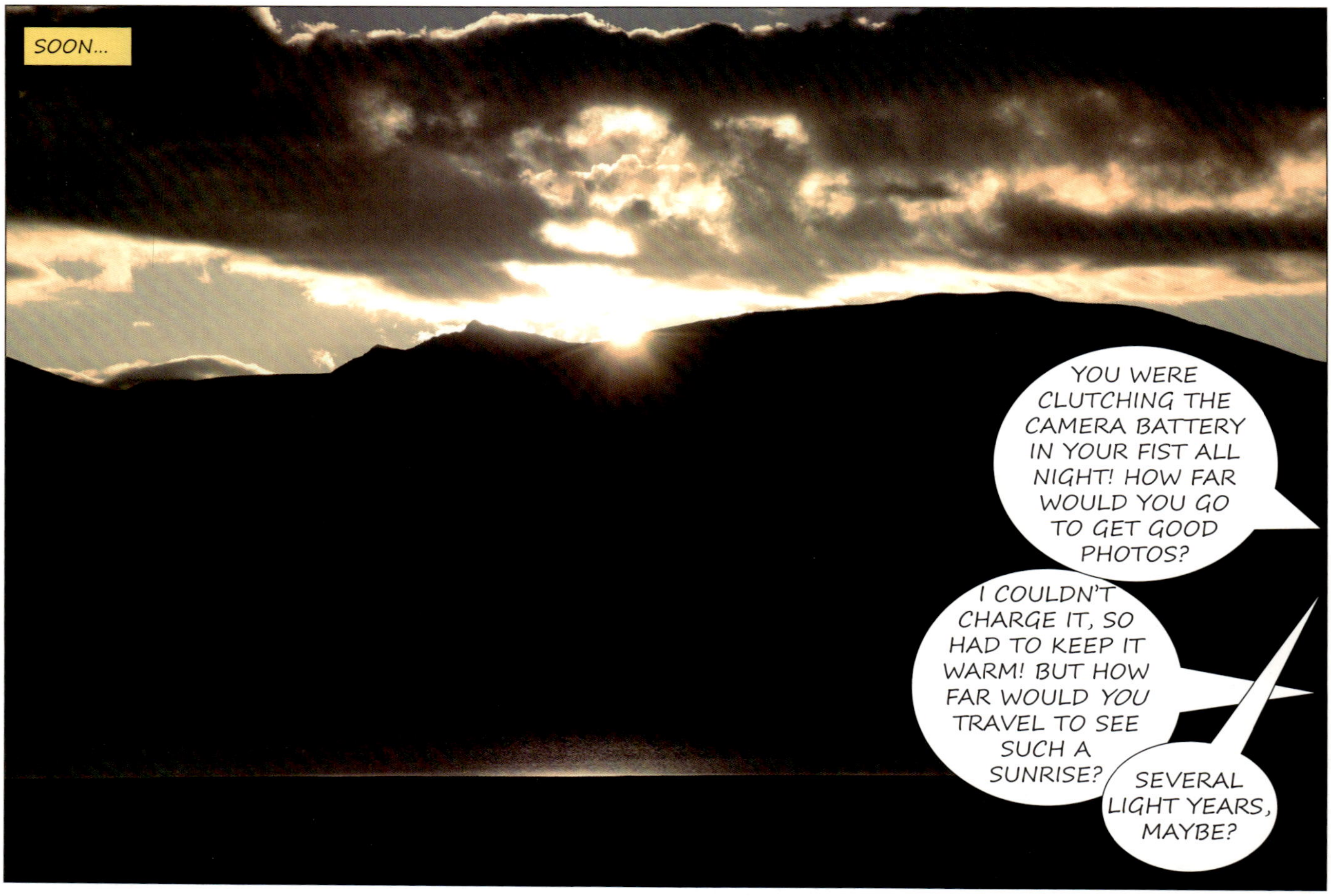
SOON...
YOU WERE CLUTCHING THE CAMERA BATTERY IN YOUR FIST ALL NIGHT! HOW FAR WOULD YOU GO TO GET GOOD PHOTOS?
I COULDN'T CHARGE IT, SO HAD TO KEEP IT WARM! BUT HOW FAR WOULD *YOU* TRAVEL TO SEE SUCH A SUNRISE?
SEVERAL LIGHT YEARS, MAYBE?

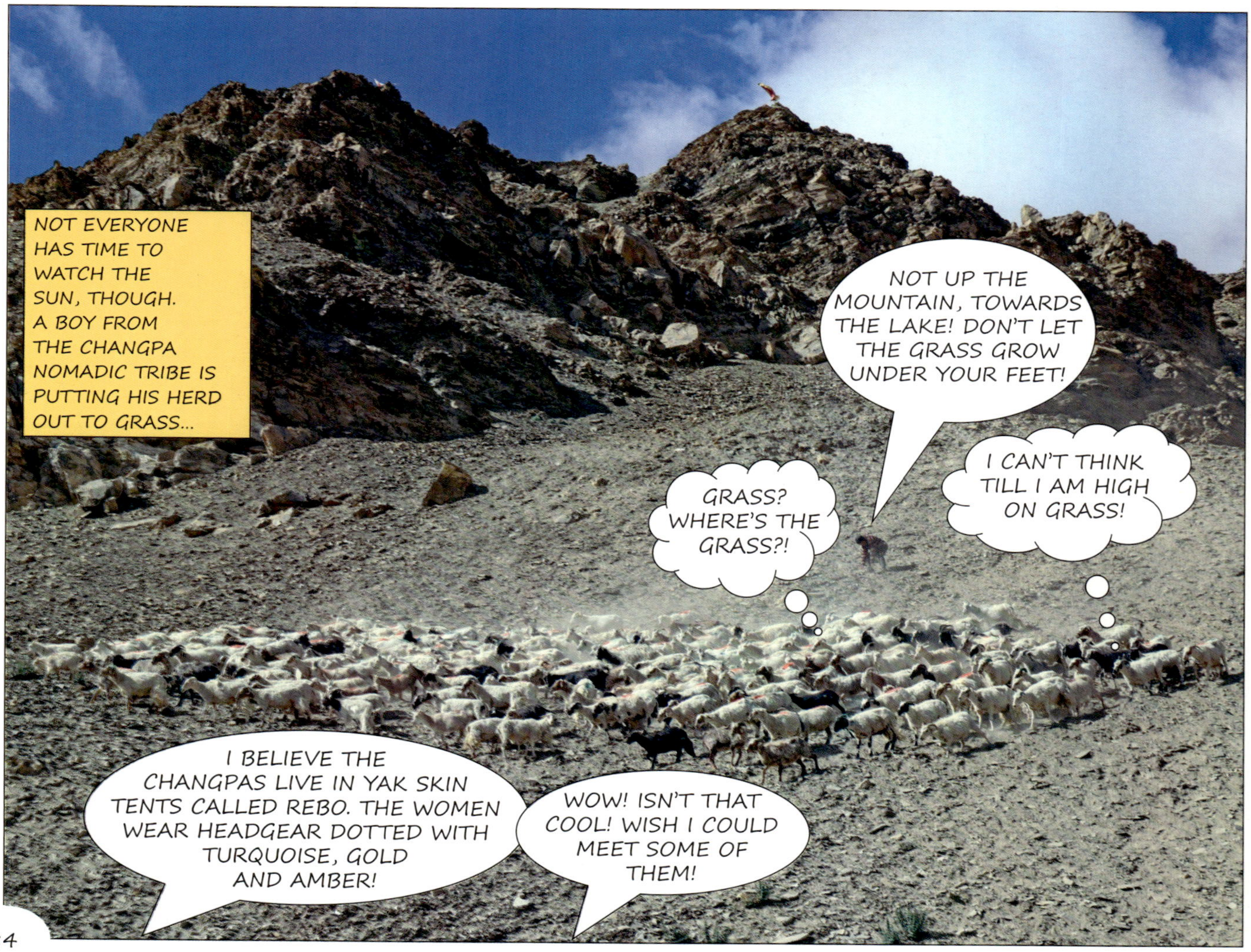
NOT EVERYONE HAS TIME TO WATCH THE SUN, THOUGH. A BOY FROM THE CHANGPA NOMADIC TRIBE IS PUTTING HIS HERD OUT TO GRASS...
NOT UP THE MOUNTAIN, TOWARDS THE LAKE! DON'T LET THE GRASS GROW UNDER YOUR FEET!
GRASS? WHERE'S THE GRASS?!
I CAN'T THINK TILL I AM HIGH ON GRASS!
I BELIEVE THE CHANGPAS LIVE IN YAK SKIN TENTS CALLED REBO. THE WOMEN WEAR HEADGEAR DOTTED WITH TURQUOISE, GOLD AND AMBER!
WOW! ISN'T THAT COOL! WISH I COULD MEET SOME OF THEM!

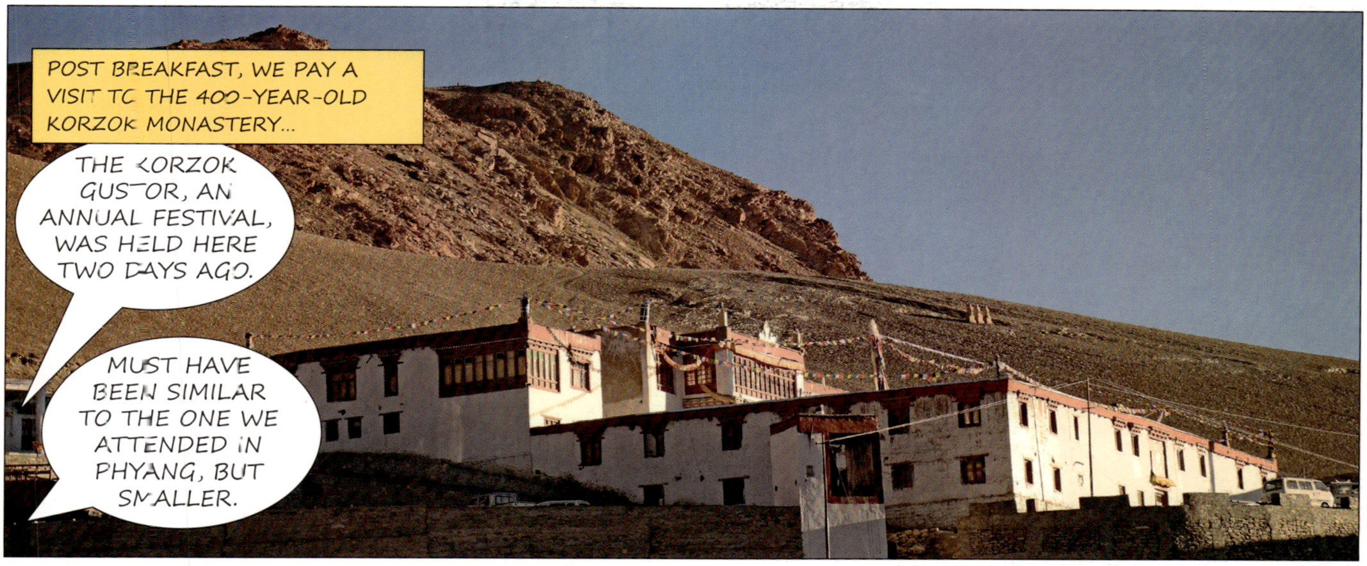
POST BREAKFAST, WE PAY A VISIT TO THE 400-YEAR-OLD KORZOK MONASTERY...
THE KORZOK GUSTOR, AN ANNUAL FESTIVAL, WAS HELD HERE TWO DAYS AGO.
MUST HAVE BEEN SIMILAR TO THE ONE WE ATTENDED IN PHYANG, BUT SMALLER.

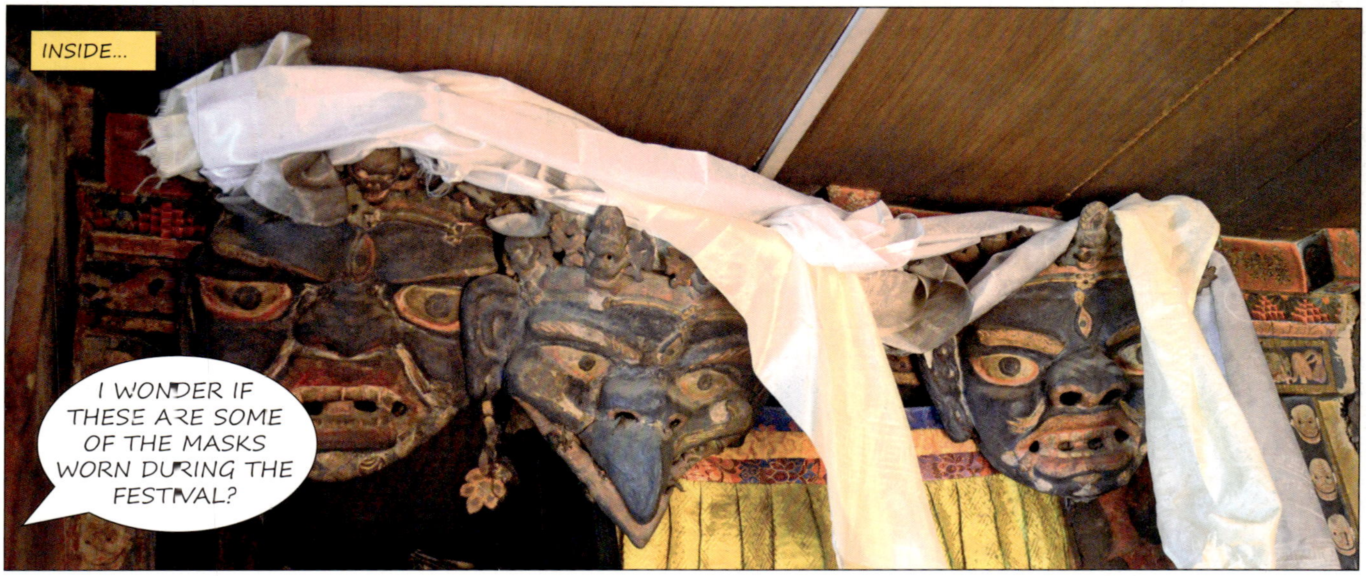
INSIDE...
I WONDER IF THESE ARE SOME OF THE MASKS WORN DURING THE FESTIVAL?

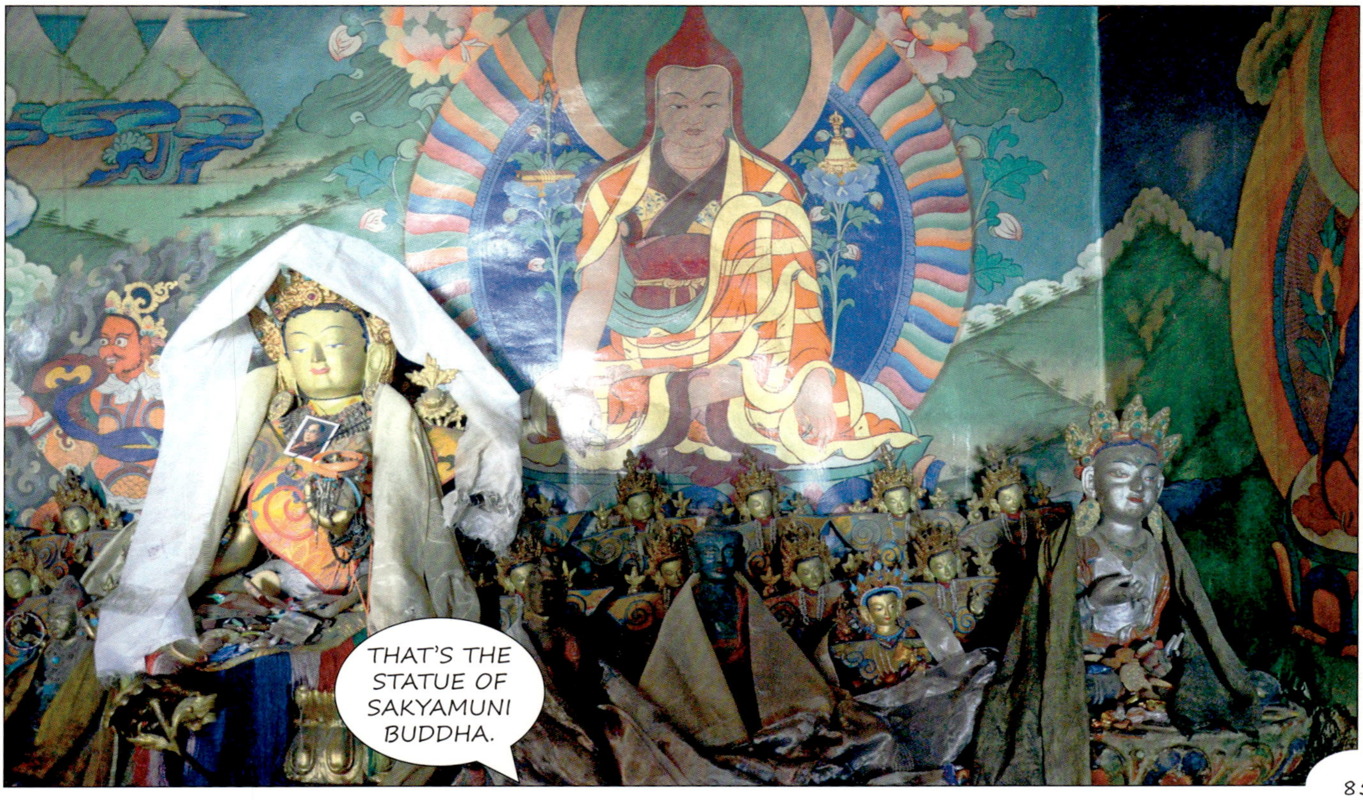
THAT'S THE STATUE OF SAKYAMUNI BUDDHA.

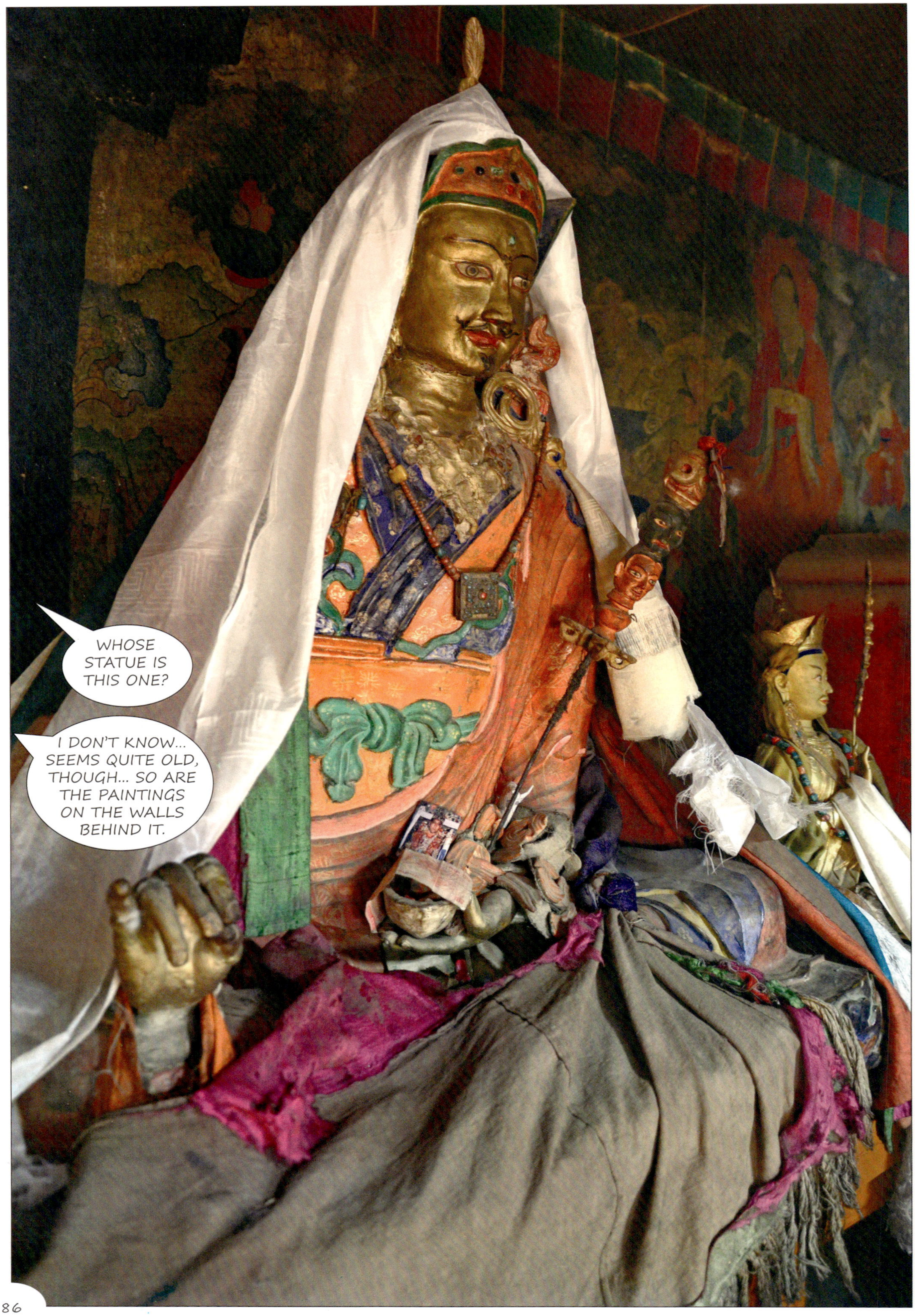
WHOSE STATUE IS THIS ONE?
I DON'T KNOW... SEEMS QUITE OLD, THOUGH... SO ARE THE PAINTINGS ON THE WALLS BEHIND IT.

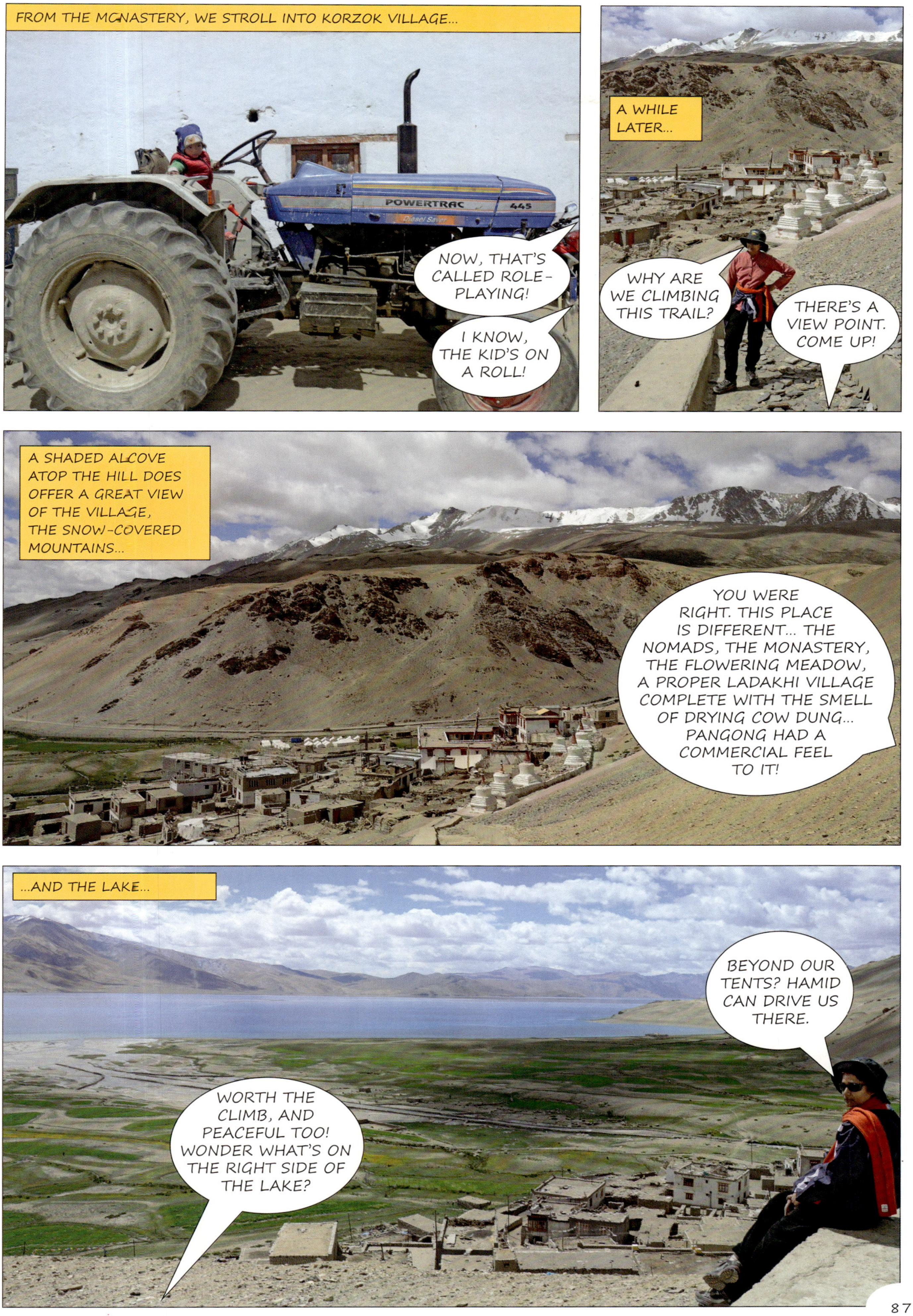
FROM THE MONASTERY, WE STROLL INTO KORZOK VILLAGE...
POWERTRAC 445
NOW, THAT'S CALLED ROLE-PLAYING!
I KNOW, THE KID'S ON A ROLL!
A WHILE LATER...
WHY ARE WE CLIMBING THIS TRAIL?
THERE'S A VIEW POINT. COME UP!
A SHADED ALCOVE ATOP THE HILL DOES OFFER A GREAT VIEW OF THE VILLAGE, THE SNOW-COVERED MOUNTAINS...
YOU WERE RIGHT. THIS PLACE IS DIFFERENT... THE NOMADS, THE MONASTERY, THE FLOWERING MEADOW, A PROPER LADAKHI VILLAGE COMPLETE WITH THE SMELL OF DRYING COW DUNG... PANGONG HAD A COMMERCIAL FEEL TO IT!
...AND THE LAKE...
WORTH THE CLIMB, AND PEACEFUL TOO! WONDER WHAT'S ON THE RIGHT SIDE OF THE LAKE?
BEYOND OUR TENTS? HAMID CAN DRIVE US THERE.

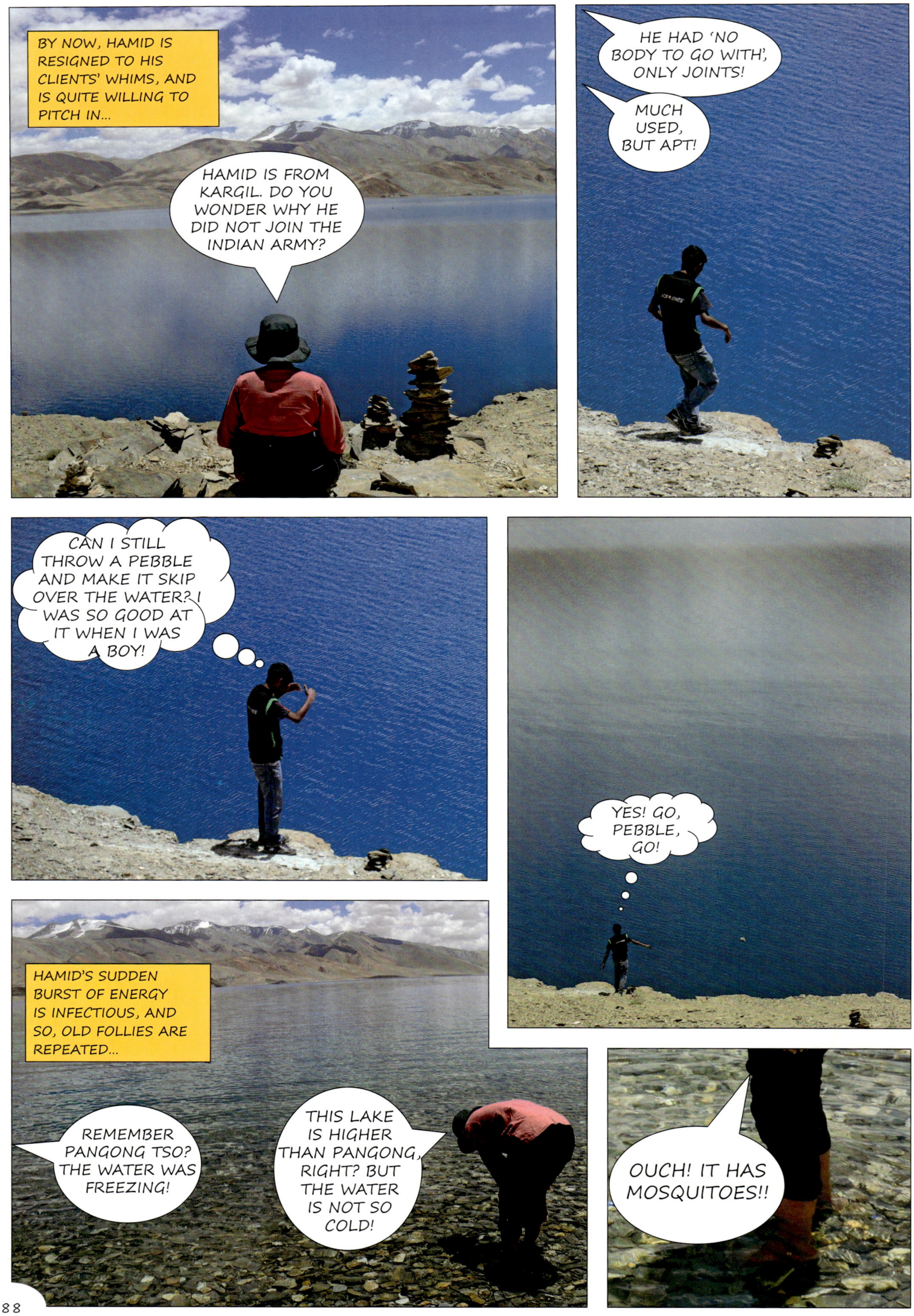
BY NOW, HAMID IS RESIGNED TO HIS CLIENTS' WHIMS, AND IS QUITE WILLING TO PITCH IN...
HAMID IS FROM KARGIL. DO YOU WONDER WHY HE DID NOT JOIN THE INDIAN ARMY?
HE HAD 'NO BODY TO GO WITH', ONLY JOINTS!
MUCH USED, BUT APT!
CAN I STILL THROW A PEBBLE AND MAKE IT SKIP OVER THE WATER? I WAS SO GOOD AT IT WHEN I WAS A BOY!
YES! GO, PEBBLE, GO!
HAMID'S SUDDEN BURST OF ENERGY IS INFECTIOUS, AND SO, OLD FOLLIES ARE REPEATED...
REMEMBER PANGONG TSO? THE WATER WAS FREEZING!
THIS LAKE IS HIGHER THAN PANGONG, RIGHT? BUT THE WATER IS NOT SO COLD!
OUCH! IT HAS MOSQUITOES!!

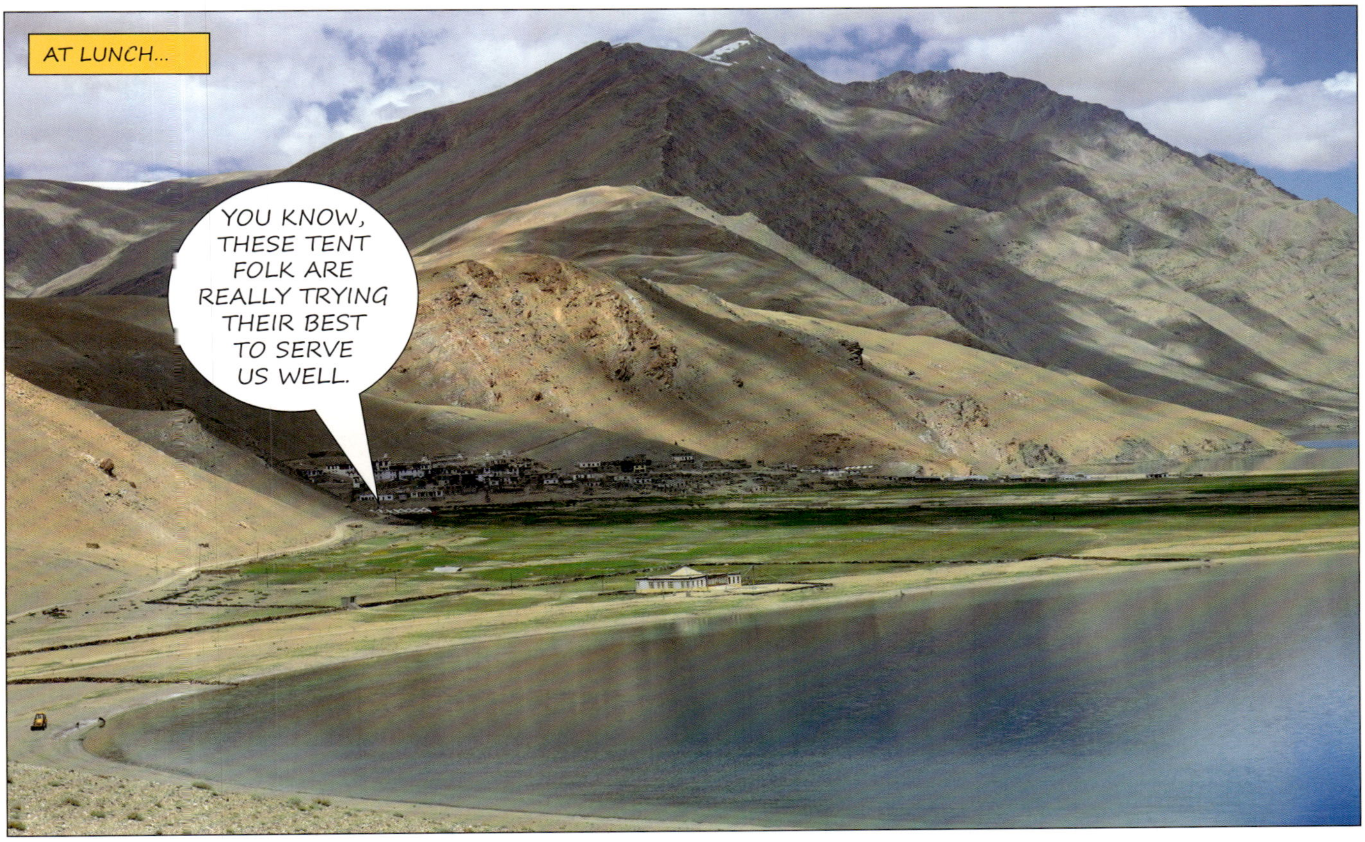
AT LUNCH...
YOU KNOW, THESE TENT FOLK ARE REALLY TRYING THEIR BEST TO SERVE US WELL.

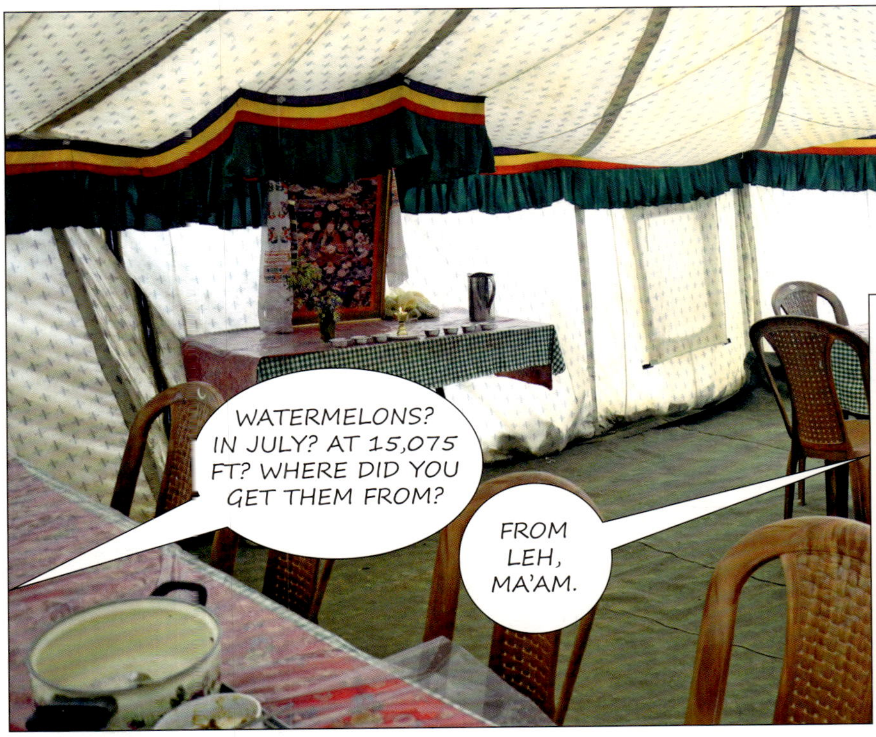
WATERMELONS? IN JULY? AT 15,075 FT? WHERE DID YOU GET THEM FROM?
FROM LEH, MA'AM.

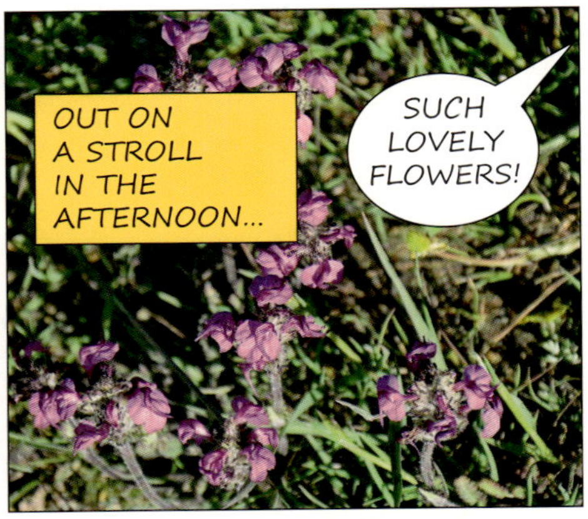
OUT ON A STROLL IN THE AFTERNOON...
SUCH LOVELY FLOWERS!

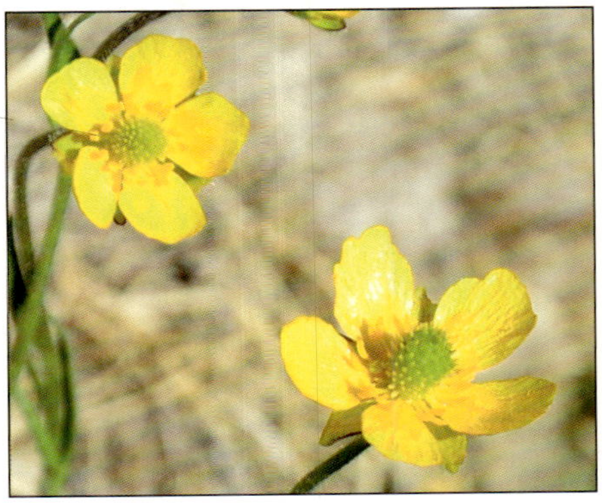

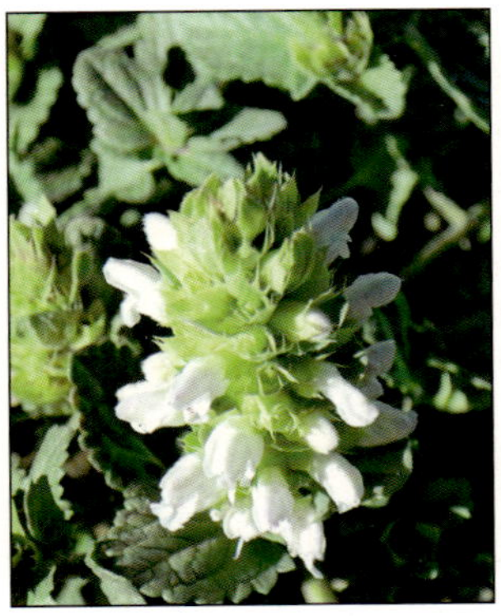

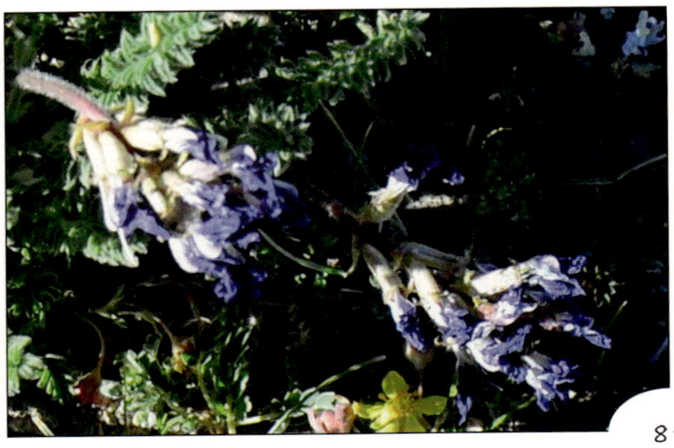

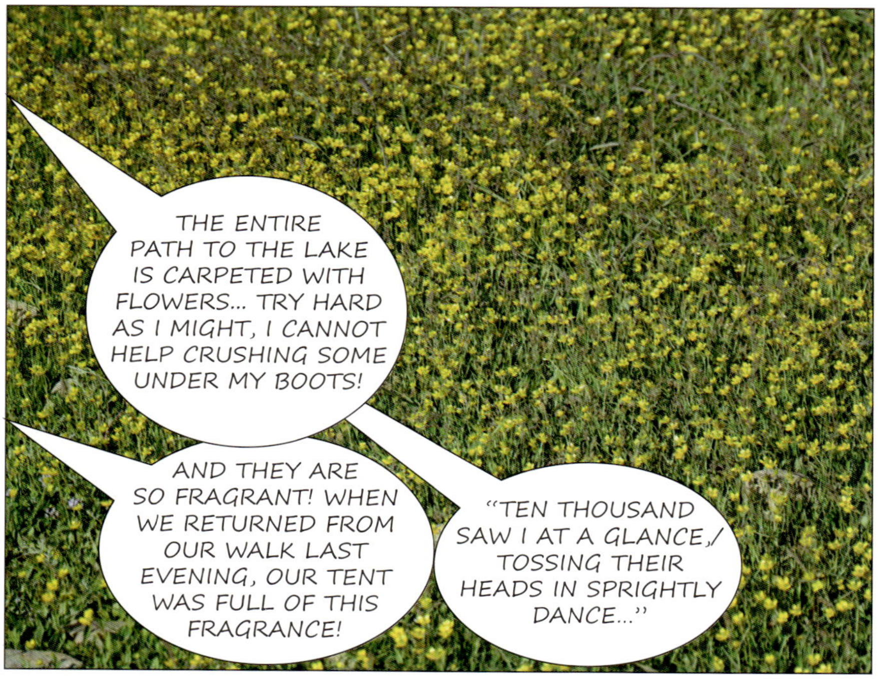
THE ENTIRE PATH TO THE LAKE IS CARPETED WITH FLOWERS... TRY HARD AS I MIGHT, I CANNOT HELP CRUSHING SOME UNDER MY BOOTS!
AND THEY ARE SO FRAGRANT! WHEN WE RETURNED FROM OUR WALK LAST EVENING, OUR TENT WAS FULL OF THIS FRAGRANCE!
"TEN THOUSAND SAW I AT A GLANCE,/ TOSSING THEIR HEADS IN SPRIGHTLY DANCE..."

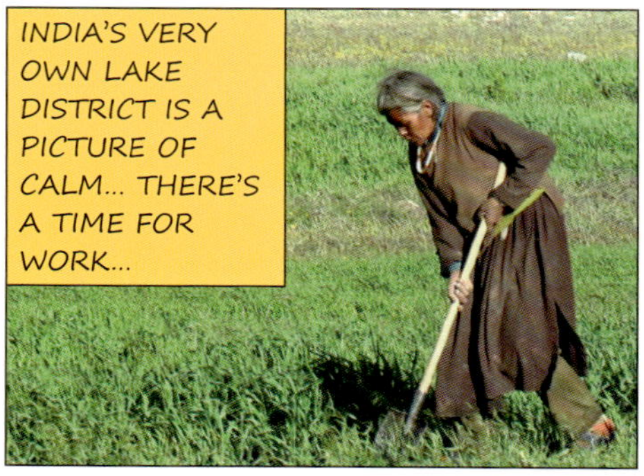
INDIA'S VERY OWN LAKE DISTRICT IS A PICTURE OF CALM... THERE'S A TIME FOR WORK...

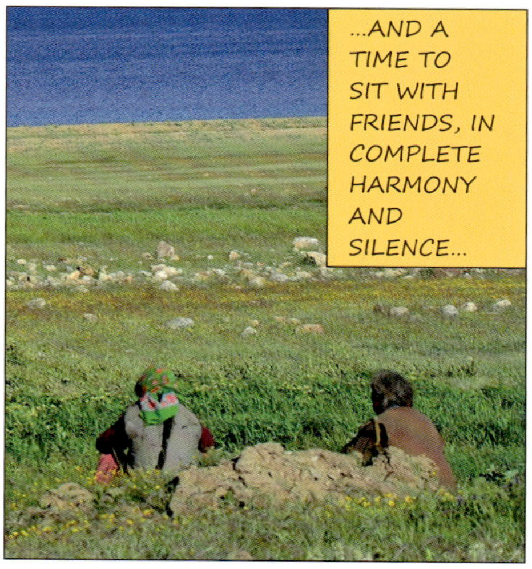
...AND A TIME TO SIT WITH FRIENDS, IN COMPLETE HARMONY AND SILENCE...

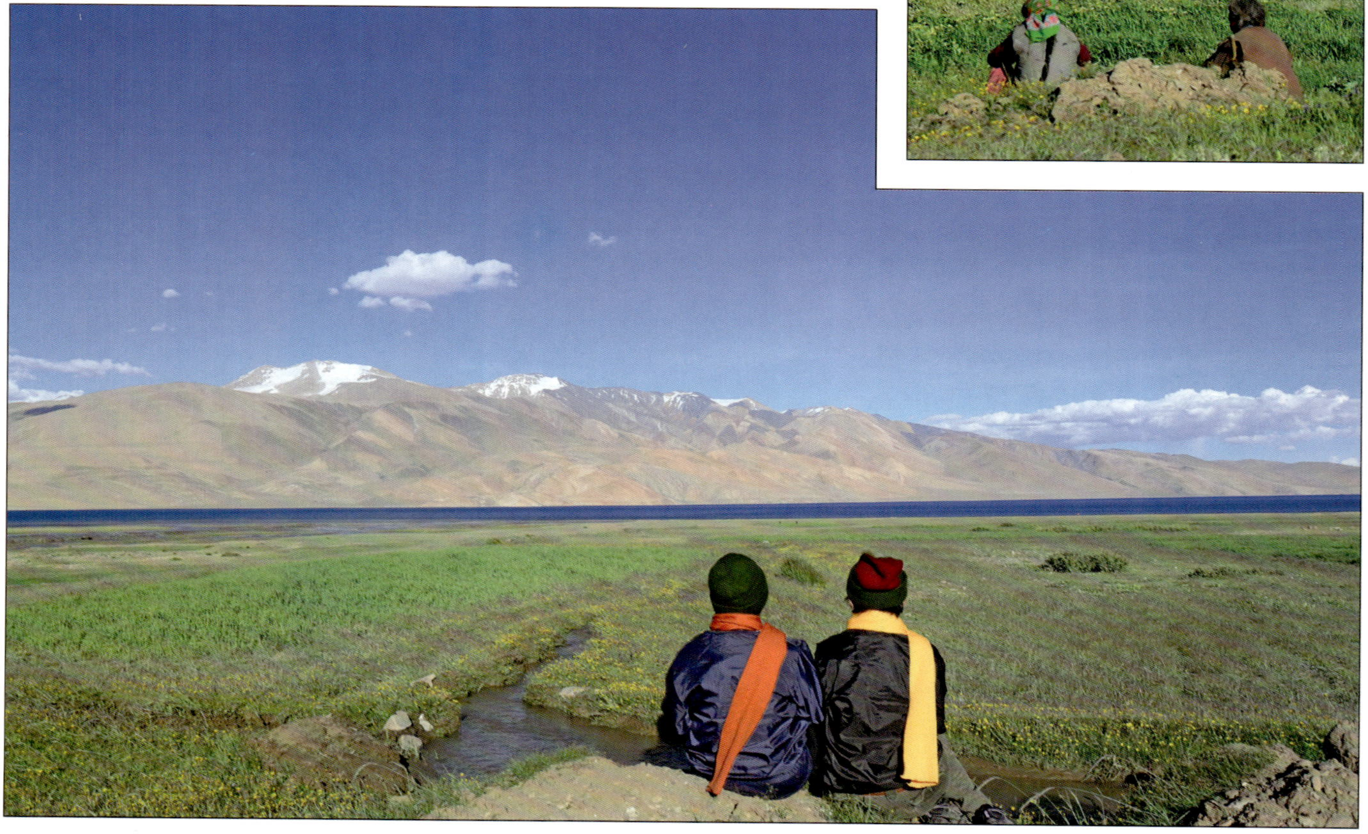

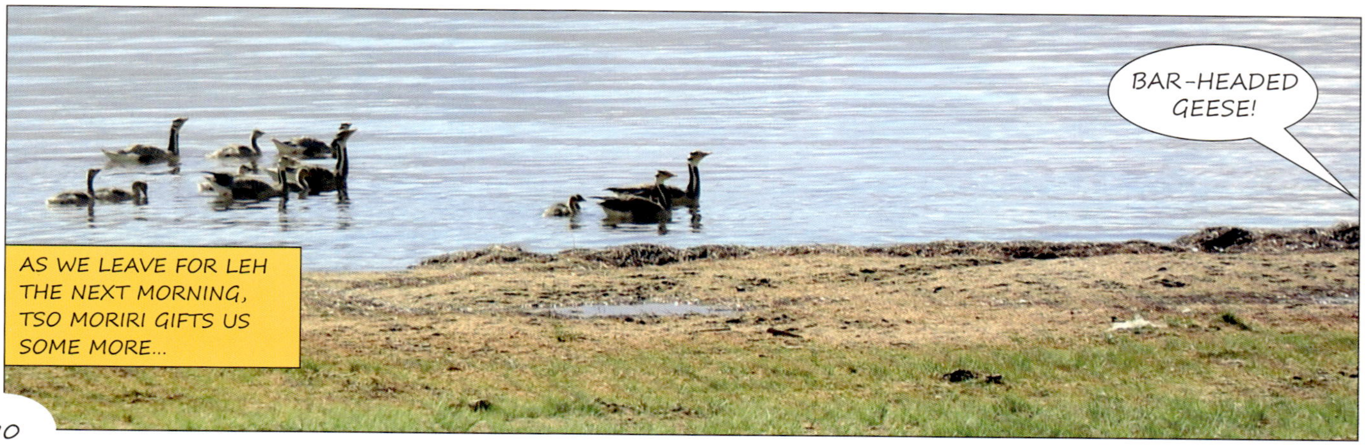
BAR-HEADED GEESE!
AS WE LEAVE FOR LEH THE NEXT MORNING, TSO MORIRI GIFTS US SOME MORE...

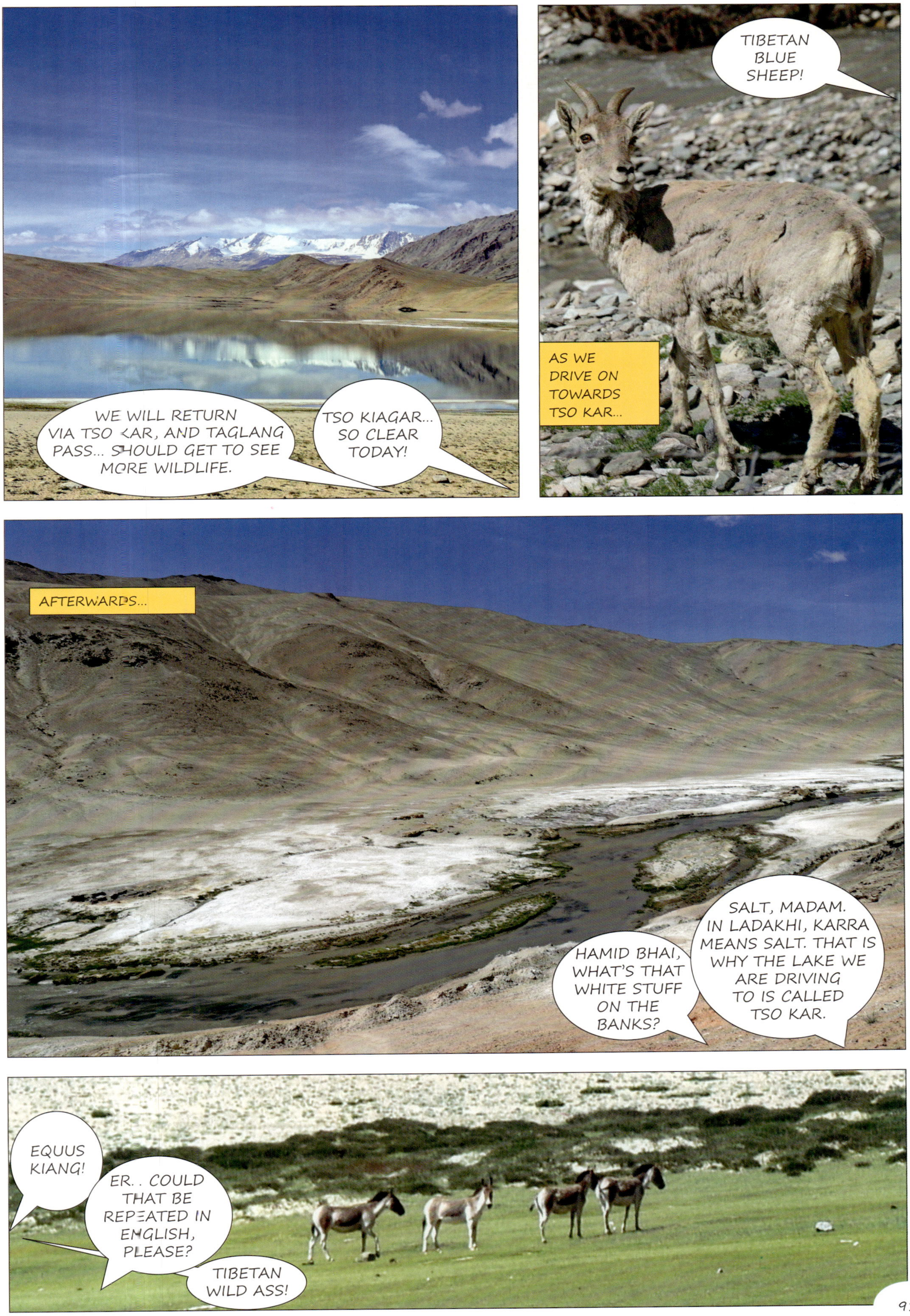
WE WILL RETURN VIA TSO KAR, AND TAGLANG PASS... SHOULD GET TO SEE MORE WILDLIFE.
TSO KIAGAR... SO CLEAR TODAY!
AS WE DRIVE ON TOWARDS TSO KAR...
TIBETAN BLUE SHEEP!
AFTERWARDS...
HAMID BHAI, WHAT'S THAT WHITE STUFF ON THE BANKS?
SALT, MADAM. IN LADAKHI, KARRA MEANS SALT. THAT IS WHY THE LAKE WE ARE DRIVING TO IS CALLED TSO KAR.
EQUUS KIANG!
ER.. COULD THAT BE REPEATED IN ENGLISH, PLEASE?
TIBETAN WILD ASS!

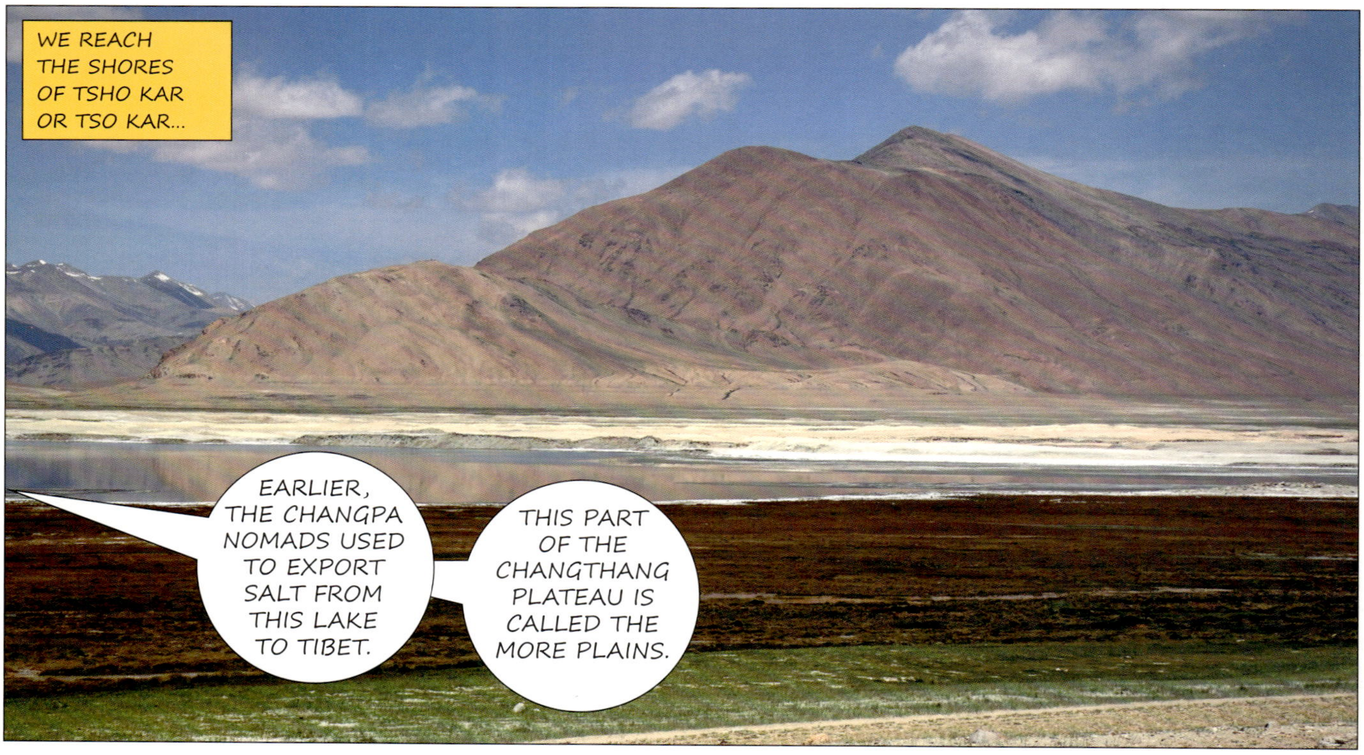
WE REACH THE SHORES OF TSHO KAR OR TSO KAR...
EARLIER, THE CHANGPA NOMADS USED TO EXPORT SALT FROM THIS LAKE TO TIBET.
THIS PART OF THE CHANGTHANG PLATEAU IS CALLED THE MORE PLAINS.

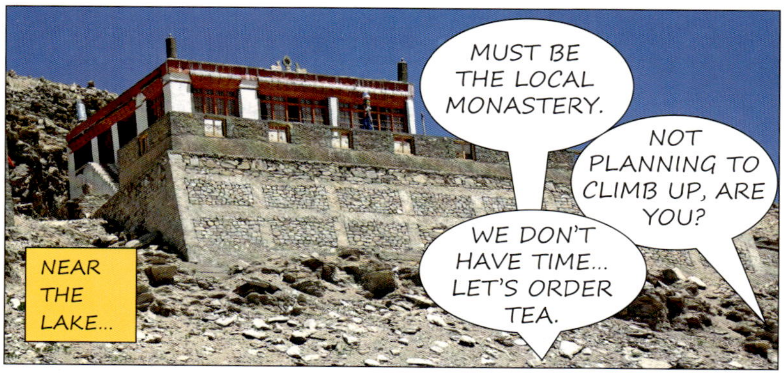
NEAR THE LAKE...
MUST BE THE LOCAL MONASTERY.
NOT PLANNING TO CLIMB UP, ARE YOU?
WE DON'T HAVE TIME... LET'S ORDER TEA.

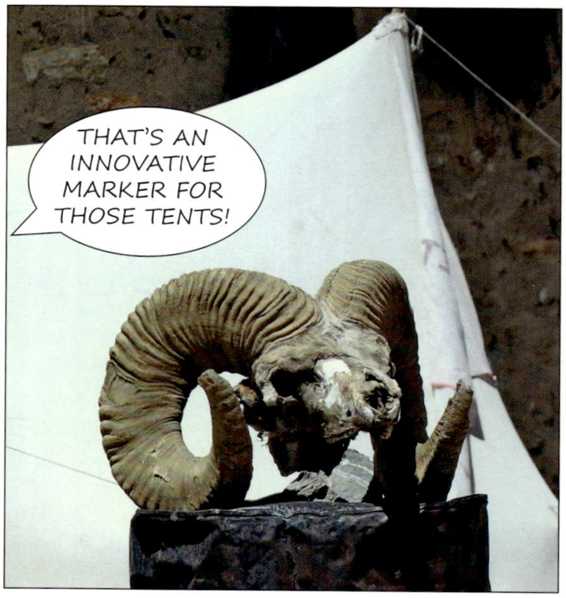
THAT'S AN INNOVATIVE MARKER FOR THOSE TENTS!

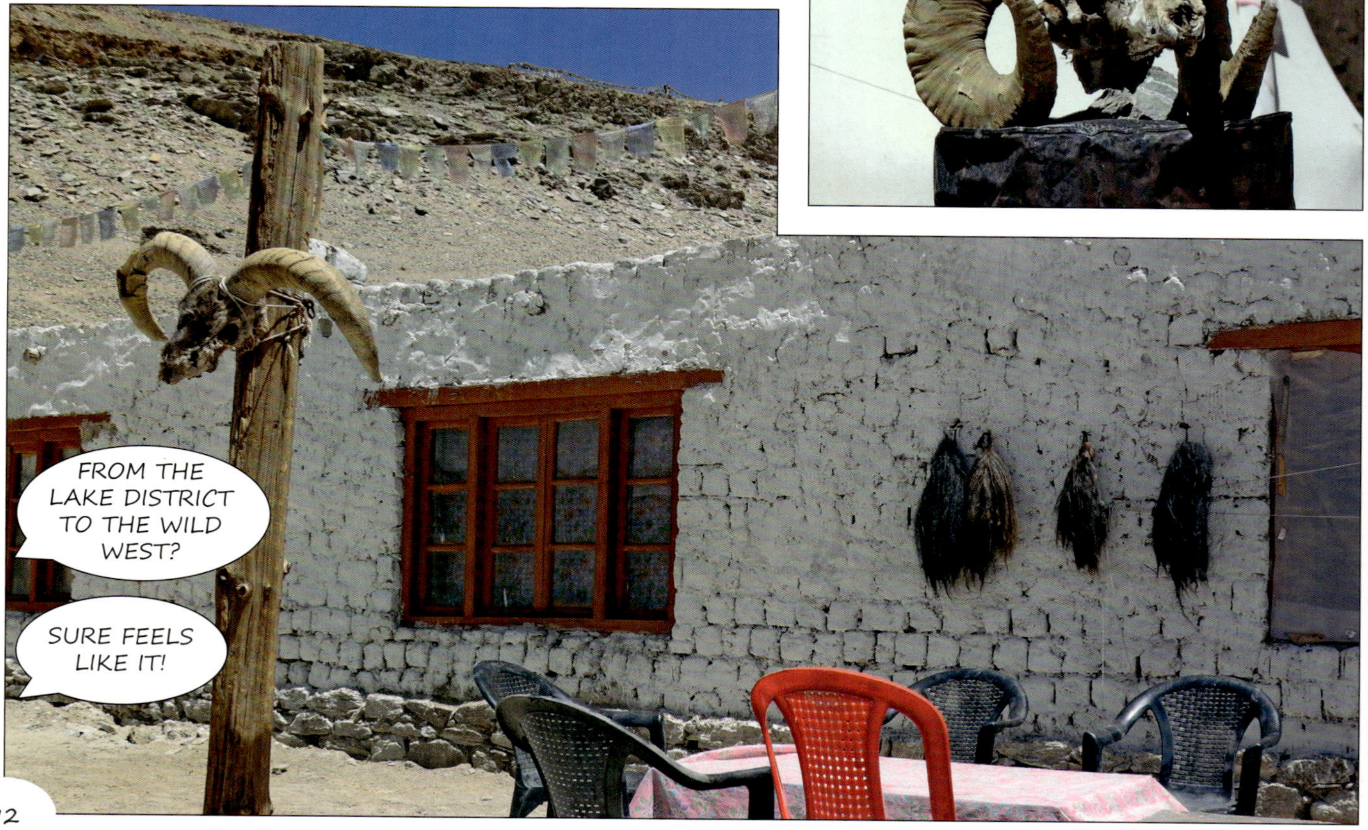
FROM THE LAKE DISTRICT TO THE WILD WEST?
SURE FEELS LIKE IT!

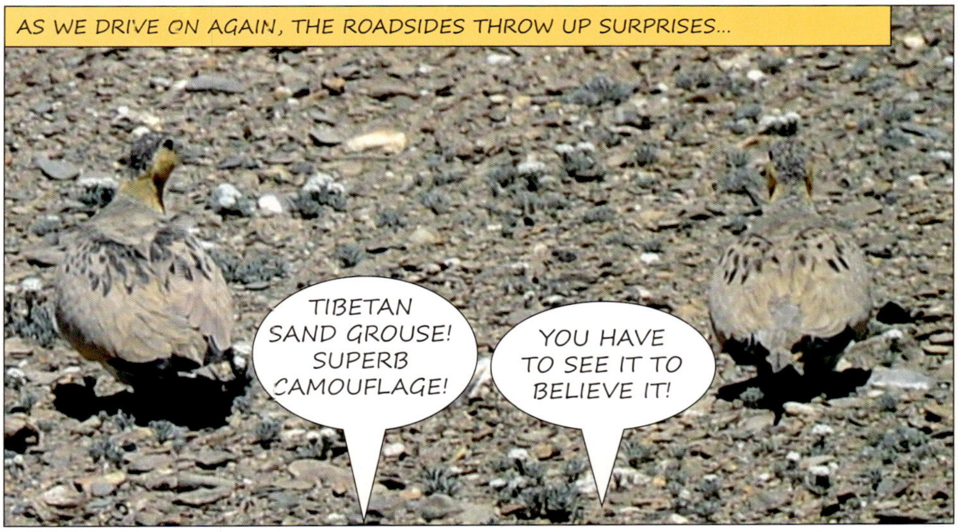
AS WE DRIVE ON AGAIN, THE ROADSIDES THROW UP SURPRISES...
TIBETAN SAND GROUSE! SUPERB CAMOUFLAGE!
YOU HAVE TO SEE IT TO BELIEVE IT!

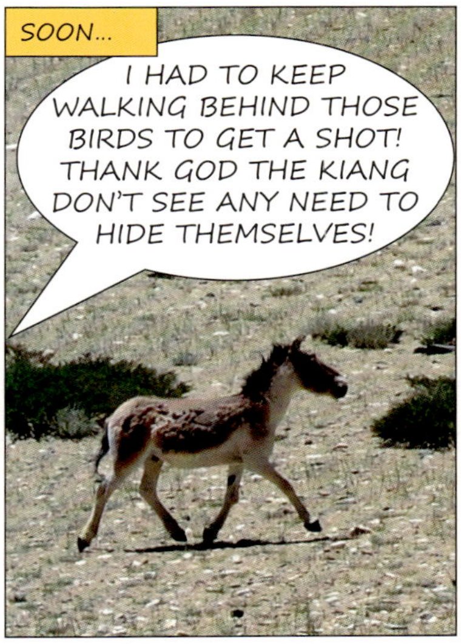
SOON...
I HAD TO KEEP WALKING BEHIND THOSE BIRDS TO GET A SHOT! THANK GOD THE KIANG DON'T SEE ANY NEED TO HIDE THEMSELVES!

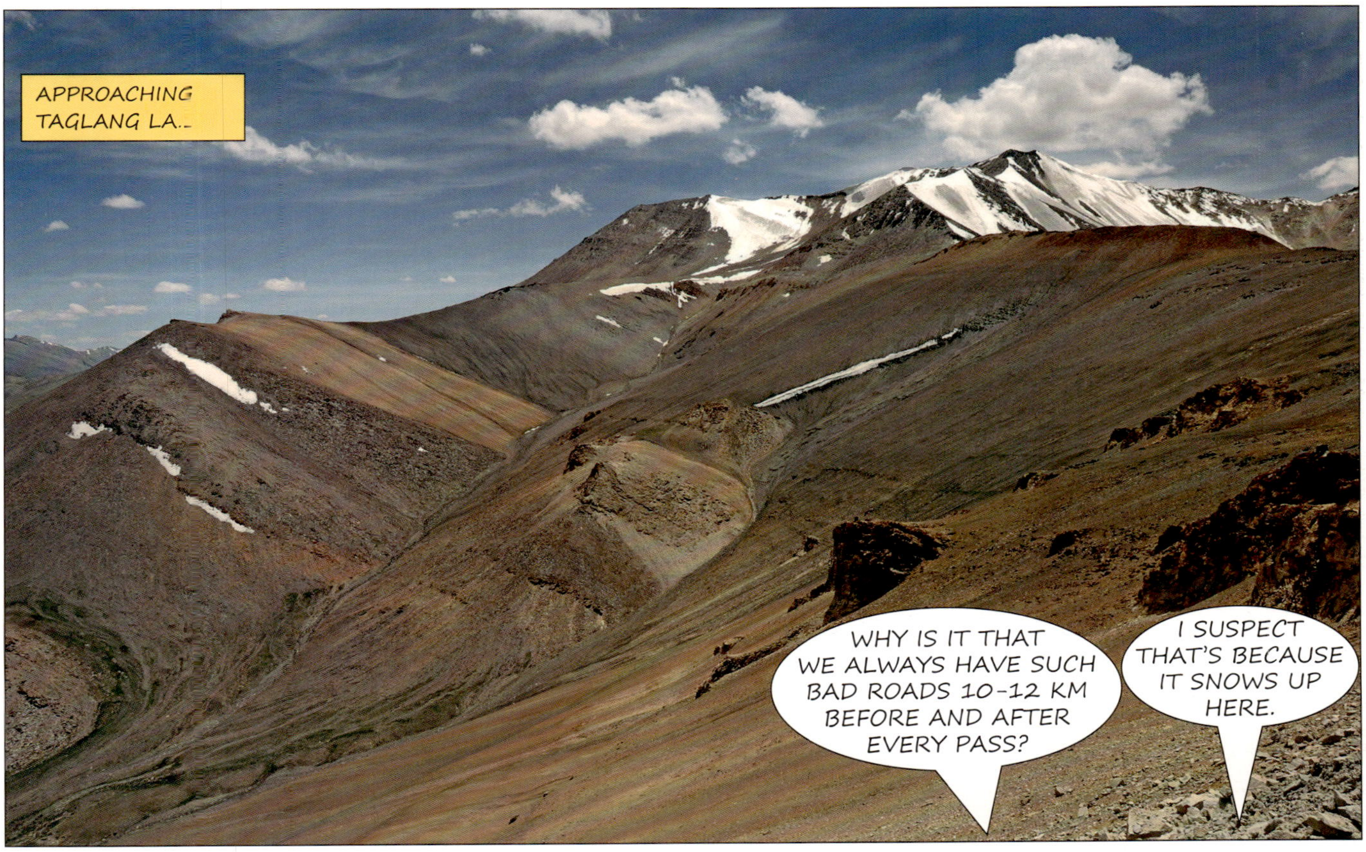
APPROACHING TAGLANG LA...
WHY IS IT THAT WE ALWAYS HAVE SUCH BAD ROADS 10-12 KM BEFORE AND AFTER EVERY PASS?
I SUSPECT THAT'S BECAUSE IT SNOWS UP HERE.

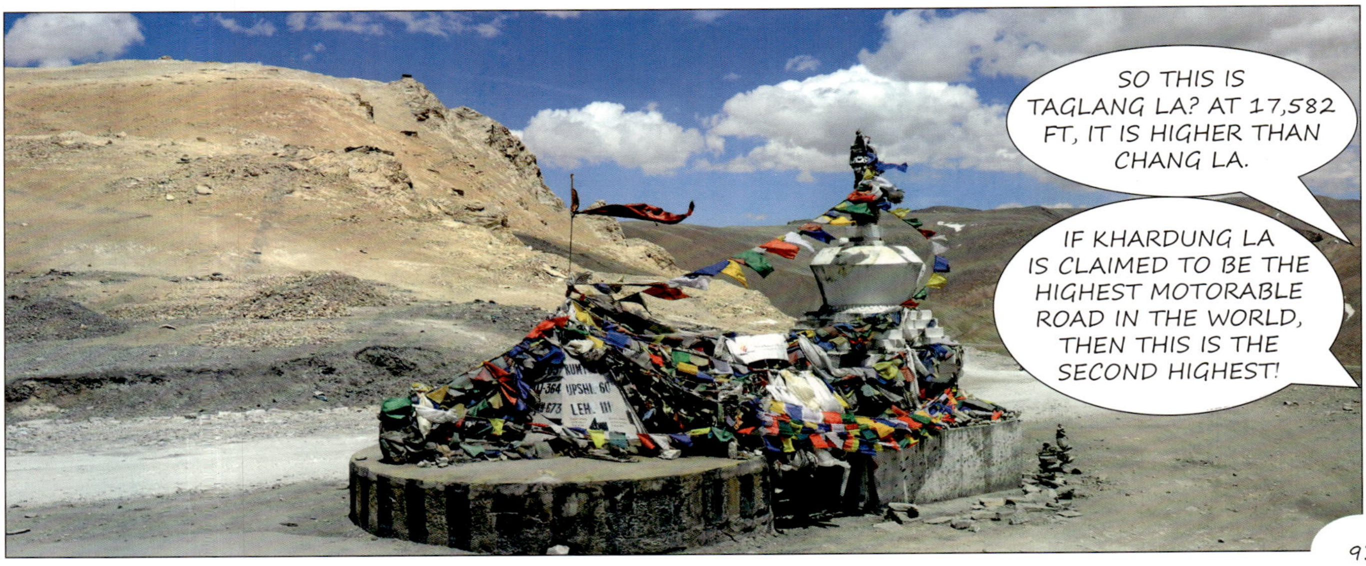
SO THIS IS TAGLANG LA? AT 17,582 FT, IT IS HIGHER THAN CHANG LA.
IF KHARDUNG LA IS CLAIMED TO BE THE HIGHEST MOTORABLE ROAD IN THE WORLD, THEN THIS IS THE SECOND HIGHEST!

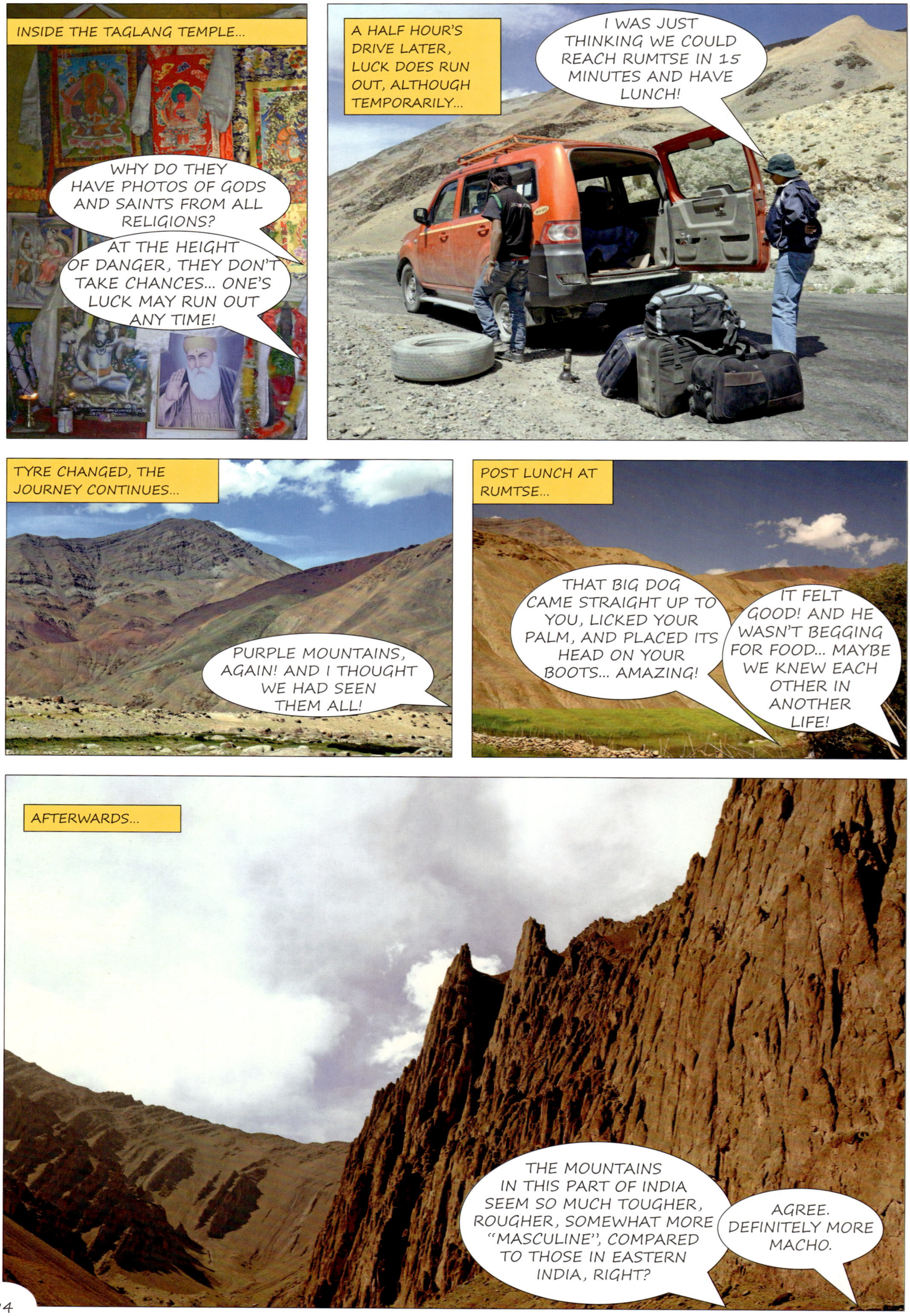
INSIDE THE TAGLANG TEMPLE...
WHY DO THEY HAVE PHOTOS OF GODS AND SAINTS FROM ALL RELIGIONS?
AT THE HEIGHT OF DANGER, THEY DON'T TAKE CHANCES... ONE'S LUCK MAY RUN OUT ANY TIME!
A HALF HOUR'S DRIVE LATER, LUCK DOES RUN OUT, ALTHOUGH TEMPORARILY...
I WAS JUST THINKING WE COULD REACH RUMTSE IN 15 MINUTES AND HAVE LUNCH!
TYRE CHANGED, THE JOURNEY CONTINUES...
PURPLE MOUNTAINS, AGAIN! AND I THOUGHT WE HAD SEEN THEM ALL!
POST LUNCH AT RUMTSE...
THAT BIG DOG CAME STRAIGHT UP TO YOU, LICKED YOUR PALM, AND PLACED ITS HEAD ON YOUR BOOTS... AMAZING!
IT FELT GOOD! AND HE WASN'T BEGGING FOR FOOD... MAYBE WE KNEW EACH OTHER IN ANOTHER LIFE!
AFTERWARDS...
THE MOUNTAINS IN THIS PART OF INDIA SEEM SO MUCH TOUGHER, ROUGHER, SOMEWHAT MORE "MASCULINE", COMPARED TO THOSE IN EASTERN INDIA, RIGHT?
AGREE. DEFINITELY MORE MACHO.

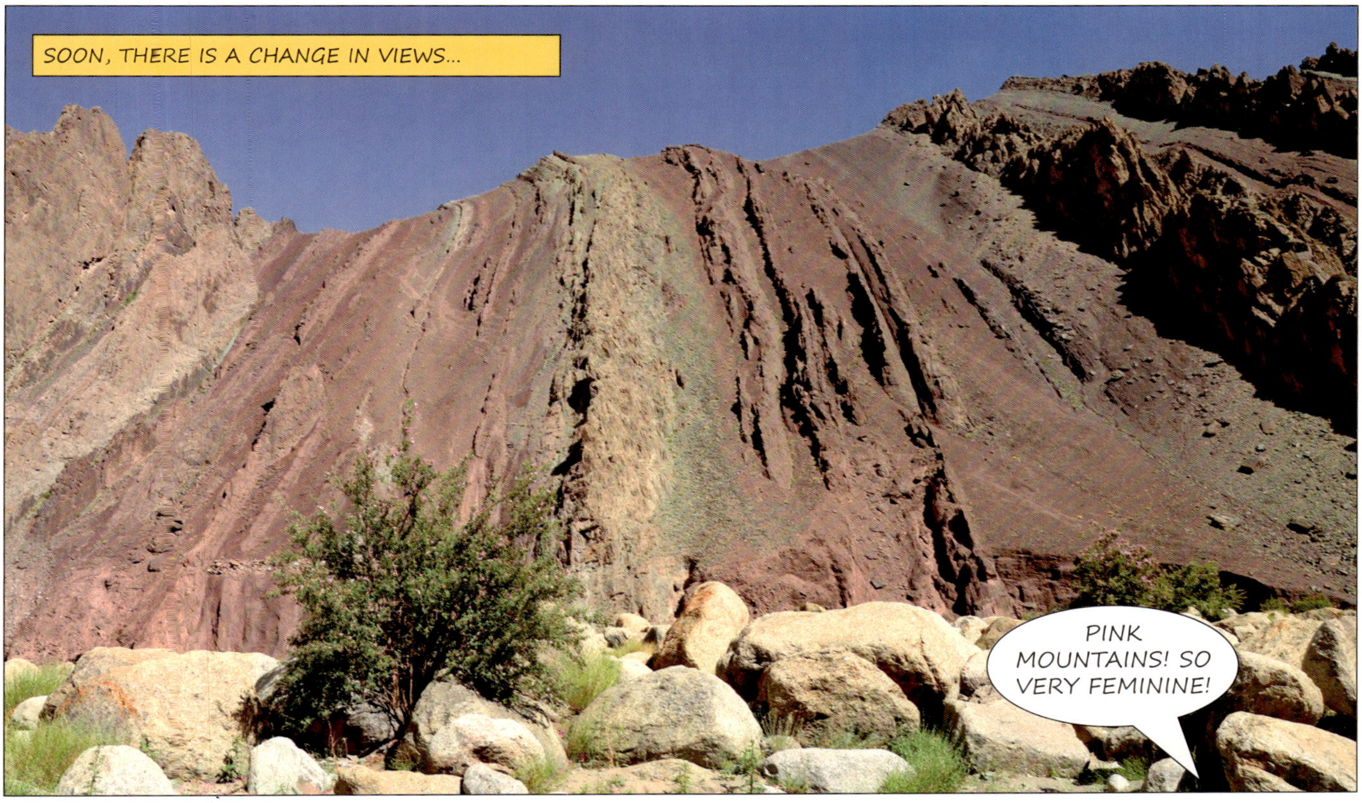
SOON, THERE IS A CHANGE IN VIEWS...
PINK MOUNTAINS! SO VERY FEMININE!

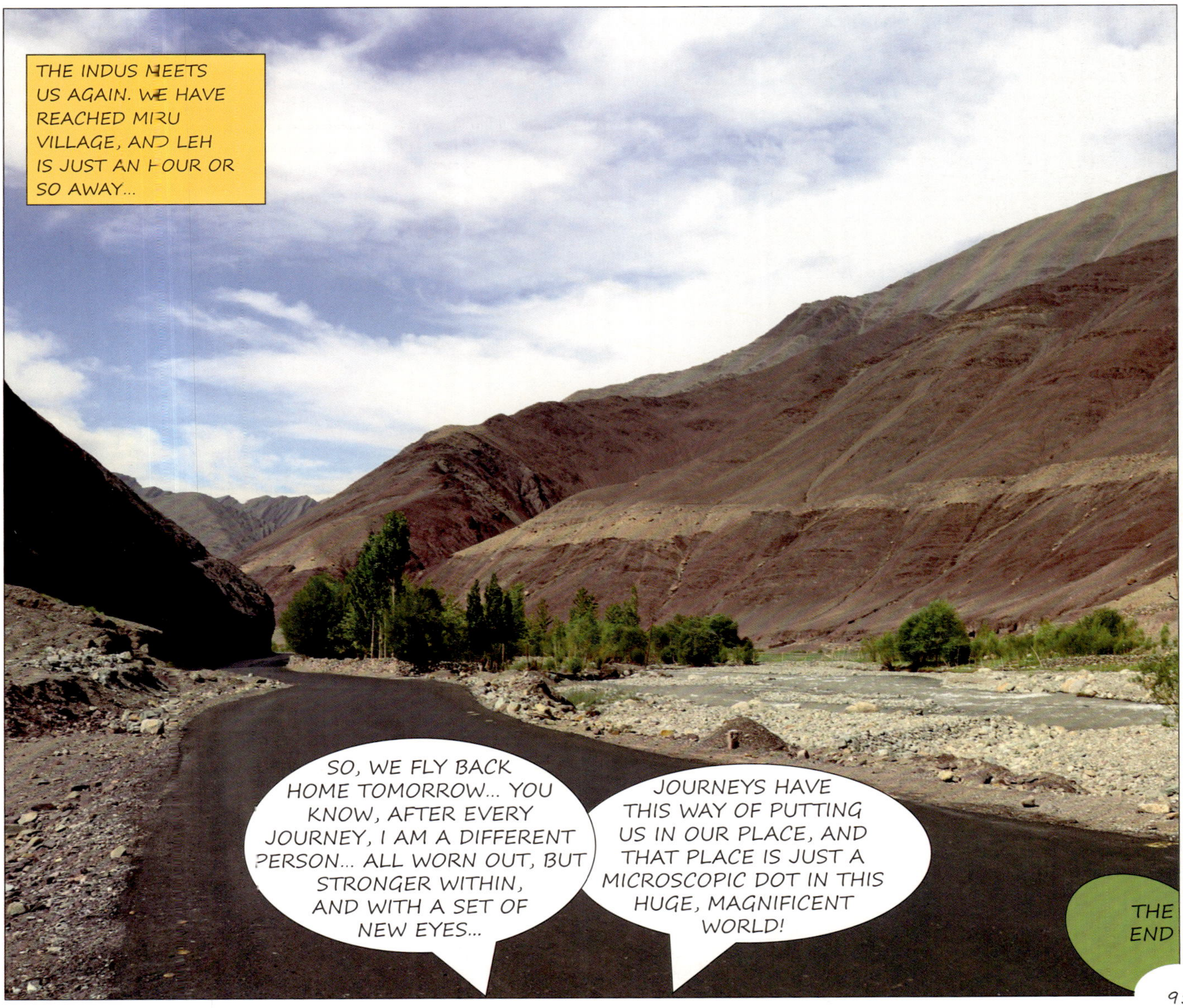
THE INDUS MEETS US AGAIN. WE HAVE REACHED MIRU VILLAGE, AND LEH IS JUST AN HOUR OR SO AWAY...
SO, WE FLY BACK HOME TOMORROW... YOU KNOW, AFTER EVERY JOURNEY, I AM A DIFFERENT PERSON... ALL WORN OUT, BUT STRONGER WITHIN, AND WITH A SET OF NEW EYES...
JOURNEYS HAVE THIS WAY OF PUTTING US IN OUR PLACE, AND THAT PLACE IS JUST A MICROSCOPIC DOT IN THIS HUGE, MAGNIFICENT WORLD!
THE END

Acknowledgements

It is not often that one gets to count one's blessings, and I am happy to have this chance to do so.

Thank you Sumita Rakshit, for your unquestioning company on all my journeys. Without you, this book would not happen.

Thank you Swati Dasgupta, for hosting us at your home, driving us down to the airport for that pre-dawn flight from New Delhi to Leh, and for the kebab rolls you made and packed for us. Thank you again for patiently reviewing this book.

Thank you Shirin Bhattacharya, for taking time out after office to do an audience-analysis.